INVESTING IN SILVER

INVESTING

Transworld Publishers Ltd
a National General Company

IN SILVER
Eric Delieb

INVESTING IN SILVER
A Corgi Book 0552 98534 1
Originally published in Great Britain by Barrie & Rockliff, The Cresset Press,
2 Clement's Inn, Strand, London, W.C.2
Text set by Harrison & Sons (Westminster) Ltd, 20/22 Bedfordbury, London,
W.C.2
Colour pages printed by L. Van Leer & Co. N.V., Amsterdam
Text and Covers printed in Great Britain by Jarrold & Sons Ltd, Cowgate,
Norwich
Printing History
Barrie & Rockliff Edition published 1967
Second impression 1970
Corgi Edition published 1970
Copyright © Design Yearbook Ltd, 1967
Corgi Books are published by Transworld Publishers Ltd, Cavendish House,
57–59 Uxbridge Road, London, W.5

The writer would like to express his deep indebtedness to the anonymous
collectors who kindly allowed him to illustrate articles from their collections,
and to the following for kind advice and assistance: Captain T. E. Barlow,
D.S.C., H. E. Brocksom, Esq., H. A. Cooper, Esq., Miss Susan Hare, Librarian
to the Worshipful Company of Goldsmiths, Rev. W. A. Hepher, M.A., Richard
Kingston, Esq., E. Kish, Esq., Dr. and Mrs. David Lawrence, B. Lenga, Esq.,
Mrs. Eugene R. Miles, Mrs. William Bennett Munro, Maurice Newbold,
Esq., John R. Rayment, Esq., John Simon, Esq., D. G. B. Wilmot, Esq., and
the Wardens of the Worshipful Company of Goldsmiths.

With the exception of the photographs on pages 11, 42 (centre), 112 (top
right) by Raymond Fortt, A.I.B.P., A.R.P.S., 120 (top), 135 (top) by Photowork,
Ltd, and 10 (centre), 19 and 32 by Christopher Ashdown, and those from
the American and Goldsmiths Company collections, all the illustrations are by
Peter Parkinson, A.I.B.P.

CONTENTS

The prices quoted throughout this book are estimated on the basis of typical figures paid during 1967. They should be taken as no more than a guide to future prices, as it is (and remains) impossible to forecast changes with any accuracy. Similarly the effect of devaluation of the £ in November 1967 cannot be expressed in terms of an exact figure, although it has led in general to an accentuation of the existing upward trends.

DEDICATION

Proverbs XXXI 10–12.

INTRODUCTION

It is a safe assumption that at no time during the present century has there been such interest and movement in the field of antique silver as in the second half of the 1960's, with prices soaring ever higher, and attention veering away from 'museum interest' to appeal to a wide public of small collectors. The days of the important art-collector of the J. Pierpont Morgan— William Randolph Hearst class are seemingly over, although the contemporary American collections, notably the Munro Collection at San Marino, California, and the Miles Collection of Cleveland, Ohio, are outstanding. A whole range of lesser connoisseurs is actively engrossed in the medium, both as researchers and actual buyers. So great is the thirst for knowledge that almost any book published attracts a massive readership.

The present volume is designed to fill a double need: on the one hand, to provide would-be investors with a modicum of knowledge in their chosen subject, and on the other, to examine aspects connected with silver which many of the major works of reference have neglected to mention. Most of the classic writers, Jackson among them, have all but ignored the existence of the *small* piece of antique silver, and this book sets out to examine and analyse not only their early origins but to distinguish between the ordinary examples and the important specimens, giving much attention to 'condition' and restoration as well as to historical background.

In his approach, the writer has concentrated more on social than technical aspects, and has sought to introduce material relating to the domestic conditions of the period involved, and thus to bring a feeling of 'belonging' and continuity with ages past. He has deliberately omitted all attempts at analysis of hallmarks, methods of manufacture, biographies of individual silversmiths, etc., as he feels any further attention could not possibly emulate the sterling efforts of such learned contemporary authors as Judith Banister, Richard Came, A. G. Grimwade, J. F. Hayward, The Hughes', Mrs. Jane Penrice How, Gregor Norman-Wilcox, Charles Oman Jonathan Stone and Gerald Taylor naming but a few. These talented antiques journalists are ably represented by important works of reference and any attempt at repetition would be merely tautologous.

In his research strategy, the writer has adopted the method, used with marked success by many authorities, notably Penzer, of attacking the subject from an oblique approach, apparently irrelevant to the topic under discussion, but embracing such interesting aspects as mediaeval spellings and the earliest references to various articles of silver in English mediaeval literature. Many other fascinating sidelights have been revealed in subjects which other writers have studiously ignored, chiefly because the obvious sources yielded little.

The attention to investment has been tackled with diffidence: it is recognised that many people might object to overt discussion of prices, (especially

George III Baby Rattle:
Maker: Hester Bateman, London, 1790.
Maker's mark on mouthpiece, other marks near ivory handle. With eight bells set in two tiers, and faceted mouthpiece-cum-whistle, bright-cut all over with foliate motifs.
5".
Baby Rattles are known from very early times. The wonderful Keijser Collection of Amsterdam contains hundreds of fine specimens dating from the Ancient Egyptian epoch to Dutch, English, French and German examples of the 17th, 18th and 19th Centuries. English rattles are mentioned as far back as 1519 by William Horman '*Vulgaria*': 'I wyll bye a rattell to styll my baby for cryenge' and the great English essayist Joseph Addison (1672-1719) wrote in one of his essays, in *The Spectator Papers* that 'I threw away my rattle before I was two months old, and would not make use of my coral until they had taken the bells away from it'.

dealers' prices as opposed to those of the saleroom) feeling that unscrupulous persons might take advantage of such information to 'push' prices up or to coerce the collector into paying far more than the actual article is worth. This objection might have been justified in the not-too-distant past, when prices were comparatively low, both in the saleroom and in the antique shops. Today, with the great interest in all forms of antiques, the public as well as the trade is remarkably well informed on all aspects connected with values. Any objection on the grounds that some traders might increase their prices in keeping with those quoted in these pages, (ignoring the fact that they are for superlative specimens in fine state) is further discounted by the recent practice by many small antique shops of sending their acquisitions to the metropolis in any case, only retaining those articles which they may require for their regular customers.

Prices have been mounting steadily for the past decade, in fact, careful research has revealed that the values of most antique items have quadrupled, Queen Anne and George I articles have multiplied by five, Charles II and earlier by as much as ten, and articles by the 'name silversmiths'—Lamerie, Storr and the Batemans—by equally impressive amounts. While it is not attempted to compile such magnificently reasoned deductions as those in Gerald Reitlinger's monumental *The Economics of Taste*, (Volume II) with their balanced analyses of fashions and trends in collecting over many years, these are nevertheless examined in the section at the end of each chapter where a survey devoted to assisting the investor is appended. The writer has

George III 'Bosun's Call':
Maker: Joseph Taylor, Birmingham, circa 1790. (No date-letter.) The 'Keel' wriggle-engraved, otherwise plain.
4½".
The origin of the Bosun's Whistle harks back to the Ancient Greek galleys, and the custom of the Boatswain to set the pace of the rowing by piping the rhythm on a flute. The earliest English reference to the 'Bosun's Call' is recorded in 1671, but for many years before this date the article was known as a 'Mariner's Whistle'. In the year 1574, for instance, the sum of three shillings and fourpence was paid for the hire of a 'Mariner's Whistle' during revels at Court.

concentrated his attention on those articles which, being of apparently unimportant size, have not until recently attracted the notice of the collectors, and being thus undervalued, still permit sizeable appreciation. He has not, however, neglected mention of the important vessels and other articles, and many of these are both illustrated and discussed.

Some attention is also devoted to the delicate question of repairs and restorations which tend to worry some would-be investors, and such subtle anomalies as 'box-lid insertions' and the removal of out-of-period enrichment are examined. A chapter devoted to rare items illustrates many unusual manifestations of the Georgian silversmith's art; the work of several famous makers is profusely illustrated—Hester Bateman and her family in particular—such charming relics of the past as silver toys, magnificently conceived caddy-spoons, Old Sheffield Plate items, even a lady's folding parasol which packs away into a tube 8" long, all appear within these covers.

In the main, the writer has attempted to impart some of the pleasure and fascination which antique silver holds for him. It is true that as a dealer, he has perhaps more opportunity to examine and admire these beautiful objects, but he loves his calling far beyond his normal day's work and the results of his researches are gladly offered to all who share his sentiments.

George IV 'King's Messenger's Pendant':
No maker's mark, King's head and lion passant only, circa 1820. Formed as finely chased and cast Greyhound with suspensory loop.
1¾".
The 'Four Messengers of the Great Chamber in Ordinary' were already in existence in 1454 at the reign of Henry VI; there were always four in the early years, but in 1641 there were 40. The earliest appointment was in 1485. Apart from carrying messages at home and abroad, the King's Messengers arrested persons for high treason and kept them in custody. The Silver Greyhound is figured as one of the Royal Badges, the House of Lancaster used it and Henry VII had two silver greyhounds as the supporters in his Arms. In 1689 a bill was delivered to the Jewel Office from Their Majesties' Goldsmith Robert Vyner for '20 Messenger Badges, curiously chased and gilt with a Cristal over the Armes and supporters on each badge. Weight: 106 ozs. 3dwts. 2 grains: £127.10.3.'
The first silver 'Greyhound Badge' or pendant is mentioned in 1758 in the Lord Chamberlain's books. The George III examples were large but the William IV specimens were smaller.

THE SPOON

The English silver spoon is, in the face of today's universal admiration of the fine arts in general and antique silver in particular, perhaps the most important item in the silver collector's cabinet. It represents almost the only remaining article originating in the 16th or early 17th Centuries whose price is still not altogether prohibitive: there is a vast difference between the £500, $1,400, which a fine Henry VIII apostle or maidenhead spoon might be expected to cost and a comparable 'hollow-ware' article such as a wine cup or a salt-cellar which could cost upwards of £4,000, $11,200. Many people can thus only envy those fortunate few who are able to possess these fine *chefs-d'oeuvre* which really belong in museums and national collections, and even the affluent connoisseur finds that the demand far exceeds the supply.

Left
Charles I Sliptop Spoon: London, 1627. No Maker's mark.
Centre
Elizabeth I Apostle Spoon: Subject: St. Jude.
Maker: 'A Crescent enclosing a Mullet', London, 1592.
6¾″.
Weight: 1 oz. 10 dwts.

Right
Elizabeth I Apostle Spoon: Subject: St. James the Greater.
Maker: 'A Bird's Claw', London, 1568. Silver-gilt. Rough cast terminal with nimbus of cast 'Saint Esprit'.
6¾″.
Weight: 1 oz. 17 dwts. An exceptional weight, spoons of this type are usually 1 oz. 15 dwts.

So the early spoon, if it is of fine state, venerable age and with clear hall-marks, is an attractive acquisition and an excellent investment. This pristine condition is important, as the collector must put himself in the place of the future purchaser: he himself would not like to pay a high price for an inferior article, and it is only fair that the advantage of quality be passed on. Collectors should resist the temptation of indiscriminate purchase simply because 'the price is right', and should remember that the antiques trade is a highly organised and erudite branch of the fine arts whose members pride themselves on their knowledge of current trends. While it is true that an occasional 'bargain' might be allowed to slip through, either from ignorance or benevolence, the general axiom of 'you get what you pay for' (as one cynical dealer once put it) is perhaps truer today than it has ever been.

Many collectors strive to build up a complete set of apostle spoons (twelve apostles and The Master) by selecting single spoons with differing finials and thus aspire to make up a series by the same maker and, if possible, of the same year. There are only a very few full sets of apostle spoons extant and their cost is very high indeed. As long ago as 1903 the superb Abbey Set was sold for the then record sum of £4900, $13,700, what they might be expected to fetch today is anybody's guess, certainly at least ten times that figure. So the singleton specimen is really the only type to interest the average spoon collector. It will be apparent that the target of assembling a full set of thirteen apostle spoons is the work of a lifetime, as these, and especially London-made examples, are few and far between and many silversmiths made them, often in three different sizes each year. The collector who derives most satisfaction is the one who spreads his purchases over a wider field, either over a set period of time—Elizabethan, Jacobean and Carolean—or for spoons bearing the hall-marks of the various provincial assay-offices.

Another benefit of acquiring singletons as opposed to sets or even pairs is that the latter command a very high price. The fact that the articles have survived together over a period of some four centuries the hazards of theft, damage or family division is a happy miracle of coincidence, and this

From a private Canadian collection:

Henry VIII Maidenhead Spoon: The terminal finely detailed, the back view showing the flowing 'tresses'.

Maker: 'A Fringed 'S'', London, 1519. The inset clearly shows the method of union of the terminal with the stem: in the early spoons, this was effected by means of a 'V' joint, the stem receiving the pointed end of the terminal. In the later specimens, the union was by means of a 'lap-joint' where the terminal possessed a projecting lug and the stem had a section cut away to receive this. Most London specimens have the former, and most provincial examples the latter.

6½".

Weight: 1 oz. 15 dwts.

phenomenon does not go unnoticed: the price is commensurate with the rarity.

The history of the spoon itself as a table accessory is obscured by the veil of time. Certainly, man used slates and shells before he thought of using metal. As to the origin of the English word 'spoon', the etymologists remind us that our Anglo-Saxon forebears employed a similar-sounding word to describe a chip of wood pressed into service as a ladle.

The collector of antique spoons is, however, not so preoccupied with etymology as with the history of their development from earliest times. Strangely the actual form of the prototype spoons, Roman or Anglo-Saxon in conception, has hardly changed over the centuries. The original Roman spoon began life as an elongated oval bowl attached to a simple wire-like stem; the 'keel-type' terminal on the back of the bowl evolved in the later English spoons into the 'rat-tail' which served both as an enrichment and a strengthener. The Roman stem emerged gradually as an hexagonal handle (as in most English late 15th, 16th or 17th Century examples) which might be surmounted by a cast finial depicting fruit, diamonds or acorns, and, of course, the famous apostle terminal.

These primitive spoons, and their immediate successors, the early French and English spoons, possessed very shallow bowls, and it is doubtful whether the latter were ever intended to contain liquids. Montaigne, in his famous essays, commented on the fact that it was fashionable in the 16th Century to raise the vessel to the lips and drink the broth; whether the fashion dictated the custom, or vice versa, is conjectural. However, it is probable that the shallowness of the bowl of the early spoon resulted in some of the lamentable damage which can be observed on many otherwise perfectly formed articles, where one side of the bowl is completely worn away; if the spoon was used only for scooping semi-solids from a bowl, the rim scraped the bottom of the vessel.

Acorn, diamond and fruitlet terminal spoons are all mentioned elsewhere. For the most part, they are out of the province of the general collector in view of their extreme age: many are unmarked or partially marked, and originate from the last quarter of the 15th Century, and the study of these inaugural versions is complicated and intricate, although students of the spoon and its history will find this a rich field of research. For the rest, attention to fully marked specimens is indicated, or, in the case of provincial specimens (which are very often only partially marked) examples from the interesting assay-offices are attractive.

Left
    James I Apostle Spoon: Subject: St. Peter with Key.
    Maker: MH Conjoined, London, 1614.
    7".
    Weight: 1 oz. 15 dwts.
    Silver gilt, finely modelled terminal.
Centre
    Elizabeth I Maidenhead Spoon:
    Maker: 'A Campanula' (Jackson, page 101.), London, 1572.
    7".
    Weight: 1 oz. 15 dwts.
Right
    Elizabeth I Moor's Head Spoon:
    Maker: D enclosing C, London, 1602.
    4⅝". Probably a child's spoon.
    Weight: 1 oz.

Another early terminal favoured by the silversmiths was the 'slipped-in-the-stalk' variety, better known as the sliptop. This spoon had an hexagonal stem, with the very tip cut away at an angle, as one might snip a rose off at the stem. There has been much conjecture about this type and some ingenious theories advanced. Some authorities have speculated on this lack of a finial by supposing that the figure was removed to satisfy the rigorous ideas of the emergent Protestant religion (The Reformation) which objected to the use of sacred figures on secular objects. But it appears to have been overlooked that the Reformation began in 1517 with Martin Luther's protest against the sale of indulgences, and by that time the sliptop spoon had been in use for at least twenty-five years.

Another theory was that during the Commonwealth the Puritans objected to the use of sacred terminals on spoons, in the same manner as they removed the statues of saints in churches. The reply to this suggestion is given quite categorically by the famous Commander How in his magnificent and monumental *English and Scottish Silver Spoons*: 'The placing of a mark high on the stem proves conclusively that sliptop spoons thus marked were fashioned in this form and were never intended to have finials'. This complicated analysis needs explanation. All London sliptops are marked as follows: the Leopard's Head is struck in the bowl, like the other figure terminal spoons, but unlike the apostle spoon which is marked fully on the lower part of the stem-back near the bowl, the sliptop has always had its date-letter struck at the top of the stem. If, therefore, a sliptop dated 1501 has this date-letter in the position cited, the spoon never had a finial, otherwise it would have been marked near the bowl.

Another, more simple answer to this problem is that the sliptop terminal was by far the easiest and cheapest form to produce, as well as, possibly, the most graceful.

The most renowned of all the English figure-terminals is that group of religious emblems embracing the apostle, maidenhead and Virgin and Heart finials. Again, the origins of their design are obscure. A reasonable assumption would have been that they were introduced at the time of the Byzantine Empire, for apostolic iconography abounds on Byzantine plate, but a searching review of most works on the subject has revealed nothing approaching an apostle terminal, and such spoons as do exist resemble the Roman wire-stem with a 'keel-like' terminal on the back of the bowl. Little is known of the silversmithing of the Middle Ages, but some authorities believe that the motif came to England from the continent in the middle of the 15th Century, or that the terminal was copied from the portrayal of martyrdom on English rood screens in churches. Thus, some apostles are depicted bearing the instrument of their martyrdom: St. Simon Zelotes with his saw, St. Bartholomew with his flaying knife and St. James the Less with his fuller's bat (a type of clothworker's hammer). Some apostles are shown with the emblems of their office: St. Peter holds the Keys of the Kingdom of Heaven, and St. Matthew grasps the money-bag which symbolises his work as Herod's tax-gatherer.

Most apostle spoons have a nimbus or halo on their heads, which takes the form of a flat disc, sometimes pierced to simulate rays, sometimes cast to the same effect. There are exceptions to this rule; the famous Abbey Set, for instance, have uncapped finials, The Master's nimbus is cast or engraved with the Saint Esprit or Holy Dove symbolising the Holy Spirit, and He holds the Orb and Cross.

Apostle spoons were popular christening gifts in the 16th Century and this is undoubtedly the reason for the multiplicity of such types. The finial either represented the patron saint of the giver or the name saint of the baby. If only one spoon was given, it could be the apostle whose anniversary came nearest to the christening. St. Paul, though not one of the apostles usually depicted, is frequently found on London spoons, as he is the patron saint of the City of London. The very wealthy gave a complete set of thirteen spoons, or a variation might be the gift of one of the four evangelists. Godparents evidently took pride in their gifts. An interesting inscription on one spoon reads:

> Rich. Elnor. Joane
> At Ye Font Stone
> Their word did give
> How Yu shouldst live

The practice of giving apostle spoons as christening gifts began to wane towards the middle of the 17th Century, and this may account for the disappearance of the type not long afterwards.

The maidenhead and the Virgin and Heart finials are frequently mistaken for each other, although the latter variety is the rarer. The maidenhead is formed as the bust of a lady emerging from the calyx of a fleur-de-lys or an iris, and represents the Virgin Mary. Because there is no nimbus, the features are often worn completely away, so as to be totally unrecognisable. The Virgin and Heart specimens are very similar to the maidenhead except that the figure appears to be holding something in her hand; in some of the cruder examples, this appears to the uninitiated as a flaw in the casting. These little spoons (they are generally about 5″ long) first made their appearance during the closing years of the 15th Century, but the majority of specimens date from about the first quarter of the 17th.

The final terminal in this religious group is the type commonly termed the 'moor's head': this is, in reality, a representation of the Holy Child, and, as it usually surmounts a small spoon, was most probably intended for a child's use. Curiously enough, while many small-size sliptops and moor's head examples have been noted, no apostle spoon of similar proportions appears to have existed, although it would have been natural for a christening gift to be scaled down to the recipient's requirements. Any doubt that these spoons were used by young children is dispelled by the fact that many bear unmistakable tooth marks.

Of the remaining cast terminals on spoons, the lion sejant is perhaps the most attractive, being formed as a seated or crouching heraldic lion. The London-made examples usually take the form of the 'lion sejant affronte', that is to say, the animal faces to the front. Occasionally, the lion supports an heraldic shield between its paws. Provincial lion sejants are usually rough cast and have protruding jaws and grinning teeth; they resemble a dog rather than the King of Beasts.

By far the most prolific of all the cast terminals is the sealtop spoon, which takes its name from the fact that the baluster (originating as a gothic column in Tudor architecture) is topped by a circular disc, which might or might not bear the engraved initials of the owners. Quite massive hexagonal balusters appeared on the early examples, but these gradually thinned down to the 'double-baluster' type common to most mid-17th Century sealtops. The early spoons were quite small, but subsequent arrivals developed into coarse and cumbersome articles, the handling of which, at table, must have been quite uncomfortable.

Following the era of cast terminals, the English spoon commenced the long transition from the narrow hexagonal stem to the widening 'Puritan' type, eventually culminating in the so-called 'Old English' handle of the 18th Century. In retrospect, there were infinitesimal changes from the very beginning, with the stem widening imperceptibly until the spoon became a pleasant article to hold and capable of containing a good volume of liquid.

The only remaining vestige of the earlier types was the rat-tail which was simply an extension of the short union at the back of the bowl, where the handle was originally soldered on. This 'tongue' gradually spread down almost the whole length of the bowl and was eventually struck in a die to simulate the rat-tail; the early trefid spoons (the top of the stem has three lobes) had a rat-tail which ran half way down the back of the bowl. The earliest noted specimen (dated 1664) much resembled the famous 'puritan' of the Commonwealth (which possesses a sturdy slightly tapered stem and still has the date-letter struck high on the handle like the sliptop) in that it had a rudimentary rat-tail.

William III Dessert-size Trefid Rat-tail Spoon:

Maker: William Scarlett, London, 1700. With 'lace-back' enrichment on back of bowl.

5¾".

As the century drew to its close, the hitherto severely plain surfaces acquired a form of primitive enrichment known as 'scratch-engraving' which consisted of stylised acanthus foliage and sometimes posturing amorini and cherubs as well as mythological birds. The front of the stem might be die-struck with foliate motifs and these might be repeated on the back of the bowl in beautiful scrolling ornament; this last type is known as the 'lace-back' probably because the intricate designs resemble the delicate needlework of the Stuarts.

The trefid terminal gave way to the 'dognose', which is almost the same, with the exception that the notches of the lobes have disappeared, and the latter in turn developed into the rounded-end terminal of the Hanoverian conception which no longer had a flat stem, but one in which the face became ridged, a kind of reversed rat-tail.

The spoons became heavier in gauge and the rat-tail was more prominent. At this stage of its evolution, the spoon was wrought in Britannia Standard metal (95·8% as opposed to the normal 92·5% standard in use before 1697 and after 1719) and is much brighter in colour, as well as silkier to the touch.

The rat-tail disappeared about 1725 (although out-of-period examples are occasionally encountered) and the 'heel' or 'dewdrop' unions became fashionable. Some George II specimens have heavy heels, others, like the Aberdeen spoons, have a type of double-ringed heel. The marking sequence was struck on the bottom of the stem, and did not rise again until 1781.

At about the middle of the 18th Century there was a revival of the die-struck motifs on the backs of the bowls, but now the emblems had a political or heraldic significance rather than a purely decorative one. Tablespoons bearing the Arms of some of the City Livery Companies have been noted: The Vintners' Company, the Mercers', and finally the splendid Arms of the Goldsmiths' Company appear struck in deep relief. In the case of the last, a series of such spoons was struck in 1773 by the London silversmith Robert Salmon for the use of newly admitted Freemen of the Company who presented them as mementoes of the occasion. Large size spoons of the 'picture-back' variety, as these articles are known, bear most of the motifs found on the smaller teaspoons, but the latter are far more common.

It has not been considered necessary to examine late Georgian and other tableware, as once the rat-tail terminal was shed, the spoon form remained more or less static. The stem became the centre of attention, and a great variety of decorative motifs was applied to it. Of these, the most attractive was perhaps the famous 'Onslow' cast terminal, which consisted of an architectural volute or 'knurl'; this, like the early figure terminals, was spliced on to the stem. The Hanoverian 'rounded-top' stem gave way to the 'Old English' type but there were also feather-edged, beaded, bright-cut and reeded handles and these, in turn, evolved into the 'fiddle-pattern' (although it had existed since the 1670's on French tableware). There followed the opulent 'King's and Queen's pattern' which embodies elaborate shell motifs, and various rare enrichments such as the 'Rose ornament' which consists of trailing rose tendrils, the 'Naval motif' which incorporates an anchor, and many other obscure patterns. Pity the poor owner who tries to match these specimens: it might be almost easier to match a set of Elizabethan apostle spoons!

The Teaspoon

English teaspoons in general were produced from the 1670's, but for the most part were simply smaller versions of trefid rat-tail table-spoons. They differed in one important detail: unlike the large variety, early teaspoons are seldom fully marked: at best, all they might possess is the maker's mark and the lion passant. Some fully marked specimens however have been noted, but these are of exceptional rarity. Strangely, George I and II specimens are also only partially marked, and the marks are 'bottom struck', that is, near the back of the bowl.

Perhaps the most uncommon stem encountered is the 'twisted cable' type which is surmounted by the usual dognose terminal but has a section of stem convoluted. The mark (generally a lion's head erased) is struck on the back of the terminal.

The teaspoons of the 18th Century picture-back variety, that is, with die-struck motifs on the back of the bowls, were produced by a multitude of silversmiths, yet all appear to originate from the same *atelier*, so closely do they resemble each other. But of course, all bear different makers' marks and were produced over a period of some thirty years.

The logical inference would therefore be that pattern-books were available and were hired out to all workers who thus drew their inspiration from them. These handbooks of ornament were common to most European countries, and the French, in particular, based their embellishment on many of these fine drawings.

Opposite
Top
From a private collection.

William and Mary trefid three-pronged fork: the slightly rounded shoulders hinting at a date of circa 1690, there being no marks. Of sturdy gauge and scratch-engraved with contemporary initials.
(7¼" in length).

Charles I very small child's sliptop spoon: maker's mark obscured. Date-letter struck at top of stem in keeping with the marking position of larger specimens. London, 1640.
(4½" in length).

James I silver-gilt provincial apostle spoon: of fine proportions and very heavy gauge. The mark, 'a rose barbed and seeded' is variously ascribed to Southampton and Carlisle, circa 1620. Subject: St. Peter with nimbus. Struck in bowl and three times on back of stem. Ex. The Marquess of Breadalbane's collection.
(7¾" in length, weight: 1 oz. 19 dwts).

Charles II puritan spoon: made in the first year of the Restoration by Stephen Venables, London, 1660. A full description of this type will be found in this chapter (6¾" in length).

James I sealtop spoon: with very small 'seal' terminal. By the celebrated London maker: 'A Crescent enclosing a Mullet', 1622. This silversmith's mark is first recorded in 1553, and this particular spoon must be one of the last pieces from this workshop; it is probable that this was a father and son partnership, otherwise a working life of seventy years is implied.
(6" in length).

Charles II puritan spoon: of very unusual type. It was originally made in London by the maker whose mark is 'WC pellets above, a mullet below in plain shield', and subsequently overstruck by John Peard of Bideford (an earlier ascription was Barnstaple) circa 1670. Peard's mark is overstruck on the leopard's head in the bowl, and appears in addition to the lion passant and the London maker's mark on the back of the stem. There is no date-letter. The top of the stem has been hammered in a mould to give it the characteristic West Country tapering terminal, and is pricked with a floral motif of provincial influence.
(6⅜" in length).

Centre
George II large heavy soup ladle: the hollow curving-back handle with cast and chased 'eagle's head' terminal, the deep oval bowl of 'fig-shape' form. By George Wickes, London, 1743. This specimen is one of a pair, being marked 'No. 2', and is ex. the Marquess of Breadalbane's collection.
(15" in length, weight: 10 ozs. 14 dwts; engraved on back with original weight: 10 ozs. 18 dwts; the article has thus lost four pennyweights, or just under quarter of an ounce in two centuries of polishing. It has, however, acquired a magnificent patina).

Bottom
From the collection of Dr. David Lawrence.

Pair George II large sauceboats: the massive bodies supported on four cast 'seaserpent' feet and with similar type cast handles. The rims are finely shaped and there are generous spouts. The engraved ornament consists of fine scrolling cartouches containing intertwined cyphers. By the eminent Huguenot silversmith Aymé Videau who was apprenticed to David Willaume in 1723 and became a Freeman of the Goldsmiths' Company in 1733. Dated London, 1735.
(6⅛" by 4" by 3" high, weight: 35 ozs).

16

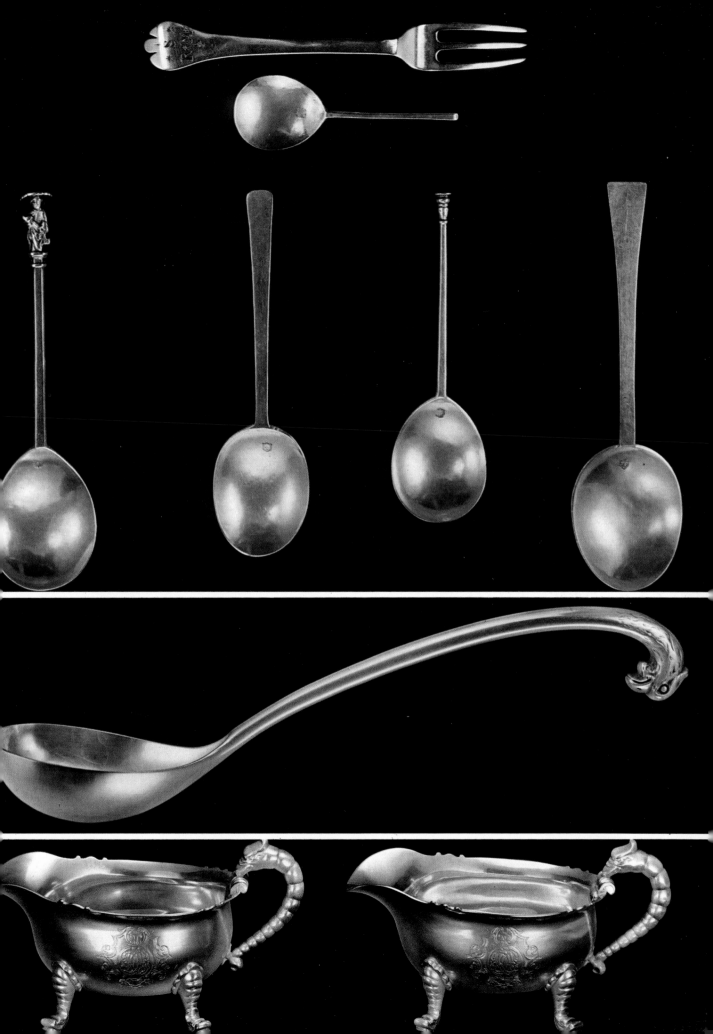

From the collection of H. A. Cooper, Esq.

James II oval tobacco box: the lid engraved with portrait of William Sancroft, Archbishop of Canterbury. By Pierre Harrache, London, 1686. This box is fully described in the chapter on 'The Box'.

($3\frac{1}{2}$" by $2\frac{3}{4}$" by $\frac{7}{8}$" deep. Weight: 4 ozs. 2 dwts.)

William and Mary set of six 'scratch-engraved' trefid teaspoons: with acanthus motif on back of bowl embracing the 'rat-tail' terminal, and similar motif on front and back of stems. By Jean Harrache, London, circa 1690. Engraved with contemporary initial 'C' on back of stems.

($4\frac{3}{8}$" in length).

Charles II silver-gilt trefid teaspoon: with 'ridged' rat-tail on back of bowl. By SH pellet below in shaped shield, London, 1679. Fully hall-marked teaspoons of this date are very rare.

($4\frac{3}{8}$" in length).

Charles II scissor-case: the top scratch-engraved with scrolling acanthus foliage and 'female and satyr's mask' enrichment, the stem with acanthus diaper motifs and ball terminal on base. Three-lugged hinge and 'snap' fastener and suspensory loop. Unmarked, circa 1680. The scissors accommodated by these articles are usually of the 'travelling' type, with 'finger-loops', which fold inwards on a pivot so as to slide into the narrow opening of the case.

($3\frac{3}{4}$" by $1\frac{1}{2}$" at the top).

A careful perusal of many fine art catalogues both in museums and libraries has failed to reveal any English pattern-books produced before 1760. In their absence, the hypothesis must be made that the motifs were invented by one craftsman and there upon ruthlessly plagiarised by his contemporaries; as new subjects were introduced, these too were universally copied.

The earliest die-struck motifs were simple in conception: spoons were struck with scrolling rococo shell ornament, escallop shells, baskets of fruit and vases of flowers, and sprigs of foliage. There were also some cast variations with emblems consisting of farm-yard themes: a hen with her chicks, a turkey with hers, a swan with her cygnets.

By far the most sinister aspect of the picture-back was the 'political allusion': the enemies of King James II brought about his downfall in 1688, and for a century thereafter British politics abounded with secret societies. The Jaco-bites, as the King's followers were known, were mercilessly persecuted, both in his own time, and during the 1745 Rebellion in which Bonnie Prince Charlie tried to regain power. The more obvious relics depict Charles Stuart in a variety of media, glass, enamels, etc., but the subtle way to hide one's allegiance to the Cause, yet at the same time reveal one's sympathies to potential allies, was to take one's tea, or, indeed, one's wine, in vessels or with teaspoons bearing enigmatic political emblems. There were so many clandestine groups that many defeat identification to this day: all that may be safely assumed is that some of the emblems on picture-backs are so obscure in origin, that they *must refer* to some 'unlawful' activity.

The rarest of this 'political emblem' group is the cast 'rose' teaspoon: the bowl is formed as serrated leaves, the stem with two little buds nestling on it (emblematic of the Two Pretenders). Another uncommon variety is the cast and shaped 'acorn-bowl' which might have an 'oak-leaf' spray on the back of the bowl and a representation of St. Sebastian on the front of the stem. The 'oak' motif appears on all the Jacobite relics, and harked back to the miraculous escape by Charles II in the Boscobel Oak in 1651. The motif was

Set of six Charles II Trefid Rat-tail Spoons:
   Maker: Sir Jeremiah Snow, London, 1681.
   $7\frac{1}{4}$". Sets of six spoons are very uncommon, although pairs and sets of four are occasionally encountered.

subsequently worn on Restoration Day, May 29th, from 1660 onwards. Furthermore, the 'Oak-leaf' was a true Stuart emblem; it was the custom of the clans in battle or on any great occasion to wear in their bonnets a badge of evergreen or a flower. Thus, the Mcgregors wore a sprig of ivy, the Macdonalds heather, and the Stuart clan, an oak leaf.

The Hanoverians considered the motif offensive, and in 1716 some soldiers who wore it on May 29th, were severely beaten up in Hyde Park, and several persons were committed to prison for doing so. The St. Sebastian motif is

Detail: Back of William & Mary Trefid Rat-tail Spoon: showing very fine 'Lace-back' ornament consisting of 'swans' necks and vine-leaf' motifs.
Unmarked, circa 1691 (date 'pricked' on stem).
7¼".

less certain, but it has been tentatively suggested that he might have been the patron saint of the Jacobites.

Another veiled emblem is the 'cockerel' type: the key to this allusion is to be found in the concluding verses of the 13th chapter of St. Mark's Gospel: 'the servants of the absent Master are bidden to watch for his return, which may occur at midnight, or at cock-crow'. The 37th verse of this chapter was inscribed on King Charles I's watch.

Other spoons bore patriotic emblems: specimens invoked prosperity on British agriculture: the 'harvest-back' variety depicted crossed rakes, pitchforks and scythes, a barrel at centre, topped by the rakish hat of a farmlabourer and set in a scrolling foliate cartouche. There were also the 'wheatsheaf' surmounting the word 'plenty' and a milkmaid with her pails on a yoke about her shoulders.

One of three Queen Anne Rat-tail Teaspoons:
Maker: Louis Cuny, London, circa 1705. Of sturdy gauge and finely marked with maker's mark and lion's head erased.
4⅝".

Current events might also be immortalised. A victory at sea could be commemorated with the striking of a galleon in full sail, and banners flying. Various heraldic emblems recalled Royal events: it is believed, for instance, that the coming of age of the Dutch King William V in 1766 was recorded by the issue of the 'Stork with a serpent in its beak' variety, as the Arms of the city of The Hague contain this device. The succession to the Princedom of Wales by George William Frederick (later George III) on the death of his father, Frederick, George II's son in 1751 was commemorated by the 'Prince of Wales Feather' motif, the Royal Crown was struck to celebrate the Coronation of George III in September 1761, and the attractive 'dove with olive branch' was probably struck to mark the termination of the Seven Years War in 1763, or it might be connected with the 'Olive Branch' petition from the American Colonists to George III in 1775 which failed when the King refused to see Richard Penn their emissary.

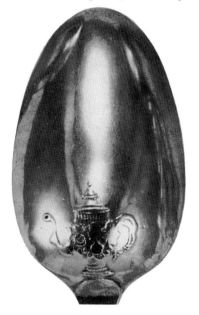

Left
George II Picture-back Teaspoon:
Subject: A Scrolling Shell.
Maker: Thomas Wynne, London, circa 1750.
4½".

Centre left
George II Picture-back Teaspoon:
Subject: A Scroll.
Maker: Elias Cachart, London, circa 1750.
4½".

Centre right
George III Picture-back Teaspoon:
Subject: A Wheatsheaf, surmounting the word 'Plenty'.
Maker: Thompson Davis, London, circa 1760.
4½".

Right
George III Picture-back Teaspoon:
Subject: A fully rigged Galleon.
Maker: Joseph Preedy, London, 1793.
Being dated after 1781, this spoon has a full set of marks struck at the top of the stem.
5".

A mysterious motif which has not been explained, was the 'teapot' back: the emblem resembled the florally enriched reversed pyriform teapot fashionable in the 1760's; this is perhaps the rarest of all the picture-backs, but unless, once again, it is a Jacobite allusion, its origin is extremely obscure.

Perhaps the most famous picture-back theme of all is the 'I love liberty' motif found on teaspoons dating from the late 1760's. This recalls one of the most sensational *causes célèbres* of the 18th Century when the notorious gutter-politician and journalist John Wilkes was arraigned on a charge of scurrilous libel on the Government of the day for its foreign policies in his paper 'The North Briton'. Wilkes's imprisonment resulted in the national outcry 'Wilkes and liberty' and his release was commemorated by the issue of a wide variety of articles in glass and silver depicting the theme of 'freedom'. On teaspoons, the incident is portrayed as an open birdcage, upon the top of which sits a

Left
George III Picture-back Teaspoon:
Subject: A Pyriform Teapot.
Maker: Charles Hougham, circa 1770.
This subject believed to be the rarest of all 'Picture-backs'.
4⅜". One of a set of six.

Right
George III Picture-back Teaspoon:
Subject: A Dove with an Olive branch in her beak.
Maker: Elizabeth Tuite, London, circa 1775.
4¾".

bird with outstretched wings, the whole surmounted by the motto: 'I love liberty'.

The last picture-backs emanated from the mid–1790's, and, as such, were fully marked at the top of the stem-back. The later varieties all have 'bright-cut' (a method whereby a richly carved effect was achieved by gouging out the surface metal) or engraved foliate motifs on the front of the stem.

The Mote-spoon

One of the most puzzling of all the smaller spoons is the type variously known as the 'stirrer spoon', 'mote spoon', 'mulberry spoon', and 'olive spoon'. The article is well known to collectors: it possesses a long tapering stem topped by a barbed spike, and, in the earlier specimens, the wire-like stem is soldered to the back of the bowl very much like the Roman spoon, the union with the bowl forming the rat-tail. In the later examples, a die-struck rat-tail appears, first full length, and gradually half length, disappearing about 1730. The oval bowl is generally pierced: the early types are simply 'punch-pierced', that is with holes all over the surface, but with no definite motif, the later versions with geometric or architectural motifs. Fully marked specimens are almost unknown, the usual marks are a maker's mark and the lion's head erased on the earlier examples and a maker's mark and a lion passant on the later ones. The former variety are usually marked on the back of the bowl, the latter 'bottom-marked' on the back of the stem.

Only one thing is certain: the pierced oval bowl facilitated the straining of liquids. On most other aspects, the experts disagree. Some believe the barbed terminal to have been used for spearing lemon pips in hot punch, others held that the spike was prodded down the spouts of teapots to clear the accumulation of soggy tea-leaves. The function of the strainer bowl was similarly conjectural: it was argued that since the article was often advertised for sale in conjunction with sets of teaspoons, it must have been intended to serve as a primitive tea-strainer, or perhaps to skim the 'motes' or floating tea-leaves off the surface of the tiny teabowls; the tea-strainer proper did not come into service until the 1790's.

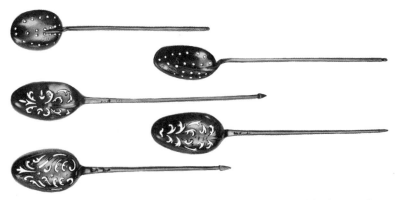

Left

William & Mary Mote Spoon:
Maker: AH Crown above, cinquefoil below, London, circa 1690. Simply pierced with holes, long wire stem soldered to back of bowl to form 'rat-tail' terminal.
5½″. An early specimen.

George I Mote Spoon:
Maker: BI Crown above, London, circa 1720. Long stem terminating in half 'rat-tail' terminal, with simple foliate piercing in the bowl.
5½″.

George III Mote Spoon:
Maker: William Cripps, London, circa 1760. Maker's mark only. Long stemmed, the bowl pierced and engraved with foliate and star motifs.
5½″.

Right

William III Mote Spoon:
Maker: LE (Script), London, circa 1697–1700. The lion's head erased mark is of this cycle. With long wire stem soldered to back of bowl to form 'rat-tail' terminal.
5½″.

George I Mote Spoon:
Maker: HS, London, circa 1725. Long stem terminating in 'rat-tail'. With simple foliate piercing in bowl.
5½″.

George II Mote Spoon with Marrow Spoon handle:
Maker: Frederick Kandler, London, circa 1740. Maker's mark only. The bowl finely pierced with geometric and foliate motifs.
6¾″.
Weight: 1 oz. 10 dwts.

American Mote Spoon:
Maker: Pygan Adams, New London, Connecticut, circa 1740. With long tapering stem, die-struck on back of bowl with 'raying-shell' motif, and pierced in centre of bowl with diaper motif and tiny crosses, and around the rim with foliate piercing. Small 'barb' at terminal. Engraved with contemporary initials.
6¼″.

All these conjectures might be correct, as also might the objections to these theories: that the curved spout of the contemporary teapot would not accommodate the straight stem of the spoon, that mulberries did not require the services of a strainer-spoon, that the article had nothing to do with olives.

The origin of the 'olive-spoon' ascription might have arisen from the use of strainer-spoons in the excclesiastical anointing of the sick, and in baptism, with Holy Oil, which was, in fact, olive oil. This was probably strained for the same reason that sacramental wine for the communion was strained, namely, to remove impurities and flies. Large strainer-spoons for the latter have been noted by various writers: some are obviously adaptations of secular Elizabethan spoons with later pierced bowls (earlier specimens would have had simple punch-pierced bowls) others, being of contemporary date to the piercing, were probably ordered specially for the purpose.

Some of the mote-spoon types (the most reliable ascription) have finely pierced bowls: one outstanding specimen noted has the quite superb Coat-of-Arms of a noble family with full supporters, the whole surmounted by a helmet, all pierced within an area of one and a quarter inches. Others have die-struck picture-back motifs such as escalop shells, squirrels and birds. A fine American example by the noted New London, Connecticut, silversmith Pygan Adams, circa 1740 has been included in an otherwise entirely English group, chiefly because of its rarity.

Of the remaining 'Special Purpose' spoons, the 'suckett spoon *cum* fork', the basting spoon, the marrow spoon and the medicine spoon, all merit the attention of the collector: all are attractive in conception and appearance, but with the possible exception of the basting spoon, which could be of service in the modern kitchen, the other varieties now merely serve to emphasise the revolution in culinary fashions and methods regnant in the 20th Century.

The Suckett-spoon

The candied fruit addict of the 1960's uses a plastic spear to spike the stem ginger he adores: the sweet-toothed Stuart of the 1660's employed a silver implement, with a spoon at one end and a twin-tined fork at the other. The suckett spoon is thus only a collector's curio, and, in any case, was of such fragile construction that it must have been very difficult to use at all!

The later versions of the suckett spoon (Elizabethan specimens have been noted, but the majority are of the late Charles II period) are slightly more sturdy in gauge, and may have three tined forks. They generally have scratch-engraved foliate motifs on the stems, front and back, and acanthus foliage surrounding the rat-tail on the back of the bowl. Fully marked suckett spoons are very uncommon; most have only a maker's mark, struck on the back of the stem. They are quite small, no more than five or five and a half inches long, and, as has been stated, of very thin gauge silver. The bowls of the early types are almost spherical, but tend to become more oval as the century draws to its close.

Charles II Suckett-spoon:
Maker: BR in Monogram, circa 1675. (Jackson, page 136, line 11). Formed as primitively wrought 'twisted-in-the-middle' stem, surmounted at one end by a short rat-tailed spoon bowl, and at the other by an equally primitive two-tined fork, cut from the same stem.
5⅞".
Weight: 10 dwts.

The Basting Spoon

The basting spoon was, as its name implies, a kitchen utensil. The earliest known examples date from the late 1670's, and have long trefid handles and deep pierced or partially pierced spherical bowls. These gave way to un-pierced oval bowls, and subsequent versions had hollow tapering tubular handles which terminated in a thick rat-tail along the back of the deep bowl. The former were marked along the back of the stem, the latter were either marked inside the bowl or on the back of the stem near the union with the bowl; there might be a maker's mark and a lion's head erased on the side of the bowl.

Queen Anne and George I basting spoons had heavy bowls and massive stems. Some had a marrow-scoop handle incorporated in the stem. The dognose terminal, as in most other contemporary spoons, was succeeded by the Hanoverian 'rounded-end', and the later George II and III specimens might have a die-struck shell motif on the back of the bowl.

James II Rat-tail Basting Spoon:
Maker: IK Rosette below, London, 1686. With tubular 'slipped-in-the-stalk' handle, and deep, oval bowl. Engraved on back with contemporary crest. Fully marked on back of stem and with maker's mark and lion passant on side of bowl.
12".
Weight: 8 ozs.

The Marrow Spoon

Marrow spoons, and their near relations, the marrow scoop, are still widely in use in France and Switzerland where bone marrow is considered a succulent delicacy. The English marrow spoon was simply an adaptation of the trefid rat-tail spoon, with a hollowed-out stem, the earliest specimens being of the 1690 period. Many are silver-gilt, but as there appear to be no caustic properties in bone marrow, which might corrode the surface of the silver, it is probable that the gilding was for decorative purposes only.

The Queen Anne marrow scoops sometimes had attractive 'faceted stems', and George I examples have been noted which had reversed bowls, that is, the two ends faced away from each other. The early Hanoverian specimens had flat stems between the ends.

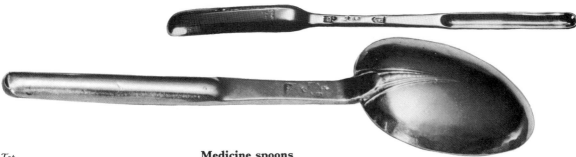

Queen Anne Marrow Scoop:
Maker: John Broake, London, 1712. With 'chamfered faceted' bowl and stem. 8½".
Weight: 1 oz. 15 dwts. A fine specimen with superb hall-marks.

William & Mary Marrow-spoon:
Maker: ID a sexfoil above, crescent below in shaped shield, London, circa 1690. Of Dessert-size, heavy gauge spoon, with 'beaded' rat-tail terminal on back of bowl, the hollowed-out stem serving as marrow scoop. Silver-gilt. Early Marrow Spoons are rare.
5⅝".
Weight: 1 oz. 15 dwts.

Medicine spoons

Those interesting and curious medicine spoons of the 18th and early 19th Centuries no longer have a use in a pharmaceutical world where accurate scientific measurement has superseded haphazard hand-gauging of potions and mixtures. The double-ended spoon with the differently sized bowls at either end of the stem emerged in the 1760's. The little shortened stem spoon which was gradually adapted as the prototype tea caddy-spoon first appeared during the mid-fifties; both were used for liquid measurement. A late development, but fascinating in conception, was the famous 'castor-oil-spoon'. This was formed as a closed-in receptacle with a hollow self-handle: the unpalatable purgative was poured into the spoon, the thumb of the giver placed over the opening at the end of the handle, thereby arresting the flow, the spoon placed in the child's mouth, and the liquid released. The inventor of this curious instrument was one Gibson, but examples by other silversmiths have been noted. The first castor-oil-spoons date from the late 1820's and the type was still in use in the 1850's.

Victorian Invalid Feeding-spoon:
Makers: J. & J. Aldous, London, 1839. Formed as very large 'castor-oil-spoon', with ivory mouthpiece.
8¾".
Weight: 4 ozs.

George IV Castor-oil-spoon:
Maker: John Reilly, London, 1825. Unusually small, with short oval bowl and tubular hollow handle.
3½" by 2½".
Weight: 2ozs. 10 dwts.

George III Medicine Spoon:
Maker: John Lamfert, London, 1766. With two spoon-bowls at either end of stem, the larger probably for mixtures, the smaller for powders.
This spoon was formerly in the Collection of her late Royal Highness, the Princess Royal, and bears her crest in the bowl.
7½".
Weight: 2ozs. 15 dwts.

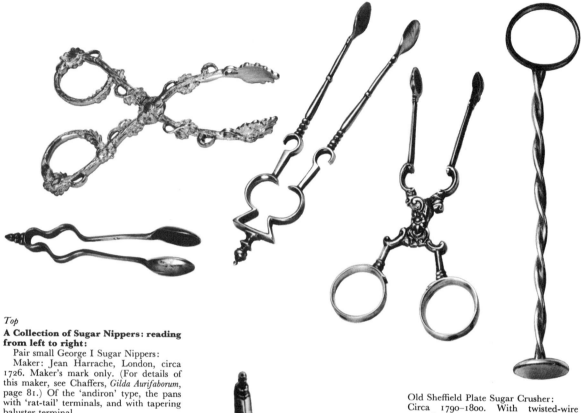

Top

A Collection of Sugar Nippers: reading from left to right:

Pair small George I Sugar Nippers:
Maker: Jean Harrache, London, circa 1726. Maker's mark only. (For details of this maker, see Chaffers, *Gilda Aurifaborum*, page 81.) Of the 'andiron' type, the pans with 'rat-tail' terminals, and with tapering baluster terminal.
3¾″.

Pair George IV Sugar Nippers:
Maker: Edward Farrell, London, 1829. Silver-gilt and ornately enriched with cast foliate motifs, the pans formed as leaves.
3¾″.

Pair George I Sugar Nippers:
Maker: Thomas Parr, London, circa 1720. Maker's mark and lion passant only. With slender baluster stems and engraved shell pans, the faceted terminal rising into spherical form.
4¼″.

Pair George II Sugar Nippers:
Maker: Walter Brind, London, circa 1750. Maker's mark and lion passant only on handles. Of 'scissor-type' with floral boss and 'shell-shaped' pans.
4½″.

Bottom left

Pair George I Sugar Nippers:
Maker: Thomas Parr, London, circa 1720. Maker's mark and lion's head erased only. Of the 'andiron' type, silver-gilt, the top finely hinged, the baluster stems terminating in circular pans. With acorn terminal.
4″.

Old Sheffield Plate Sugar Crusher:
Circa 1790–1800. With twisted-wire stem and simple 'loop' handle, the terminal being a flat circular plate with reeded motif on top. Used in crushing loaf sugar.
5⅜″ by ⅝″ diameter of terminal.

Early references to *sugar* occur as far back as 1340 where in the *Ayenbite of Inwyt*, a translation by Dan Michel of Northgate, a monk of the cloister of St. Austin of Canterbury, of a French ethical work, the following reference is made: 'Thet is the zuete sucre and of guod ssmak'. The 'sugar loaf' is first mentioned in a source of 1440 'Item 1 layf de sugir', and another of 1491 contains '6 loves of sewger'. The *Paston Letters*, written between 1422 and 1509, and containing much interesting contemporary material, include the quaint request: 'I pray yow that ye woll vouchesaff to send me an other sugor loff, for my old is do'. The earliest reference to *sugar tongs* occurs in William King's '*The Art of Cookery in imitation of Horace's Art of Poetry*', 1708: 'For want of Sugar-tongs or Spoons for Salt'. The early nippers were all formed as 'andirons', indeed, it is believed that these were adapted from the toy fire-irons which form part of the miniature Charles II 'fire-grates', to serve as sugar-lifters.

Bottom right

Pair George I Sugar Nippers:
Lion Passant only, circa 1720. Of the 'andiron' type and with 'pin' spout-cleaner, the baluster terminal of which forms the terminal of the Nippers. With 'rat-tail' terminals on the pans. The pans are pierced, and it has been suggested that these are late 'ember-tongs' but in that case the presence of the 'pin' is unexplained.
5″.

THE CADDY-SPOON

George III 'tumbler-cup' bowl: the deep 'hand-raised' bowl soldered to short 'Old English' handle. By Charles Chesterman, London, circa 1775, struck with maker's mark and lion passant only at the base of the stem. 2½".

George I octagonal tea-caddy: on 'stepped' foot and with pull-off lid surmounted by octagonal baluster terminal. By Glover Johnson, London, 1716. Fully marked on body and on bezel of lid. Height: 5".

In order to explain the varied shape and form of the 18th Century tea-measuring devices, it is first necessary to examine the early evolution of the containers used as receptacles. Tea as a prepared leaf arrived in England in the early years of the Restoration. As stated elsewhere, it originated in China; the herb came packed in large chests, and accompanying these, a number of small porcelain pear-shaped and octagonal vessels. These primitive containers were the forerunners of the tea-canisters, or *tea-caddies,* as they were to be known, curiously named for a type of Malayan measure (comprising one and one-fifth of a pound) known as a *kati.* These vessels were generally decorated with the 'blue and white' Chinese motif, and floral and foliate designs, possessed small circular lift-off lids, and were necessarily quite small, as tea in the first instance was exorbitantly expensive and was taken sparingly. Indeed, a contemporary periodical, *The Female Spectator* declared that 'a tea-table cost more to maintain than a nurse with two children'.

The form of the Chinese porcelain vessels must have appealed to the imagination of the English silversmiths, as they soon began to copy the style, altering it a little. The pear-shape took on an octagonal appearance, and the octagonal type was simplified into either of two shapes: a rectangular 'bottle' with flat sides and canted corners and a domed lift-off lid, or a rectangular plan with baluster or octagonal shaped sides and a 'stepped' lift-off lid (see below). Either way, the lift-off lid was retained, but the vessels gradually assumed the characteristic 'bottle with octagonal corners' common to the Queen Anne—George I periods. As long as the domed or stepped lift-off lids were in existence—usually with sliding panels at the top or in the base to facilitate the transfer of the tea into the caddy—there was no need for any other measuring device as *the tea was poured into the lid and thence transferred into the teapot.* It was only when, towards the middle of the 18th Century, the caddies assumed the form of rectangular vessels with flat or slightly domed hinged lids, or cast vase-shaped containers with large domed lids, that it became imperative to introduce a new type of ladle with which to measure the tea.

In the later tea-vases, the method was comparatively simple: a cast shell-bowl spoon with a curling volute terminal, usually of the 'Onslow' type, was suspended from either of the upturned cast handles, although there is no proof that these spoons were used exclusively for tea. In the former, however, there was no such provision. It was at this juncture that the ingenuity of the English silversmiths manifested itself: rather than devise an entirely new ladle, they adapted an existing variety. For the early period of its life, the tea-caddy spoon, or *caddy-spoon* as it will henceforth be designated, was merely a development of the short stemmed 'medicine-spoon' which resembled a truncated teaspoon, and which was originally used for dispensing potions. It was, for many years before its adaptation, an item in many a personal necessaire. The most prolific maker of this type of spoon was George Smith, who first entered his mark at Goldsmiths' Hall in 1739 and whose work continued to appear for another forty-five years.

By 1750 the tea-caddy had become an ogee-sided rectangular container, often enriched with chinoiserie repoussé or engraved embellishment, and although the vessel was by this time large enough to accommodate a measuring spoon, it was not until the early 1780's (when fully marked oval bowled short stemmed spoons appeared) that this occurred. Until 1781, there was no accurate method of dating, as from the mid-1750's until that date, teaspoons and other small spoons were 'bottom marked' that is to say, the only marks to appear on the back of the stem, near the union with the bowl, were the maker's mark and the lion passant. In 1781 the marking sequence was increased to incorporate the date-letter and the whole was applied in a straight line near the top of the stem.

Paradoxically, although London led in the manufacture of fine silverware, there are very few fully hall-marked London caddy-spoons before 1783, although a few 1781 specimens have been noted. Such spoons as do exist evolved from the 'medicine-spoons' and possess slender handles with that type of 'shield-top' terminal known as the 'Old English' type. This form of terminal

George III 'medicine-spoon' type: formed as shortened stem, with oval bowl spoon. The 'Old English' handle engraved with 'A Duchess' in mid-Georgian script. By George Smith, circa 1755–60. Silver-gilt. 3⅜".

appeared on all but a few of the earliest caddy-spoons proper. An interesting specimen of the early adaptation of the 'medicine-spoon' with the words 'A Duchess' engraved on the stem appears on this page; this is believed to refer to a type of mid-Georgian tea-measure.

With the advent of the 'Adam Period' when classical Roman motifs were adapted by the famous Adam Brothers from the archeological discoveries at Herculaneum and Pompeii to enrich contemporary domestic architecture and furnishings, the Roman pre-occupation with the scallop or *pecten shell* was exploited, and this new motif also influenced the style of the early caddy-spoon: the form of the convoluted bowl allowed a goodly measure of tea to be scooped from the caddy and was also decoratively attractive. It is, however, probable that the 'shell-motif' had occurred to the designers much earlier, when, at the end of the 17th Century, the Chinese importers who packed the tea-chests, included large exotic sea-shells, probably of the escallop variety to serve as efficient and convenient tea-ladles. The motif was therefore merely revived, and as careful study has revealed, the shell-bowl caddy-spoon embraces the widest possible range, and the interesting exhibition which the Society of Caddy-spoon Collectors held at Goldsmiths' Hall in 1965 contained, as the catalogue shows, no less than sixty different examples of this type alone.

George III silver-mounted conical conus-shell: By Matthew Linwood, Birmingham, circa 1790. These silver-mounted specimens are rarely struck with more than the maker's mark on the back of the handle. 3".

As has been stated, the early caddy-spoons were formed as pecten shells. At first the handles were simple, with short 'Old English' type terminals and shallow bowls, but as the 18th Century drew to its close, and the advent of the Industrial Revolution heralded the age of the machine, working in precious metals became more adventurous. Styles became more elaborate, the convolutions of the bowl were more sharply defined and handles first lost some of the delicate bright-cut and engraved enrichment and then assumed the 'fiddle-pattern' that is, a shaped terminal resembling the body of a violin. The majority of shell-bowls were produced in London, but the earliest specimens, with the sole exception of the 'medicine-spoon' type, appear to have originated in Sheffield, and the first fully marked spoons from that Assay-office bear the dates of 1777–9. These spoons generally took the form of deep shell-bowls with flat 'escutcheon-type' self-handles, that is, the handles were 'shield-shaped' and part of the bowl, not soldered on as were some of the early London examples. The embellishment might consist of 'feather-edging' (a type of slant engraving) or punched bead ornament. Sheffield caddy-spoons were usually marked on either side of the bowl or on the front of the handle.

The Birmingham Assay-office was opened in 1773 after the great industrialist Matthew Boulton and other prominent citizens had petitioned Parliament that it was anomalous for a city such as Birmingham, with its massive silversmithing interests, to have to send articles to London or Chester for assay and hall-marking. It is probably for this reason that the Birmingham-made caddy-spoons tended to be more fanciful, not to say attractive, than their London counterparts: the provincial craftsmen, feeling the need to compete for custom

George III 'cast-back' 'strutted' oval bowl: with 'picture-back' motif on back of bowl. By George Smith, London, circa 1775. Maker's mark and lion passant only at the base of the stem. 3″. This cast specimen antedates any other cast example by at least fifteen years, as the first fully marked cast caddy-spoon noted was dated 1790. Moreover, the enrichment, consisting of a 'picture-back' motif is seldom found on a caddy-spoon.

with their long established metropolitan cousins, went out of their way to produce interesting shapes and charming designs. Most of the classical types, the 'Eagle's Wing' exclusively, and the 'Jockey-cap' almost so, originated in Birmingham. The inventive silversmiths also specialised in a wide variety of foliate motifs, particularly leaves—tea, ivy, oak, vine and acanthus—enriched with the most delicate ornament: engraved, embossed or matt-chased.

A close examination of the famous 'Eagle's Wing'—which is by no means as rare as might at first be imagined—reveals that it is often of flimsy lightweight silver, probably because a heavy gauge would not successfully survive 'die-stamping', the method of production. The handle is formed as the bird's neck, which terminates in a sharply hooked beak, and the bowl is formed out of the eagle's 'feathers'. With the solitary exception of one specimen by Joseph Taylor, all the others noted were by Joseph Willmore, although it is believed that Matthew Linwood also produced a few examples. The Hepher Collection contains one cast London 'Eagle's Wing' by Barnabus Blackburn dated 1878, but it is probable that this was cast from a crisp Birmingham specimen of Georgian extraction.

There were three cycles of production: most Georgian specimens dated from 1814 to 1817, the William IV spoons from 1830 to 1835, and the early Victorian variety from 1837 to 1840. Some are silver, but most encountered were silver-gilt. The marks are variously distributed: some were noted in the repoussé feathers, hardly visible to the naked eye, others are struck on the back of the bowl, and yet others have been observed struck along the back of the handle.

The 'Hand' is a very interesting example of Georgian ingenuity: by the early nineteenth century when it originated, both the public and the trade were tired of the out-moded shell-bowl caddy-spoon, and it became imperative, if public interest was to be maintained, to design a new type of tea-measuring device which would somehow combine beauty with practicability. The Hand was the result. This also was made by being struck in a die and usually comes from the workshop of Josiah Snatt of London, but one Birmingham specimen by Samuel Pemberton dated 1799 has been noted which, like the deep 'fist-shaped' example on page 36, appears to be 'hand-raised from the flat'. Both the latter have 'fiddle-pattern' handles but the Snatt versions usually have short 'cuff-like' handles enriched with bright-cut or engraved foliage or an owner's monogram. Some writers have sought to imply that the

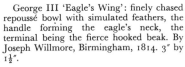

George III 'Eagle's Wing': finely chased repoussé bowl with simulated feathers, the handle forming the eagle's neck, the terminal being the fierce hooked beak. By Joseph Willmore, Birmingham, 1814. 3″ by 1½″.

scalloped or shaped handle is meant to represent a lace cuff, but in all probability, this is merely a variation in design.

The 'Jockey-cap' is another famous type and a large number are known. For some reason, only those marked on the peak are thought to be genuine, but in fact, with few exceptions, specimens marked on the side or inside the crown are also perfectly good. Four distinct varieties exist: the plain segmented cap engraved and bright-cut on the peak and sometimes with a 'snowdrop' or 'star' motif engraved on the top of the crown, which is generally by Joseph Taylor of Birmingham; the 'ribbed' cap and peak, which also emanated from Birmingham, but which, strangely, has never been noted with a maker's mark; the sturdy London-made examples which were usually plain or lightly engraved, and the die-stamped Birmingham specimens which were enriched by geometric designs overall, and also from Taylor's workshop. There were also a few filigree or 'simulated filigree' Jockey-caps, but these will be discussed in the relevant section dealing with this pleasant medium.

As was stated above, the 'Eagle's Wing', though uncommon, is certainly not as rare as is generally believed: it has been roughly estimated that between one and two hundred specimens survive. The distinction of 'exceptional rarity' is shared by about ten examples. some dating from the last decade of the 18th Century, the remainder from the first half of the 19th.

Undoubtedly the rarest of all the caddy-spoons are the following:
      (a) The cast and chased 'Serpent and Shell'.
      (b) The 'hand-raised' Harebell.
      (c) The 'Piscatorial' variety.
      (d) The 'Giant Mandarin'.
      (e) The cast 'Rocaille-motif' group.

The presently unique 'Serpent and Shell' is in the famous Lewer Collection at the Holly Trees House Museum at Colchester, Essex: it is completely unmarked, but the work is reminiscent of the finest casting of the 1820 period. This little spoon—it is three inches long—depicts a sinuous serpent coiled in a cockle-shell. The serpent forms the handle and the shell forms the bowl. It is a masterpiece of miniaturisation and of the finest quality.

The 'Harebell' must also rank as near-unique, as no other similar example has ever been noted or documented. It is delicately formed, with the *corella,* or whorl of petals enriching the 'hand-raised' bowl, with a wire-stem handle and a small stem-leaf. It is by Thomas Willmore of Birmingham (the father of the more famous Joseph) and is dated 1791.

The 'Piscatorial' specimens of which only two types are known, comprise the Scottish 'Salmon' and the unique 'Carp'. The salmon—a specimen by William Auld of Edinburgh is in the Lewer Collection and is dated 1796—is formed as a cast elliptical bowl with a wedge-shaped fishtail handle. The whole spoon is enriched with delicate 'scale-motif' engraving with an eye and a slit representing the mouth at the top of the ellipse. The 'Carp' is in the

Hepher Collection and is by William Pugh of Birmingham, 1807. This little 'gem' is quite small, being no more than two and a half inches long, of irregular oval shape, with a fronded fishtail forming the handle and dorsal fins on either side of the bowl, which is repoussé with 'scale-motifs', and also has an eye and a mouth.

The 'Chinese Mandarin' is a massive cast spoon: it takes its name from the portrait of a Chinese Mandarin in ceremonial dress and conical hat which appears in the bowl, the dignitary holding a tea-plant in his hand, and the

From a private collection:
George III heavy cast 'Chinese Mandarin': the bowl depicting the Mandarin holding a tea-plant, set in a scrolling cartouche and surmounted by floral motif handle. By Edward Farrell, London, 1816. 3¼″ by 1⅞″ wide. Weight: 4 ozs. 2 dwts.

Victorian cast and chased 'Chinoiserie-revival' spoon: subject: 'Figure-terminal' showing a Lady in a Crinoline holding a parasol, the bowl formed as matt-chased rocaille shell. By John Figg, London, 1841. 2½″.

Victorian 'Figure-terminal' spoon: formed as a Fisherman in contemporary dress proffering a raying shell. Finely cast and chased. By John Figg, London, 1854. 3½″ by 2″.

Victorian silver-gilt cast and chased 'escallop-shell': the back with matt-chased 'raying' motifs, the interior delicately gilded, the 'valve' scratched with owner's initials. By George W. Adams, London, 1869. 2⅜″ by 2¼″.

In the first edition of this book I stated that these fine cast caddy-spoons were by John Foligno. The writer was misled by Jackson's erroneous ascription. As far as may be ascertained, there *never was* a silversmithing family of this name. Jackson's first mention of '?John Foligno' appears on page 228, and has been identified as John Cope Folkhard. The second, on page 232, is in reality that of John Figg, Plate Worker, of 25 St. John's Street, Clerkenwell, who first entered his mark on 31st July, 1834, and his son, John, entered the same mark in 1880. Jackson's ascriptions go further: in the 'Names of London Silversmiths', pp. 262 (3 lines from the bottom) he mentions both J. Foligno, and 264 (last line) Edward Foligno. Now, A. G. Grimwade, in his *Treasures of a London Temple* (an account of the vestments of the Queen Anne Spanish and Portuguese Synagogue of Bevis Marks) lists a silver Sanctuary Lamp presented by Edward Foligno in 1876, but on closer examination, the lamp is by Thomas Smiley, Plate Worker. Thus, the Foligno Family did exist, as their name is engraved on the lamp, but how Jackson connected them with silversmithing is highly enigmatic.

whole is set in a scrolling cartouche and surmounted by a floral cast handle. Two variations of this spoon are known: one late George III example which is dated 1816 and the other of the William IV period dated 1830. Both are by the well-known London caster-silversmith Edward Farrell from whose workshop emerged some of the finest rococo-revival articles of the 19th Century.

The 'Rocaille-motif' group embraces such fine spoons as the 'Fisherman and Shell' dated London 1854 by the celebrated artist John Figg who also produced the superb little 'Lady in the Crinoline' of the Chinoiserie-revival period; the 'Limpet-shell' by William Trayes of London 1830 which reproduces an exact replica of a limpet with its characteristic roughly-cast exterior; the 'Mussel-shell' by Francis Higgins, London, 1852 and an 'Escallop-shell' by George W. Adams London, 1869.

Perhaps the finest piece emanating from the 19th Century (and there are many excellent specimens from this period) is the George III 'simulated filigree' specimen illustrated which bears the Arms of England and France struck on either side of a 'Dove and Olive-branch' motif, made, it is believed, to celebrate the ending of the War between the two nations in 1814. It is by the famous Birmingham partnership of Cocks and Bettridge who worked between 1806 and 1820 and who between them produced a great many outstanding examples. They specialised mainly in fine enrichment, but also issued some remarkably fresh designs.

An attractive type was introduced in the last decade of the 18th Century with the arrival of a colony of Italian immigrants who brought their native speciality of filigree working in silver wire to the London district of Clerkenwell —already inhabited by many famous craftsmen—and who produced a whole series of fine caddy-spoons between 1790 and 1830.

Their advent in London is not generally known, and for this reason many collectors have for years steadfastly refused fine specimens in filigree work in the mistaken belief that these were of oriental origin. There *were* Indian or Chinese filigree articles, but were usually of a much finer wire and of a darker colour as the standard was generally lower; there is also a greater complexity of whorls and loops which can be detected as un-English in conception. The Anglo-Italians soon adapted themselves to English design, as after a few years, it was no longer possible to distinguish their work from the earlier English examples—filigree as a medium stems not, as may be imagined, from the early 19th Century, but from the first years of the Restoration—and they then produced many fine caddy-spoons: shells, shovels and scoops, leaves, pear-shaped bowls, circular bowls, often as good as, or even better than their silver counterparts. It is interesting that one of Birmingham's oldest and best-known silversmiths, Samuel Pemberton, used filigree inset panels in many of his spoons, so it is possible that Italian wire-workers also settled in Birmingham. There is evidence that Matthew Boulton also produced filigree items.

As has been stated, filigree originated in England in the mid-1660's: a titled lady advertising in a journal of 1668 listed a 'cabinnett of cristall and philigrin' which she had lost, and the London Gazette of 1682 asked for information regarding some 'Coco-nut Cups set in fillagreen' which had been stolen, while in 1721, the same paper advertised 'Fine chac'd Philigrews and Household Plate'. Some fine little lace-shuttles, small boxes, perfume bottles, etc., are occasionally encountered which are of undoubted 17th Century origin, but except in the most rigid articles, the delicate wirework was too fragile to accept a hall-mark, and there is therefore no exact method of 'pinning down' the date except by style.

The only two exceptions to this rule, namely that filigree articles are never marked, were noted on caddy-spoons: one fine 'Jockey-cap' had a tiny plaque set inside the crown, probably to receive an owner's monogram, and the maker, Joseph Taylor, had struck his mark on this. The other instance was noted by a careful researcher who spotted a minute date cut into the back of the handle which read '1791' in a neat copperplate hand.

Caddy-spoons were made in a great variety of shapes and with delicate, moderate or opulent enrichment. Circular 'frying-pan' bowls—which resembled the well-known kitchen utensil—and pear-shaped 'pastern-bowls' —similar to a horse's hoof in design—were two uncommon shapes. There were scoop and shovel bowls, acorn and thistle bowls, cruciform bowls— mostly in Old Sheffield Plate, a medium which comprised many fine examples chiefly copied from silver types—facetted bowls from the famous Bateman Family, incorporating Adam themes, plain bowls and repoussé bowls, pierced bowls—of the 'mote-spoon' type with geometric or star motifs—cast and engraved bowls—the list appears never ending.

Further decorative motifs included 'simulated filigree' where the pattern was not worked by hand, but struck in a die, which exactly reproduced the intricate wire loops and whorls: embossed themes from classical mythology: a shepherdess seated in a pastoral setting holding a dog on a leash, or a shepherd reclining against a tree in an Arcadian tableau. There were elaborately rocaille motifs comprising shells, marine plants and architectural designs,

George III 'simulated filigree': the oval bowl struck with the Crown of England and the Fleur-de-lys of France on either side of a 'Dove and Olive-branch' motif, with similar 'self-handle'. By Cocks and Bettridge, Birmingham, 1814. 3¼".

George IV 'Quatrefoil' 'simulated filigree' spoon: the bowl die-stamped with whorls and loops. With wire tendril handle. By Taylor and Perry, Birmingham, circa 1825 (no date-letter). 3".

matt-chased rose and violet petal bowls, 'oriental' type bowls incorporating Chinese motifs—a Mandarin holding a dish of tea in his hand, and a coolie carrying a yoke with boxes of tea across his shoulders.

Finally, there was the famous 'Figure-terminal' group in which both the 'Lady in the Crinoline' and the 'Fisherman with Shell' appear, the figures forming the handles. There are certainly many more which have not as yet come to light: clever researchers are at work and new types become known almost daily. The caddy-spoon was long neglected as an art-form, primarily because the trade looked with disdain at 'small articles', but the Renaissance of the Arts which followed the Second World War has brought with it a revival of interest in these small 'collectibles', and today they are as eagerly sought as many of the major articles.

The finest makers included the whole Bateman Family from Hester downwards—embracing the brothers Peter and Jonathan who worked together for only three months in 1790 when the latter, the husband of the famous Anne died, and the great Paul Storr, who made only a few caddy-spoons—in fact, in view of his pre-occupation with massive opulence it is surprising that he made any at all! The fine silver-gilt 'Strawberry-leaf' specimen on page 30 came from his busy *atelier*. Then there were the industrious casters: Farrell, Foligno and the Foxes, father and son, all of London; the ingenious 'toymakers' Phipps and Robinson whose chunky elliptical cast 'Roman Leaves' are so eagerly sought, the prolific makers of spoons (of all shapes and sizes) Eley and Fearn who produced the unusual deep 'fist' shown.

The Birmingham silversmiths have already received some acknowledgement: Cocks and Bettridge, Thomas and Joseph Willmore, Joseph Taylor and Samuel Pemberton were all fine craftsmen, but perhaps Matthew Linwood was the virtuoso of them all: his silver-mounted caddy-spoons, for instance, achieved a summit of craftsmanship. There were sundry makers from other provincial cities such as Thomas Watson and Peter Lambert of Newcastle, Daniel Holy, Richard Morton and Tudor and Leader of Sheffield, James le Bass, Samuel Neville and John Osborn of Dublin, and William Cunningham, George Fenwick and John Ziegler of Edinburgh.

The provincial caddy-spoons, with the possible exception of the Irish examples—which tended to be somewhat larger than their English or Scottish cousins, perhaps in keeping with the Hibernian tea-caddies which were also of greater capacity than the English vessels—were of graceful proportions. The Scottish varieties, in particular, could achieve an austerity which was, however, well balanced by the fine 'lines' and general excellence of construction. Most were of the 'raying-shell' bowl type with 'fiddle-pattern' handles, but a few had pleasant oval bowls with 'Old English' handles.

The less prolific assay-offices—York, Exeter, Chester and Glasgow—also struck a few 'fiddle-pattern' spoons, but for the most part, provincial caddy-spoons emanated from Birmingham and Sheffield. Perhaps some of the most attractive of all the spoons are those where the silver is 'married' to an allied material. One superlative specimen noted consisted of an oval bowl set in the centre with a panel of translucent cornelian. It was in a spoon by Joseph Taylor dated 1804, and when the light struck this wonderful amber gem, all the genius and inventiveness that went into the production of this and all the other marvellous creations were amply justified: it achieved the apotheosis of the silversmith's craft.

THE SPOON & THE INVESTOR

As was stated at the beginning of the chapter, singleton spoons, if of good quality, constitute a very good investment for the collector who enjoys a feeling of continuity with history. A careful study of current prices has revealed that, in keeping with most of the other items of antique silver which this volume examines, spoons have quadrupled in value over the past decade; a tendency which, without wishing to enter upon the question of 'inflationary trends', is nevertheless quite a gratifying reward for a modest sum invested.

The English spoon was, for many years between the wars, sorely under-valued, even allowing for differences in the purchasing power of the pound sterling, and in view of the relative lack of interest in this medium until recent years, it has still not reached its peak. There are a few important collectors, but these are, for the most part, concerned with items of exceptional interest, such as pre-16th Century specimens or the rarer terminals. More recently, the Tudor period has attracted the attention of medium-range investors, as it is, after all, a turning point in English history. Further, in purchasing such a spoon one may still acquire a decent article, while a vessel of comparable date commands a price suited only to the deepest purse.

It should be explained that the breadth of the 'brackets' cited in pricing the various articles is necessary, as there are several factors which can affect the value of a spoon besides the necessary proviso of 'fine state'. It is perfectly possible for a collector to purchase a good Elizabethan apostle spoon or a maidenhead specimen for a very small sum, and very occasionally a connoisseur will boast that as a result of his business acumen he has acquired a beautiful early spoon for £25, $70 (the story varies with the honesty of the teller) and this might well happen. The opportunities for such low-priced purchases seldom occur in the metropolis, where the dealers, mostly buying from the saleroom to replenish their stocks, maintaining imposing establishments and employing qualified specialist staff, cannot afford to sell for such small figures. The only chance would arise where a small country shopkeeper, with no such worries as high rent and rates has bought the article privately for a price which may be small, but adequate in the eyes of the seller.

In case every collector immediately rushes to the country, it should be pointed out that this course is no longer feasible as most country dealers, intoxicated by the vision of high prices paid in the metropolitan salerooms, send most of their articles to auction. These latter sources are still attentive to their regular customers, of course, so lower priced articles are still perfectly possible. It is for this reason, namely, the wide difference in prices of the same article but from different origins, that the wide price brackets are given.

A good quality Tudor apostle spoon today sells for around £500, $1,400. It should be stated immediately that this and all the following prices and values are actual *dealers' prices*, and not saleroom figures, as these are frequently confusing and do not give an accurate picture of values, at any rate as far as antique silver is concerned. Elizabethan and Carolean spoons command between £300 and £450, $850–1,250 for apostle terminals depending on age, quality and condition. Maidenhead terminals of this era are somewhat rarer and might cost upward of £350, $1,000. Sealtops are the most common terminal encountered and would fetch up to £250, $700. Sliptops sell at around £400, $1,100 for Elizabethan specimens and up to £300, $850 for the Stuart examples. Charles II sealtops fetch between £150 and £250, $425–700 depending on condition, date and quality of terminal. All the prices quoted are for London-made spoons: provincial specimens are lower in value, possibly by as much as half in some cases, but are also good articles to acquire as they are frequently of fine workmanship and attract investors with a limited budget.

Of the more uncommon terminals, lion sejants of London origin are priced at between £350 to £500, $1,000–1,400 for Elizabethan specimens, and

Top

George III 'wing-shaped' filigree caddy-spoon: the ribs composed of scrolling filigree segments and with a light cable gadroon around edge. Wire-loop handle. Unmarked, circa 1800.
(3½" in length).

George III large oval bowl caddy-spoon: with short 'Old English' bright-cut handle, and engraved in the bowl with 'wriggle' ornament. By John Beldon, London, 1795. This spoon was formerly in the collection of her late Royal Highness, the Princess Royal.
(2¾" in length).

Centre

George III bright-cut 'jockey-cap' caddy-spoon: enriched on the peak with foliate motifs, the cap segmented and bright-cut on the crown. By T. W. Matthews, London, 1808. Fully marked on upperside of peak.
(2½" in length, by 1½" in diameter).

George III 'hand' caddy-spoon: of light gauge metal, struck in a die to simulate the 'fingers'. With bright-cut 'cuff' handle. By Josiah Snatt, London, 1805. In the first edition the writer wrongly attributed this to Joseph Sanders. This was the result of another Jackson error; there is a John Saunders in the Plate Register at Goldsmiths' Hall, circa 1775, but there are two Snatts: Josiah, of 4 Fan Street, Aldersgate Street, entered in January 1798, who was working to circa 1823, and Susanah, presumably his wife, also of the same address, entered in 1817. (Her mark is SS in a cut-corner rectangle.)
(3" in length).

Bottom

George III silver-mounted small stag-cowrie shell forming caddy-spoon, with 'separated' fiddle-pattern handle. By Matthew Linwood, Birmingham, circa 1790. Silver-mounted specimens are never fully marked, at best, they might have a maker's mark and a lion passant.
(3" in length).

Victorian cast 'mussel-shell' caddy-spoon: the silver-gilt handle formed as cast 'lily-leaf' tendril. By Francis Higgins, London, 1852.
(3" in length).

From the collection of Rev. W. A. Hepher.

Top

George III 'fist-hand' caddy-spoon: a very unusual variation of the 'hand' specimens; the deep bowl with finely shaped 'fingers' and with 'Old English' handle. By Eley and Fearn, London, 1800. This specimen ante-dates all the other 'hand' caddy-spoons by five years, and is, moreover, by the above makers and not Josiah Snatt, who appears to have monopolised the type.
(3½″ in length).

George III 'medicine spoon' type caddy-spoon: formed as an oval bowled, shortened stem specimen, with slender 'Old English' handle. By Thomas Nash, London, circa 1760-65. This type of spoon is generally accepted to have been the first type of caddy-spoon as opposed to the perforated bowl ladles which were suspended on the outside of the 'Rococo tea-vases'. Between circa 1755 and 1760-65 there was no really satisfactory method of tea-measurement and it was then that the 'medicine-spoon' was adapted for use.
(3½″ in length).

George III oval elliptical bowl caddy-spoon: with short 'heart-shaped' handle. By William Pugh, Birmingham, 1807. This type is known as the 'fish-type' as it greatly resembles the very rare 'Carp' specimen also by this maker; the difference being that this specimen is completely plain, and the other is repoussé with 'fish-scales' and fins.
(3″ in length).

Centre

George III sideways oval bowl caddy-spoon: enriched in centre with 'simulated filigree' ornament. With separated 'Old English' bright-cut handle. by Cocks and Bettridge, Birmingham 1809. The 'filigree' is actually created by being struck in a die.
(2½″ in length).

George III 'tulip bowl' caddy-spoon: the serrated edge bowl engraved in the centre with 'basketweave' motif; with curling shaped bright-cut handle. By Cocks and Bettridge, Birmingham, 1817.
(3″ in length).

Bottom

George III silver-gilt caddy-spoon: known as the 'Roman leaf' the bowl cast and with 'broken branch' loop handle. By Phipps and Robinson, London, 1818. The term 'Roman leaf' has been adopted to describe the classical lines of the bowl which resemble a Roman lamp.
(3″ in length).

George III circular bowl caddy-spoon with 'star-shaped' filigree panel in centre. Bright-cut 'Old English' type handle. By Samuel Pemberton, Birmingham, 1799.
(3″ in length).

George III semi-ovoid caddy-spoon: the conical bowl pierced as 'tea infuser'. With 'fiddle-pattern thread handle'. By Eley and Fearn, London, 1805.
(3″ in length).

£300 to £400, $850-1,100 for Stuart examples of the James I—Charles I period. Moor's head specimens are very uncommon, and might realise anything between £300 to £500, $850-1,400 each.

Something should be said of saleroom buying. Spoons can be deceptive articles unless one really understands the 'pitfalls', not only about 'fakes' (of which more will be said below) but also about marks and general condition, and a good price might depend on one or all of these factors. This specialised knowledge is available to the dealer, who, wishing to assist and interest his customers, will impart it willingly, but is not so obvious to the newcomer bidding against the dealers. While it is not desired to dissuade members of the public from buying in the open saleroom (many fine acquisitions are made there, often of great interest) care should be exercised by beginners, as the saleroom is a highly complex organisation dominated by erudite, and occasionally sardonic, people who might influence a novice to overbid them on poor quality articles.

Attention should be paid to the terminals on apostle, lion sejant and sealtop spoons: there are a few (very few) forged specimens in circulation which have had rough cast terminals soldered on to genuine sliptop spoon stems, done at a time when an Elizabethan sliptop spoon was of little consequence. Careful scrutiny, however, can reveal the solder line where the two pieces are joined. The genuine article has either the 'V-shaped' notch of the London examples or the 'lap-joint' of the provincial specimens. At this juncture, it must be stated that the Goldsmiths' Company is an extremely watchful body with sensitive 'feelers' throughout the trade and any fraudulent or suspicious article is immediately impounded and destroyed. There are, in fact, very few outright 'fakes' in the open market, and most of these are so painfully obvious to all but the most unseeing collector, that would-be investors need have no great fear of them. A little study will tell them what to look for and what to avoid.

Unless the spoon is of provincial origin, it ought to have the full series of marks struck in the proper marking position. Collectors should familiarise themselves with the early marking sequence, and it is recommended that they acquire a copy of 'Jackson'—*English Goldsmiths and their marks,* first published by Batsford in 1921 and subsequently reprinted on two occasions. A new lithographed edition has recently appeared. Serious investors could also purchase Commander and Mrs. How's wonderful *English and Scottish Silver Spoons,* printed in 1952, and quite expensive, but when preparing to spend appreciable sums in a new medium, such an outlay would be well justified.

Spoons, in many instances, have had a good deal of use, and this tends to diminish the gauge of the bowl, if not actually destroying the rim. The difference in price between a spoon which has a massive bowl and one which possesses a thin bowl might be as much as £100, $280, or even more in the very early specimens. Collectors should scrutinise the bowl for 'fire marks': these are the remaining vestiges of repair work, usually to strengthen or straighten the rim of the bowl, and while they are not important in themselves, they serve to indicate the fact that there has been some weakness to the bowl, and might thus dissuade purchase. If the article is a very rare type this attention can be overlooked, otherwise it should be seriously regarded.

The trefid terminal arrived with the Restoration and early specimens are not only attractive but well made in heavy gauge metal, usually with fine deep struck marks. Good specimens should command between £150 to £200, $420-560 each. A set of six (similar to those illustrated) is rare and might cost up to £750, $2,000. Another interesting type is the late Stuart 'laceback' which combines a trefid stem with a die-struck bowl enriched with foliate or floral motifs. This might cost between £50 and £120, $140-330 if of fine state. A good quality trefid teaspoon partially marked is worth £30, $85 and a fully marked specimen might cost as much as £75, $200. Even fine state George I 'rat-tail' spoons are fetching £15, $40 today.

Picture-back teaspoons are now attracting attention from many sources and sets tend to be somewhat prohibitive in price, but individual spoons with most of the famous motifs are a 'better buy' at about £12 to £20, $33-56 each, and it is perhaps more advisable to concentrate on these. Spoons by the famous makers, Lamerie, Storr and the Bateman Family are good investments, but only specimens by the latter are found in any appreciable quantity. Lamerie tableware is very uncommon and those few articles which reach the saleroom are usually acquired by avid purchasers for high sums. A single Lamerie spoon might bring as much as £75, $200.

A sure indication that the caddy-spoon (long considered below notice as a 'trifle') has arrived as a good medium for investment is that the salerooms are advertising single specimens as forthcoming attractions. These little articles were very undervalued until the end of the second World War. Undoubtedly the existence of a collecting society has aided the rise in interest, and consequently the prices, but the medium has enough allure in its own right to induce investment. The detailed analysis of the rare types outlined elsewhere should serve as a guide to availability and type, but even the ordinary caddy-spoon has shown a marked increase in price over the past few years.

The 'classic' examples are costly, but not more so than comparably rare larger spoons: an 'eagle's wing' might bring £100, $280 and a fish £200 to £250, $560–700 but care should be exercised in the case of the latter, as a few specimens have been noted where an example of the 'fish-type' illustrated in colour has been subsequently embossed with 'scale-motifs' and this can be detected if the embossing covers the marks, or rather goes through the handle (the marks are usually on the underside of the handle) to disfigure the marks. The 'fins' too, are soldered on (in the real specimens they are part of the bowl) and 'solder-lines' should be looked for. The majority of the plainer varieties, with the exception of the 'simulated filigree' specimens, range between £15 and £25, $40–70 and the latter cost about £30 to £40, $85–110 each. Plain bowls of the early 19th Century are about £10 to £15, $28–40 each. Collectors should avoid repaired handles and thin bowls with 'fire-marks'.

What then are the prospects for the future? It is very difficult to forecast trends in the realms of antiques—there are so many aspects to take into consideration—a momentary 'war-scare' lasting only a few weeks, might throw the delicate mechanism into confusion; a much-feared 'world-slump' could affect prices for years to come. If the general trend of prosperity and tranquillity continue, and there is hope that it will, the English Spoon at any rate, should continue to increase in value, especially if interest is maintained and developed, with new buyers entering the field. There is still a great potential in this enormously wide medium.

Top
George II cast silver-gilt 'Leaf and Bee' Teaspoon:
  Maker: Isaac Duke, London, circa 1740. The stem with cast 'insects', the bowl with chased foliage.
  4¼″.

Centre
George II 'Whiplash' handle Saltspoon: Probably of Scottish origin, circa 1740. (Unmarked.) With contemporary crest on back of bowl.
  4″.

Bottom.
George II silver-gilt Punch Ladle:
  Maker: Edward Aldridge, London, 1744. Formed as rocaille sea-shell with matt-chased enrichment. Boxwood handle.
  14″.

ARTICLES IN SILVER MOUNTS

George III cowry-shell: formed as a wig-caster with screw-off 'swivel-lid'. Bright-cut and engraved with foliate motifs. Unmarked, circa 1770.
(2½″ in diameter.)

George III olive-shell: formed as a snuffbox cut vertically and silver-mounted. The rim bright-cut and engraved and with plaque for initials. Unmarked circa 1790.
(3″.)

The post-mediaeval preoccupation with silver-mounted vessels was most probably the result of the lamentable isolation which had separated most Europeans from the rest of the world, chiefly through poor travelling communications. It was therefore entirely natural that the Renaissance should have brought a feeling of restlessness in its wake and the desire to become better acquainted with the romantic products of mysterious and far-off lands. Adventurous explorers brought fabulous natural substances back to a marvelling public: ostrich eggs from Asia and North Africa, nautilus shells from the Fiji Islands, the tapering left tooth of the male Arctic narwhal whale —for centuries believed to be the fabled 'unicorn horn' which symbolised early Christianity—and rock-crystal, elephant tusks and coconut shells from The Indies.

The art-starved goldsmiths allowed their imagination full rein: the unicorn horn was transformed into a tall cylindrical vessel which was thought to have power to prevent cramps, epilepsy and poisoning, and which would sweat and steam if the drink therein was poisoned. This magical container, therefore, was enriched with further 'unicorn-motifs', the base, ornamentation and terminal all consisted of unicorns. The nautilus shell—in life occupied by an ugly marine animal of the octopus family—was stripped of its outer shell and was revealed as a shimmeringly beautiful vessel; this was mounted into a silver-gilt frame consisting of *marine rocaille* themes: Father Neptune supporting the shell on his head, or surmounting it astride a sea-horse.

There was no shortage of rock-crystal; the natural product was mined in Europe as well as in Asia, and its common occurrence in rocks among Alpine glaciers led to the ancient belief that it was a kind of congealed water, hence the name 'crystal' from the Greek word defining 'ice'. The material has been in use for decorative purposes since the Mycenean period and is capable of receiving elaborate enrichment: some of the finest Renaissance carvings emerged from the substance. In post-Reformation times, after the destruction of many ecclesiastical monstrances, fragments of cylindrical rock-crystal were re-mounted in silver and turned into personal containers such as 'marriage caskets' given as wedding gifts to the bride.

Elephant or rhinoceros tusks were fashioned into breathtakingly beautiful ivory vessels: one superb specimen was sold at the famous Rothschild Sale in April 1937. It was a gem of gothic ornament and was mounted as a gateway composed of multi-turreted towers supported on 'flying buttresses' to embrace the main body of the massive horn. The tail was supported on its own pedestal and the jewelled lid was surmounted by a cast 'warrior' terminal. Such was the inactive state of the antiques market in the years immediately before the Second World war that this magnificent early 16th Century vessel was sold to an English dealer for £260!

The ostrich egg, though somewhat fragile, was nevertheless an ideal container: it was large enough to accommodate a goodly amount of liquor, was easily workable and, moreover, the pale-straw colour of the shell set the silver or gilt mounts off to perfection. Some eggs were mounted as tankards with lids made from another piece of shell, others were of the 'standing cup' variety—one early English 17th Century specimen stands on a base formed as three ostrich legs, with the figure of an ostrich surmounting the lid—with delicate 'strapwork' mounts to encompass the egg-shell.

So much for a general European survey: the earliest silver-mounted articles known in England are undoubtedly the Anglo-Saxon drinking vessels made from ox or buffalo horns or elephant tusks. From the beginning, the silver mounts were attached to the vessel by means of serrated fringes which helped to anchor the metal to the natural substance. Jackson in his *Illustrated History* remarks on this: 'There is one remarkable feature: the small finely cut *dancette* or zigzag moulding which borders the bands and triangles of the mouthpiece and terminal; an antetype of one of the details frequently found in plate of the latter part of the 17th Century, and sometimes referred to as peculiar of that period, but, in fact, one that we find used on many occasions at varying intervals between the Anglo-Saxon and the late Stuart periods'. In Stuart enrichment, the type is known as 'vandyke edging'.

In the great *Bayeux Tapestry*, the scene which depicts King Harald drinking with his Anglo-Saxons at Bosham contains two drinking horns—one in actual use—which have these characteristic silver mounts, namely, the lip-mount and the terminal at the tail; under a strong glass', the serrated rim may be discerned. The mediaeval period produced silver-mounted horns which possessed attractive bird's claw or animal paw feet, in addition to the other mounts, a feature which permitted the vessel to stand full of liquor until required. The terminals consisted of human, animal or grotesque monsters' heads, or ball-terminals. Some specimens bore engraved contemporary mottoes on bands encircling their middles, or the owner's name around the rim.

The most favoured of all the 'natural substance' vessels was the coconut: the word '*coco*' in both the Spanish and Portuguese languages signifies 'a grinning face'. This is taken to refer to the face-like appearance of the base of the shell, rarely seen, as the portion having the 'eyes' or 'branch-attachments' is frequently cut away because of possible weakness at this spot. The species of nut known as the *Cocos nucifera* was first noted by the Portuguese in India, indeed, many of the early writers knew it as 'The Nut of India'. The Portuguese historian Oviedo Y Valdes (1478–1557) in his extensive work *La General y natural historia de las Indias* (translated by Richard Eden in 1555) says the following: 'This frute was cauled Cocus for this cause, that, when it is taken from the place where it cleaueth there are seen two holes, and aboue them two other naturall holes, which altogether, doo represent the gesture and fygure of the cattes cauled *Mammone*, that is, munkeys, when they crye: which crye the Indians caule *coca*'.

Although it was extremely brittle to work on, the shell, when stripped of its outer husk and polished, could accept intricate carving, and Elizabethan specimens with fine enrichment were mounted into large standing cups. These greatly resemble silver vessels, in fact, it is believed that most silver cups which have 'straps' around the body were originally mounted with eggs or shells which were either damaged or destroyed and were subsequently replaced by metal bowls. The nuts were carved with a variety of themes: scenes from the Old and New Testaments, elaborate battle scenes, and occasional composite panels, as on a superb cup where there are three panels depicting (a) The Monogram of Queen Elizabeth I, (b) the Porcupine Crest of the Sidney Family, and (c) some military trophies. As the date of the cup is 1586—the year of Sir Philip Sidney's death—there may be some commemorative intention.

The silver mounts, of which there were generally three, were formed as bowed straps secured at the collar and base by means of 'three-lugged' rivets. All the mounted vessels were thus secured. The earlier examples stood on 'trumpet' bases, but the late 16th Century specimens of plain type sometimes had a baluster silver stem and a conical foot. Some early Elizabethan coconut cups took the form of 'flagons': the vessel then acquired a plain 'S-shaped' handle and a cast thumbpiece—in effect it resembled a 'flagon-tankard' in almost every way, except that the bowl was a silver-mounted nutshell—and was surmounted by a cast figure terminal.

From the Munro Collection in the Henry E. Huntington Library and Art Gallery: San Marino, California.
Elizabeth I coconut cup: silver-mounted. By the London maker CB in Monogram (Jackson page 106, line 6) 1586. Engraved on the three panels with (a) the Monogram of Queen Elizabeth I, (b) the Porcupine crest of the Sidney Family (whose home was the celebrated Penshurst Place which eventually descended to the Shelley Family, of whom the poet Shelley was a scion) and (c) some military trophies.
(Height 7″.)

There were also a few natural shell cups made from other vegetable material: the fruit known as the *gourd* has an irregularly shaped shell and originated in Asia Minor; a small number of gourd-cups are found in 16th Century inventories. There is a fine specimen of this type in the Victoria and Albert Museum which has painted 'moresque' motifs around the rim and a normal Elizabethan mount. The Exhibition of Art Treasures from Vienna held in London in 1949 displayed a very rare silver-mounted nut-shell: this was of the *Seychelle Palm Nut* variety and had been given by the Prince of Bantam in Java in 1602 to a Dutch admiral. The Roman Emperor Rudolf II (1552–1612) who was the greatest collector of his age, and for whose museums agents scoured the world, acquired the shell for no less than four thousand guilders and gave it to the Augsburg goldsmith Anton Schweinberger to mount. It was set in a silver-gilt frame borne by two tritons and decorated with reliefs of tritons and nereids, the cover surmounted by Neptune on a sea-horse.

From the collection of Maurice Newbold, Esq.
George I gourd ladle: silver-mounted. The elliptical rim engraved with the following inscription: 'There was a man that ow'd me spleen, and what he had I have again' and with the owner's name: 'Tho. Giles, 1726'. With simple loop handle. Unmarked.
(5″ by 2½″.)

Early George II coconut cup: silver-mounted with strapwork enrichment on rim and base, on high domed foot and with 'harp-shape' handles. Mounted with two contemporary plaques bearing the Arms of the Vernon Family of Chester and the cypher of Mary Venables Vernon, first wife of George Vernon, Esq., who assumed the title of Baron Vernon of Haslington in 1762. Unmarked, circa 1730.
(6″ high by 4″ in diameter.)

Coconut cups were popular with many European nations as well as the English and were made as late as the early 19th Century, but gradually lost their magnificence over the years. The later specimens, as in the superlative honey-coloured George II specimen shown, were of severely plain form: the example mentioned here possessed bands of pierced strapwork rising from the cast domed foot and descending from the rim. It was completely unmarked but bore contemporary engraved plaques decorated in the Hogarthian manner with foliate cartouches of architectural form and shell and 'classical mask' terminals on a diaper-motif ground, which, together with the cypher of a noble Chester family, identified it as of circa 1730 provenance. There was also a series of plain coconut cups with silver rims or occasionally with a silver lining: these were generally by the famous 'novelty silversmiths' of London, Phipps and Robinson, circa 1790–1816.

Nuts were not, however, the only popular silver-mounting media of the 17th and 18th Centuries: the Stuarts and Georgians alike loved exotic sea-shells. It is not known exactly when the shell of the stag cowry became fashionable as a mount for snuffboxes, nutmeg graters, feeding 'pap-boats', etc., but certainly the cowry has had a reputation as a charm against the evil eye, an amulet for fertility, and an insurance for long life and subsequent resurrection since time immemorial. The shell was separated from its 'teeth', that is, the base of the animal, and mounted with a flat snugly fitting lid, often beautifully enriched with bright-cutting or engraving; sometimes, the 'teeth' were mounted back into the box and formed part of the lid, thus retaining the original form.

There are hundreds of varieties of cowrie shells, all subtly different, but the majority of shell-mounted boxes emanating from the last decade of the 17th Century onwards are either of the *Cypraea Pantherina* group which originated from the Red Sea or the *Cypraea Arabica* which came from the Indian Ocean. In fact, it is difficult to 'pin' the cowry down to any one positive location as it was almost certainly passed from hand to hand by the 'caravan men' who journeyed through the deserts—specimens have been found as far from civilisation as the Gobi Desert—but it is believed that most come from the Indo-Pacific regions, being warm water molluscs.

George III provincial silver-mounted cowry-shell: formed as a sauceboat on an oval collet foot with lip, rim and double-scroll handle. Maker's mark only: Langlands and Robertson, Newcastle, circa 1790. (5½″ by 2½″ by 3″ high.)

Another attractive exotic shell which produced fine snuffboxes was the beautifully marked *Oliva Porphyria*, or olive-shell: this pale brown specimen was of the elongated kind which resembles a 'cone' without actually belonging to its group. It originated in Panama, and the markings, if viewed from below, look like a range of mountain peaks. Yet a third type of shell which took kindly to silver-mounting was the *Conus* variety. It is occasionally encountered, cut horizontally, and placed into a frame to form a Caddy spoon; Matthew Linwood of Birmingham appears to have specialised in this 'allied material', as a number of interesting spoons of both the conus and cowrie shell groups have been noted.

The conus-shell is formed as a tightly rolled cylinder, the top coming to a sharp point; the markings are not unlike those of the olive-shell, but the colouring is of a deeper reddish-brown hue. There are varieties of this group which are dangerous to man, and in fact, one specimen of the species *Conus geographus,* as this particular variety is known, is in the British Museum collection and is known to have killed a man by injecting him with its poison.

Silver-mounted glassware is among the most useful as well as possibly the most decorative group of all, and, of course, the most obvious examples fall within that classification which includes vessels for domestic use: the cruet and its serving bottles, the tea-caddy, the sugar caster, the decanter frame and the sugar bowl. The cruet in the early days was simply a small bottle or vial for liquids: the 14th Century Benedictine chronicler Ranulf Higden (circa 1299–circa 1363) in his famous *Polychronicon,* written up to 1344, describes the function of the vessel: 'A Cruette of gold with bawme (balm) brennenge in hit'—this was most probably a sanctuary lamp—and the great 17th Century lexicographer Randle Cotgrave (died 1634) the author of the first French/English dictionary, published in 1611, defined the French word 'Goutteron' thus: 'A Violl, or Cruet wherein Oyle, or Vinegar is serued to the table'.

The early domestic cruets do not appear to have survived, but are generally believed to have resembled the sacramental vessels used in the mass for wine and water. The earliest English domestic examples come from the first decade of the 18th Century, but are very uncommon at this date: Cripps in his *Old English Plate* refers to a Queen Anne cruet-stand by Benjamin Pyne, dated 1706 which contained two glass bottles with plain silver caps to serve as stoppers as well as three shaped casters with pierced tops. The superb Huguenot octagonal cruet frames are famous and normally comprised massive 'stepped' lids with scrolling handles standing away from the bottles, and the later Georgian examples emerged as finely cut glass bottles of 'shouldered type' with elegantly flowing 'Adam style' mounts.

George III four-bottle Decanter Cruet: of elongated cruciform type, with thread border on handle and on wooden base. With four contemporary cut-glass decanters. By Paul Storr, London, 1800. This is characteristic of the early Storr productions, when his apprenticeship to the Anglo-Swedish silversmith Andrew Fogelberg still restrained his style; the opulence and magnificence of his later work did not show itself until the Regency period.
(12″ by 6″.)

A number of fine cut-glass tea caddies have been noted: the finest examples were undoubtedly the magnificent deep-blue Bristol rectangular containers which would have incised 'star or foliate' motifs and silver or silver-gilt mounts consisting of acanthus or other foliate forms of decoration and pierced rim bases. Some wonderful caddies possess silver 'sleeves' of pierced form which depict 'worthies' of the mid-18th Century—one marvellous pair of these was sold in the famous Dunn-Gardner Collection sale in April 1902, which depicted famous actors of the era in their greatest roles: Macklin in the character of 'Shylock', King as 'Lord Ogleby' in *The Clandestine Marriage* at Drury Lane, David Garrick in the character of 'Macbeth' and other well-known contemporary figures in the theatrical world—on all eight sides of the frame. The glass was of the sapphire-blue type, and the regard in which these wonderful caddies were held is indicated by the price which they fetched: £380 ($1,100), at a time when (in the same sale) a pair of Lamerie tea-caddies were sold for £280 ($800), a pair of Charles I silver-gilt standing cups dated 1633 for £55 ($155), and an Elizabethan goblet dated 1583 for £235, ($660)!

Another pair of glass-mounted tea caddies noted were of the rectangular curved-side variety which bulge towards the top, much more common in silver examples of the 1760's; these glass specimens were mounted on vandyke edge bases, with scrolling feet and surmounted by silver lids rising to a dome. They were cut in the 'flat-cut' ornament and were dated circa 1770. Silver-mounted caddies continued until the first decade of the 19th Century, but became heavier, with 'hob-nail' enrichment, and mostly of oval shape. Most of the earlier mounted specimens were unmarked, but full series of hall-marks are encountered from circa 1800.

Silver-mounted cut-glass casters, or 'cruet bottles' as they were sometimes known, are found from the 1740's; they imitate the silver vessels of the period,

44

and are generally cut in 'scale-facet' or other geometrical patterns. The pierced tops are silver, but being intended for use with glass bottles, were not usually marked. The mounted sugar bowl is somewhat rarer and is not encountered until the end of the 18th Century, when delightfully bright-cut and engraved rims appear.

Pair of George III silver-mounted cut-glass Oil and Vinegar bottles: of pear-shape, the pourers formed as silver-gilt 'Eagles' Heads' and with double-scrolling handles attached. By John Linnit and William Atkinson, London, 1813.

(7″ high by 3″ in diameter at base.)

The mounted decanter frame emanated from the early part of the 19th Century: it was made of a thin plate of silver mounted on a wooden base with a solid silver frame enriched with 'reeding' or gadrooning. It might be of oval elliptical form or more commonly, of the cruciform-rectangular shape shown. The bottles were mostly.of the square-shouldered type and were heavy 'hob-nail' cut. Owing to the sacrifice of form to prismatic brilliance, cut-glass gradually lost its artistic value and emerged as massive containers completely covered with broken surfaces. A final evolution of the silver-mounted cut-glass vessels noted was a dainty little 'skep beehive' honey-pot: the body was of finely moulded and 'diamond-point' cut-glass, the silver-gilt base and mounts enriched with the 'ribbon and wreath' motif and with a charming cast 'bee' terminal. The maker was Robert Salmon and the date on the mount 1791.

Early seventeenth century 'marriage casket': formed of cylindrical portion of rock-crystal mounted with panels of finely translucent tortoiseshell, and silver-mounted. The rim contemporarily enriched with the engraved ornament known as the 'horizontal vandyke edge' which consists of cut-away 'teeth' of foliate form. On four small 'ball' feet. The hinges of three-lugged type and with snap catch. Unmarked, circa 1620.

(2½″ by 2⅜″ in diameter).

THE VESSEL

From the Miles Collection in the Wadsworth Atheneum, Hartford, Connecticut, USA.

Elizabeth I Tigerware Jug: By William Cocknidge, London, 1576. Made in German stoneware with English silver-gilt mounts. These jugs, with silver plate, were favoured prizes in the state lotteries, the first held in 1569, to finance the repair of the ports of the kingdom. Height: 9¾″.

By far the largest group of silver vessels consists of articles 'raised from the flat', that is, beaten up by hand from a flat sheet of metal into a variety of shapes. These may be spherical, cylindrical, globular and ogee, and embrace such widely differing articles as flagons, tankards, standing salts, and teapots on the one hand, and minor items including containers for mustard, pepper and sugar, to name but a few, on the other. The term 'vessel' itself is the diminutive of the Latin *'vas'*—a vase or urn—which implies the capacity to contain.

While it is proposed to examine certain articles closely, giving due consideration to their sociological and historical origins, it is not the purpose of this survey to scrutinise *all* types of vessels. Some, like the mazer-bowls, drinking-horns and ewers and dishes of the late Mediaeval period, are beyond the means of the ordinary investor-collector, being of 'museum interest' only, but there are individual items which command attention, and thus deserve to be singled out for analysis and evaluation.

The tankard is one of the oldest known drinking vessels which has undergone many changes and yet has remained basically unaltered in style over thousands of years. The earliest examples are undoubtedly the specimens dating from the Iron Age, a splendid version of which, paradoxically made in bronze, is in the London Museum, having been taken from the Thames at Brentford in Middlesex, and is known as 'The Brentford Tankard'. This is a massive vessel—it must have held six pints at least—and is in reality an oaken bucket formed of wooden staves grooved into a dowelled base and mounted with three overlapping hoops of bronze, secured by a series of bronze pins and set in the centre of the body with a small D-shaped handle. The top is lidless, but in all other respects the article is a true forerunner of the later tankards in that it was made to contain liquids, is of cylindrical form, handled for easier grasping, and finally has a turned rim in order that the drinker should not cut himself on the sharp edge; it is dated circa 100-50 B.C.

Ale was the national beverage in the middle ages: references to the liquor occur in English literature as far back as 1300 in the Anglo-Danish romantic saga *Havelok* written in a Lincolnshire dialect. A character says: 'fil me a cuppe of ful god *ale*'. In the 1535 account of the Chronicles of Scotland, mention is made not only of the drink but also of the vessel in which it was served: 'of wyne and aill *tankard* thame sic ane fill'. The early ale was a fermented liquor made from malt and water but without hops. The hopplant *Humulus Lupulus* was known in England well before the Reformation, but its use was frowned upon by some brewers as constituting adulteration. Wholesale use of the plant increased on the advent of a colony of Flemish immigrants who established their hopfields in Kent circa 1524.

The earliest English published work on the culture of hops is an old 'blackletter' pamphlet printed in 1574 by Reynolde Scot and entitled: 'A Perfite Platforme of a Hoppe Garden', and gives 'necessarie instructions . . . for all men to have which in any wise to doe with hops'.

Scholars have long speculated on the origins of the term 'tankard': some assert that it refers to the wooden tubs holding three gallons which were in use in the 11th Century to carry domestic drinking water, others that it denotes several varieties of large vessels from which quantities of liquor were once poured into smaller and more convenient vessels for personal use, but the first mention of the tankard *as a vessel in its own right* occurs in the writings of the noted English religious reformer John Wycliffe (1320-1384) in which he speaks (*inter alia*) of an 'amfer', and explains that this is 'a gloss (glass) or vessel that sum men clepen a tankard', in other words, a glass vessel known as a tankard. The term 'amfer' is interesting in itself: it is probably a corruption of the word 'anap' or *hanap* which was an Anglo-Saxon term for a cup, bowl or basin, but which, from the 11th Century was used to describe the large drinking vessels used at ceremonial feasts by the presiding dignitary or visiting celebrity. An early 16th Century reference to the tankard occurs in the translation to Virgil's *Aeneid* by the celebrated Scottish poet and divine Gavin Douglas (1474–1522) who wrote in 1513 'a mekle tankert with wyne fillit to the throt'.

Most of the early tankards are silver-mounted and fashioned from horn, ivory, stone or Venetian glass. They do not resemble the later specimens, which are of narrow cylindrical or tapering form, but possess bulbous bodies and narrow necks with handles made from the same substance as the vessel itself; the mounts are generally silver-gilt with vandyke edges, that is, serrated 'feathered' edges which turn inwards to grasp the rim of the vessel. There are also bellied stoneware jugs of the 'Rhenish Tigerware' variety, so named because they are of German extraction with a rather mottled appearance. These too were silver-mounted with domed lids, the handles and bases enriched with chased and embossed 'masks and flowers' ornament. They emanated chiefly from the last quarter of the 16th Century.

The silver-mounted stoneware specimens were not, however, the only tankards extant: in his great *Illustrated History of English Plate* Jackson illustrates (figure 977) a 'flagon-shaped tankard', which is very similar in design to the ceramic and glass-mounted examples and dated 1567. This vessel is quite small, being no more than 7½″ in height; the capacity of the article was thus curtailed, and it was not until the arrival of the tall cylindrical 'flagon-tankards' that liquor in any appreciable quantity could be imbibed.

Many paintings, mainly still-life subjects by Dutch or Flemish artists, depict studies featuring a tall tankard: whether this motif reflects the widespread use of such articles, or was merely included to provide the artist with an exercise in delineation, is problematic. Certainly, it is difficult to differentiate between flagons for domestic use and vessels which may have been intended for 'show plate' only. The great cylindrical tankards which Charles Oman identifies as a pair of 'Livery Pots' in his important study of '*The English Silver in the Kremlin 1557–1663*' (Methuen 1961) are undoubtedly magnificent pieces made for ceremonial use, as they were sent by James I in 1615 as a 'goodwill gift' to the Patriarch Filaret, the father of the Russian Tsar Mikhail. On the other hand, a small bulbous tankard is also stated to be a 'Livery Pot' and this is a much more manageable size which would be eminently suited for domestic use; this latter specimen was dated 1571.

The Elizabethan tankards were enriched with a great variety of ornamental devices, embracing naturalistic floral, foliate and animal themes applied as engraving, chasing or embossing. There might be inverted acanthus foliage and stamped or cast rims consisting of gadroons or 'egg and dart' motifs, that

By courtesy of the Worshipful Company of Goldsmiths.

Left

Elizabeth I Flagon-tankard: parcel-gilt, engraved with running border of scroll foliage enclosed by interlacing straps and geometric motifs with rosettes and pellets on a matted ground. The foot enriched with a stamped lozenge pattern and spreading base moulding with an indented border. The thumbpiece is a classical bust in relief. Engraved on the cover with the following inscription: 'THE · GIFTE · OF · THOMAS · TYNDALE · BACHELAR · 1574 ·', enclosing the donor's Coat-of-Arms, and around the neck with TO · REMEMBAR · THE · POORE.

Maker: Robert Danbe, London, 1567.
7½″ in height.
Armourers and Braziers' Company Collection.

Right

Elizabeth I Cylindrical Tankard: silver-gilt. Finely engraved with floral scrolls enclosing the donor's Arms, the Tudor rose and portcullis, and inscribed Henry James Sydney Montagu. The cover surmounted by the donor's crest, a griffon's head erased. Given to Christ's College, Cambridge, by three brothers, the sons of Sir Edward Montagu.

Maker: IH, a bear passant below in a circle, London, 1597.
9⅞″ in height. Diameter of mouth: 3¼″.
Exhibited 'Treasures of Cambridge', Goldsmiths' Hall, 1959.

is, vertical ovolos separated by an 'arrow-like' pattern. The lids were domed and usually surmounted by a 'figure-terminal': Queen Elizabeth's inventory for March 1573 contains the following entry: 'Item oone white glasse wt. strakes (streaks) downright garnished wt. silver and guilt wt. a frulling lid chased, sitting ther upon a boy wt. a dagger in thoore hande and a schilde (shield) in thother'. The thumb-piece, or 'billet' or 'purchase' as it is variously known, might be formed as a cast gargoyle, a mermaid or a voluted scroll of intertwining acorns and oak-leaves.

Charles II York Tankard: the body repoussé with foliate motifs, the lid similarly decorated. On three ball feet and with double-scroll handle. Twin-ball thumbpiece. By William Mascall, York, 1666. Marked on base and lid. 6″ by 4½″ in diameter. Weight: 15 ozs.

The tankards of James I's reign were much the same in style as their Elizabethan predecessors, but in the first years of Charles I's rule, the vessel lost its bulbous lines and acquired a conical form which was topped by a flat projecting lid. This had a most attractive cast scroll thumbpiece known as the 'breaking wave' variety: the scroll began low on the lid and rose in a gentle volute to resemble a small sea wave. The earliest specimen of this type noted was dated 1619 and the latest 1645.

Commonwealth Porringer: Very plain Puritan in style, with scrolling handles. By WH Star above, pellet below, London, 1658. 4½″ in diameter by 3¼″ high. 10 ozs.

The Civil War with all the unhappiness which followed in its wake turned men's attention away from the pleasures of the table, and thus it was not until the early years of the Commonwealth that a new influence could be detected in the design of the contemporary tankard. This innovation had been heralded in church vessels of the Charles I era and consisted of a spreading foot to the tall communion flagons, which was known as a 'skirt' and served to steady the vessel against spillage. The silversmiths of the Commonwealth, looking around for a sober yet interesting motif which would satisfy both their customers and their Puritan masters, settled on this 'skirted foot' and subsequently all pre-Restoration tankards possessed it.

In the Art Treasures Exhibition at Christie's in 1932, a London dealer exhibited a small Commonwealth 'skirted' tankard dated 1649. It was made by James Plummer of York and was enriched with four panels matt-chased, that is, small dots punched over the surface to give a shallow relief of a broken texture, depicting the Temptation of Adam and Eve and Faith, Hope and Charity. There was a mass of contemporary inscriptions round the edge of the lid, round the top of the body and on the 'skirt' of the base, of which the following is but an extract: 'When this yow see remember me' and:

> A gift I show of what I owe,
> Accept the gift and so the giver;
> The gift is small, the giver not tall,
> Take here withall the hart and all.'
>
> And when in this a health you drinke,
> Drinke yr owne and please yr selfe;
> Thinke on God and praise his name
> For this good drinke, the giver of the same.'

At about this time, namely, the mid-Commonwealth—early Restoration period, foreign influences began to assail the hitherto complacent English

Charles II Tankard: of large size. The base with acanthus motif repoussé chasing, the lid with 'swirled rose' motif. Engraved with contemporary Arms. With cast twin-dolphin thumbpiece. By EN Conjoined, London, 1681. 6½″ by 5″ in diameter at base. 15 ozs.

silversmiths. The advent of the Renaissance more than a century before had, in its turn, introduced German and Italian motifs, and now it was the Dutch craftsmen who infiltrated their designs. Working to the commission of the Protector and subsequently the King, they produced new ornamental motifs incorporating the *flora and fauna* of their native country, including, among other things, floral themes such as tulips, poppies and carnations, and domestic animal subjects: horses, cows and similar mammals.

The Scandinavians too, were not inactive, and thus from the mid-1660's drinking vessels resembled their European cousins more than ever before. One interesting aspect of this interchange of ideas was the encroachment of Danish styles upon English provincial silver, mainly from Hull, Newcastle and York. The reason for this is plain: these cities were situated near the North Sea coast which borders with the west coast of Denmark, and adventurous Danish craftsmen journeyed to England to sell their wares. It was only a matter of time before the industrious English silversmiths adopted the new Scandinavian designs, and by the end of the decade tankards reflected both the Dutch and the Danish influence.

Thus, the body of the vessel was cylindrical with a slightly rounded base; the top of the lid was almost flat, and the three feet and the thumbpiece were formed as pomegranates. The enrichment consisted of either engraved 'tulip and lily' motifs or embossed 'tulip and acanthus' themes. Many of the specimens of this type possessed 'pegs', that is, actual pins set inside the body to serve as 'capacity measures' 'The 'peg-tankard' usually had eight pins, one above another, from top to bottom: if the vessel held two quarts, there was half a pint between each pin. The first person who drank emptied the tankard to the first peg, the second drank to the second peg, and so on. If the imbiber drank short of, or below the peg, he was obliged to drink again, and thus the company was liable to get drunk very quickly. The shortcoming is reflected in the injunction issued by St. Anselm, Archbishop of Canterbury in William Rufus's day (he died in 1109) to his priests: they were enjoined not to go to drinking bouts, nor to drink to pegs. This illustrates the antiquity of the custom of 'drinking to the peg'.

How the Danish tankards came to contain pegs is not known, but one thing is certain, the English 'peg-tankards' were somehow based on the Scandinavian examples, and most, as has been stated above, were of provincial origin, London-made specimens being rare. In the latter connection, it is interesting to note that one particular drinking toast commonly ascribed to Scandinavian countries has a barbaric history as well as being the root for the name of a type of vessel: the word is 'skol', and its etymology recalls the Celtic custom of drinking mead from the skull of a slain enemy. From this inhuman cult sprang a whole series of words, the majority of which are associated with drinking vessels: the German *'schale'* the Danish *'skaal'*, the French *'ecuelle'* (a porringer) even the English *'skillet'* all drew their common root from this practice. A James I tankard dated 1614 has been noted, the thumbpiece of which was formed as a skull, but this may have been symbolic of the 'frailty of man' rather than of the 'skull cult'. The rite appears to have been widespread until the eleventh century; the great Chronicler of the Lombards,

Queen Anne Tankard: of small size. On 'skirted' foot with rib around body, the domed lid with scrolling thumbpiece. By Nathaniel Lock, London, 1705. Fully marked on side and lid, and with maker's mark on handle. 5½″ by 4½″ diameter at base. 15 ozs.

Paulus Diaconus (circa 720–circa 800) in his work 'Historia gentis Lango-bardorum' says, 'Albin slew Cuminum, and having carried away his head, converted it into a drinking vessel, which kind of cup with us is called Schala'.

Following upon the 'peg-tankards', the next innovation was the cylindrical tapering species of the 1680 period. This type had skirted bases, stepped lids, that is to say not flat-topped, but slightly domed; cast thumbpieces, usually of the 'twin dolphin' variety, and finally, and most important, a band of repoussé vertical acanthus foliage around the base. The lids might be plain, or possess an embossed 'swirled rose' or similar floral motif.

Another foreign motif to enrich the late 17th Century tankards was the famous 'Chinoiserie' design: there appears to be no satisfactory explanation for the introduction of oriental influences into English silver, not, that is, at the commencement of the third quarter of the 17th Century; the widely held opinion that the motif originated on Chinese porcelain sent to England has never been fully confirmed, and, it must be admitted, historians are rather vague on the subject. It is probable that various traveller-explorers ventured to visit China, and on their return, being impressed with the intriguing designs they had encountered, commissioned articles bearing this form of enrichment.

The motifs included posturing Mandarin figures, exotic birds, figures sitting in an arbour, flowers and trees; the latest chinoiserie-enriched article noted was a tall tapering beaker dated 1713. The motif went into abeyance until the middle of the 18th Century when the noted English architect and landscape planner Sir William Chambers (1726–1796) staged a revival of oriental-inspired decorative themes. It should be pointed out, however, that Chinese motifs had been exploited earlier in the painting of both Watteau and Boucher, the celebrated French artists, who specialised in formal garden backgrounds in the chinoiserie manner. It is probable that Paul de Lamerie drew inspiration for his famous rococo chinoiserie, in which he excelled, from this source.

William Chambers, in his turn, laid out the gardens at Kew House (which subsequently became the famed Botanical Gardens) for the princess dowager Augusta, the widow of Frederick Prince of Wales. This work was effected between 1757–62 and the lofty Chinese Pagoda which still stands in the centre of the grounds was erected in 1761. The designers of the period were preoccupied with these oriental themes, and Thomas Chippendale issued a series of designs incorporating chinoiserie motifs in his superlative furniture. Chambers published a 'Dissertation on Oriental Gardening' in 1772; so popular was this work that the revival began in earnest: it is noted chiefly on silver tea-vessels of all kinds: kettles, caddies, and pots which date from circa 1760. There was a further resurrection of the motif in the early Victorian era when some massive pieces of generally inferior design were produced. There were, nevertheless, some notable exceptions: the charming little caddy-spoon by John Foligno dated 1841 is one outstanding example.

At the turn of the 17th Century, and for half a century after that, tankards retained their tapering cylindrical shape, but other subtle changes began to infiltrate: the lid acquired a domical form, the thumbpiece became an 'open-type' handle of pierced form rather than the cast scroll of the earlier specimens, and the body, as often as not, was encompassed by a 'rib' consisting of a moulded band which gave added strength to the vessel. In the mid 1750's the tankard assumed its most familiar shape, namely, the 'ogee' or bulbous form, in which the 'line' consists of moulded convex and concave curves, set on a high circular base, generally known as a 'collet' which is soldered to the 'hand-raised' body. The lid was acutely domical, with two or three 'steps' rising towards the apex.

A rare variation noted was the charming little half-pint tankard (see right) which is really a scaled down model of the large George II specimens. As the 18th Century drew to its close, yet another variety arrived: the tapering body was enriched with reeded bands, probably in imitation of the 'hoops' which encompass a barrel; the lid became quite flat and projected slightly over the rim of the vessel. The thumbpiece was attached to the handle by a flanged hinge and the handle itself became almost square, not the elaborate 'S-shaped' grip common to all the other tankards right through the centuries. It should be added that the feet of the early tankards were very often of the

Queen Anne set of three stirrup or posset cups: with heavy rims and circular collet feet and plain 'D' shaped handles. Engraved on front with Bacchus seated on a barrel and motto 'good fellowship' in a scrolling wreath. With contemporary initials. By John Chartier, London, 1712. The purpose of these cups can only be surmised. They may have been used in field sports, but fox hunting as such did not become popular until about 1750, although Lord Arundel kept a pack of foxhounds between 1690 and 1700; most probably, they were used for handing round 'posset' which is a drink of milk curdled with wine.
(2¼″ in diameter by 2¼″ high).

George III 'travelling candlestick': formed as deep spool-shaped pans and screw-in capitals of shortened baluster form. The two parts screw together for easy packing. Reeded rims. By Thomas Heming, London, 1777.
(4¾″ in diameter, weight: 10 ozs).

George II half-pint tankard: with 'tucked-foot' and rib circling body. The domed lid with 'heart-shaped' terminal on handle. By Walter Brind, London, 1750. Marked on base, in cover and with maker's mark on handle. This is not a mug, but a scaled-down tankard, and as such, is very rare indeed. Stuart specimens are occasionally noted, but Hanoverian examples are not.
(4¼″ high by 2¼″ in diameter, weight: 12 ozs).

George III pair oval cast saltcellars: with 'ribbon and wreath' borders and 'harp-shaped' handles, terminating in four claw feet, and with cast and chased acanthus-motif on base. By Matthew Boulton and John Fothergill, Birmingham, 1777. This partnership lasted from 1762 until 1780, and was, of course, begun before the Birmingham Assay-office was opened in 1773.
(4″ by 2½″, weight 8 ozs).

From the collection of H. A. Cooper, Esq.

Pair small George II trencher salts: of octagonal rectangular form, moulded spreading bases, and exceptional heavy gauge. By James Michellsone, Edinburgh, 1729.

(2¾″ by 2″, weight: 5 ozs. 11 dwts).

George I octagonal wine strainer: the handles pierced with floral geometrical motifs, the body with 'fleurs-de-lys'. Fully marked in bowl and with lion's head erased on both handles. By George Gillingham, London, 1718. Many fine strainers have been noted but few octagonal specimens.

(7″ overall, by 3″ in diameter).

George I oval fluted spoon-tray: engraved in centre with contemporary crest. By Joseph Barbitt, London, 1723. Fully marked: maker's mark in centre and lion's head erased and date-letter on rim.

(6½″ by 3½″, weight: 3 ozs. 10 dwts).

Bottom left

George II footed baluster cream-jug: of the 'pitcher' type on collet foot and with plain 'S' handle. By PM in trefoil, mullet above, circa 1730 (not known to Jackson).

(3⅜″ by 2″ in diameter, weight: 3 ozs. 10 dwts).

Bottom right

George II cast cream-jug: of oval rectangular form of four twisted rocaille scroll feet and with recurving handle set with the head of a grotesque creature. The sides matt-chased with scrolling cartouche and diaper and shell motifs around shaped rim and under lip. Engraved with contemporary crest. By Paul de Lamerie, London, 1735. A whole series of cream jugs by this illustrious maker shares the same features: heavy scrolling feet and grotesque animal handles. Some, like this specimen, are almost 'boat-shaped', others are typically 'ewer-shaped', but all are superbly conceived and of heavy gauge.

(3⅞″ by 2¼″ by 2¾″ high, weight: 5 ozs. 10 dwts).

From a private collection:

George II tapering Beaker: on moulded collet foot, with everting rim. By Isaac Cookson, Newcastle 1739. This vessel (as mentioned on page 56) is in the 'Scandinavian Taste'. Cookson was the Master of the more prolific maker of these 'Danish-inspired' vessels, John Langlands. 4½″ by 3″ in diameter at top.

'couchant lion' type with the same motif repeated on the lid, the animal forming the thumbpiece; this theme was probably a relic of the Renaissance.

The earliest form of the Beaker is believed to have originated in the Bronze Age, when pottery vessels of the well-known tapering form have been discovered in graves of the British and North European races; in Britain, a race of nomads emerging from the Low Countries invaded the Thames Estuary circa 1800–1500 B.C. They are known as the 'Beaker Folk' for the numerous beaker-like vessels found in their tombs. An early reference to the beaker as a silver vessel occurs in the Accounts of the Black Prince, Edward, Prince of Wales (1330–1376) where the entry for the year 1348 reads as follows: '35 *magne pecie argenti, vocate Bikers*', roughly translated: '35 large items of silver, known as Bikers'. The term took its original root from various sources: in Greek it was 'bikos'—a drinking bowl, in the Romance Languages, French and Italian respectively, it was '*pechier*' and '*bicchiere*'.

It was probable that the prototype beakers were not 'raised from the flat' as were many of the later examples, but merely rolled into cylinders by the silversmith, who then soldered the tubes along the seams, inserted discs of silver into the bases and gave the articles some form of primitive enrichment. The article developed into a fine vessel: the 16th Century specimens acquired a 'skirted' spreading base, and a slightly everting, that is, an outward turning, rim; thus, it was wider at the top than at the base. It experienced various enrichments: Jackson (page 683) illustrates a massive specimen dated 1496 which has a series of projecting ribs, which as he says, look like the 'farrier's nails used by a shoe-smith for horses'. Later examples were either plain or

embellished with applied ornament, such as the famous Mercers' Company beaker which bears a bust or portrait of the Blessed Virgin, which is the badge of the Company, or tall, 'everting rim' beakers on shallow ring bases decorated with lightly incised 'moresque' ornament: this form of embellishment is found primarily on Elizabethan articles and consists of intertwining scrolling motifs of foliate form based on Roman themes dating from the early time of the empire, and not, as is generally believed, on Arabian or Moorish influences.

The tall beakers gave way to shorter examples: some, very few indeed, were of the Charles I period, and were wrought as heavy gauge vessels of severely plain tapering type, but the remainder, emerging from the reign of

Charles II absorbed the full effusiveness of the Restoration, and achieved ebullient repoussé, floral and foliate enrichment. They attained everting rims of pronounced form, and heavier circular bases. These, in turn, were succeeded by slightly more bulbous specimens, tapering gently around the 'self-base', that is, the ring bases disappeared and the vessels stood on their own bottoms. They were usually scratch-engraved in the manner contemporary to the period, with typical 'amorini or cherub' designs and with engraved vandyke edges.

Some of these latter examples were cleverly fitted as 'campaign etuis', that is, utensils used by soldiers in the field, where compactness was essential, and consisting of interchangeable components: a series of implements, such as cutlery with screw-threads on the handle-union and only one handle, compressed containers for condiments—salt and pepper, corkscrews, toothpicks, napkin fasteners and spiceboxes, all fitted into a sharkskin case, ostensibly containing only the beaker.

Finally, there was a series of out-of-period copies based on Scandinavian designs: the preoccupation of the provincial silversmiths of the cities of Hull, Newcastle and York has been mentioned above: the third quarter of the 18th Century saw the advent of beakers also inspired by the same theme, and, strangely, also emanating from Newcastle, where one noted silversmith, John Langlands, wrought a number of beakers and tankards strongly reminiscent of the Danish taste. There were also a few London-made examples of similar type, but these were altogether heavier in conception, being on 'skirted' bases and with thick 'turnover' rims. The final development in this field was the 'reeded' or hooped variety, and this type of enrichment survived until the reign of George IV.

From a private collection:

George III plain tapering beaker: the front engraved with bright-cut oval cartouche containing contemporary monogram. By Hester Bateman, London, 1788. Height: 3½".

Pair Old Sheffield Plate Beakers: formed as reeded hooped barrel. Circa 1800. The inscription reads: 'Walter Brown, Lord Provost of Edinburgh, 1827–1829' and 'From Jas. Brown to W.B.'. 6" by 3½" in diameter.

George III Tumbler Cup: of heavy gauge and small size. By Peter and Jonathan Bateman, London, 1790. As is mentioned elsewhere, Peter and Jonathan worked together for only three months before the latter died, and 'hand-raised' articles from their partnership are very rare. The 'tumbler cup' as a type appears to have originated in the second half of the 17th Century, and curiously, most specimens of this period emanate from provincial assay-offices: Leeds, York, or Newcastle, and a few from Hull—one by Abraham Barachin of that city was sold in 1935, and was stated in the catalogue to be of Queen Anne origin and thus, in view of Jackson's remark that only one other example of Queen Anne Hull extraction was known to him, of very rare provenance—possibly because they were made for travellers between these cities and the metropolis. It has always been believed that these odd articles, with the bases heavier than the sides, were designed for use in carriages, as their form would prevent them from spilling their contents. 2½" in diameter by 2". Weight: 2 ozs.

Pair George III Tumbler Cups: of very heavy gauge, and finely balanced. By Peter, Anne and William Bateman, London, 1800. 2½" in diameter by 2". Weight: 6 ozs. 10 dwts (the pair).

Charles I Tankard: of tapering form and with 'breaking wave' thumbpiece on the flat lid. With donor's Arms and inscription. Given by Thomas Eden to Trinity Hall, Cambridge as a bequest.

Maker: Orb and Star in a plain shield, London, 1635.

7″ in height.

Exhibited 'Treasures of Cambridge', Goldsmiths' Hall, 1959.

From the Elizabeth B. Miles Collection, Cleveland, Ohio, USA.

Elizabeth I Wine Cup: With band of engraved decoration around centre of vessel and 'egg and dart' border on rim of foot. The name 'Thomas Legh' engraved near the top. By AK Conjoined, London, 1571. This cup was made for Thomas Legh whose estate, Adlington Hall, in county Cheshire, dates back to Henry VI. He was Sheriff of the County in 1587 and died in 1601. Legh descendents still reside at Adlington Hall. Ex Collection Lord Swaythling. Now on exhibition in Cleveland Museum of Art.

One of the first mentions of the Goblet occurs in the famous Arthurian romance '*Morte d'Arthur*', thought to have been written about 1400, which was finished by Sir Thomas Malory about 1470 and published by Caxton circa 1485; 'The kyngez cope-borde was closed in silver, In grete goblettez overgylte'. The goblet may be defined as 'a drinking cup of bowl-shape, without handles and sometimes on a foot, with or without cover'. In some Elizabethan specimens, it is difficult to separate the goblet from the chalice, as both resemble each other, the only marked difference being that the former has a broad V-shaped bowl, which it assumed at the end of the 16th Century. The Carolean versions seemed to 'grow upwards', suddenly possessing tall baluster stems, that is, pillar-like supports enriched with knops at intervals, and slightly everting deep 'reversed bell-like bowls' embossed with acanthus foliage, the base consisting of a concave disc similarly enriched; the type is no longer referred to as a 'goblet', it has become a 'wine cup'.

The Commonwealth produced its own variation: a 'font-shaped' cup on a spreading 'trumpet' foot, punched with primitive floral or foliate designs, and this type continued in use until the last quarter of the 17th Century. The 'trumpet-foot' was occasionally embellished with a form of crude ornament which consisted of matt-chased acanthus foliage.

The Mug is yet another article whose style was based upon ancient designs. A noted philologist has suggested that the word itself might be descended from the Welsh '*mwgl*'—a cup to drink in—while the earliest mention of it as a vessel occurs in 1570. The late Stuart specimen emerged as a globular-bodied pitcher with a vertical reeded neck and a reeded S-shaped handle, and which stood on a shallow rim foot. The surface was generally matt-chased or engraved with chinoiserie motifs.

It is fascinating to note that the prototype of this Stuart mug, which it almost exactly resembles, originated in Dynastic Egypt. Among the gold and silver plate of the Pharaoh Rameses II (1322 B.C.) now in the Metropolitan Museum of New York, is a vessel which, but for the missing rim foot,

could be the twin for the Charles II type. The shape may possibly be evolved from pottery variations which gained popularity because they could easily be 'thrown' on a potter's wheel, and a primitive S-shaped handle attached.

The majority of 17th Century mugs follow the design of the lidded tankards, with the exception, of course, that they lacked the massive handle which was necessary in order to provide a suitable anchorage for the thumbpiece of the lid. An interesting variant was the little 'beaker-shaped' mug common to the

From the Munro Collection in the Henry E. Huntington Library and Art Gallery: San Marino, California.

Pair Charles I wine cups: the bell-shaped bowls supported on tall baluster stems and conical bases. Engraved contemporary initials. By W. C., London. 1630.

From a private collection:
Charles II Wine Mug: of small size, tapering sides and with plain 'S-shaped' handle with heart-shaped terminal. Struck with maker's mark four times only, GS a device above, circa 1660–70. 2¾″ diameter at top by 2″. Weight: 2 ozs. 3 dwts.

mid 1670's which was of shortened form with a plain 'S-shaped' handle and usually unadorned.

The contemporary concept of enrichment consisted of several decorative principles: there was the 'flute' or vertical, curved or oblique parallel channel applied as a continuous motif around the lower half of the body; the 'reed', or almost touching thin parallel channel horizontally encircling the centre of the vessel, and often also added to the rim, base and handle as well. Some pieces were left plain, save for a flat-chased scrolling cartouche on the side which accommodated a cypher or a Coat-of-Arms.

The actual fashioning of the vessel was usually by 'hand-raising from the flat', but some mugs were made in the same manner as the early beakers (described above) being formed as cylindrical bodies with a disc inserted into the base and a simple handle added. Where 'hand-raising' was employed, the vessel achieved a graceful line of the 'baluster' variety and possessed the added advantage of generous capacity. The circular collet foot was generally of the same circumference as the body of the mug at its widest point, and this factor gave added stability.

The 19th Century saw the introduction of improved mechanical processes— a result of the Industrial Revolution—but this boom led, paradoxically, to a nadir of design in realms where personal attention robbed the articles of mundaneness, but 'mass-production' deprived them of individuality. Nevertheless, there were some good examples even of this 'age of the machine' and the work of Paul Storr, in particular, stands out among many others.

George III tapering Pint Mug: on 'skirted' foot and with plain 'S-shaped' handle with heart-shaped terminal. By Hester Bateman, London, 1785: 4″ by 2½″ in diameter at top. Weight: 6 ozs.

From the Collection of John R. Rayment, Esq.

George I fluted pint-sized Mug: the contemporary crest in a repoussé mantelled cartouche. The spaces between the vertical flutes stamped with foliate punch-work. On circular collet foot. By William Spackman, London, 1723. 4½″ by 3″ in diameter. Weight: 12 ozs.

The ancients held the preservative qualities of Salt to be symbolic of enduring fidelity, and this belief influenced its choice for the covenant meal which was regarded as binding. Salt was believed to be possessed of a sacred character and thus created a bond of piety and guest friendship among the participants. The white mineral was also symbolic of purity and it was thought to invest the soil of the district in which it was found with a peculiar sanctity.

Early English references to salt as an additive to food both as a seasoning and a substance are found in various works: one of the earliest occurs in the primitive but highly popular Latin encyclopaedia *'De Proprietatibus Rerum'* written by the Franciscan monk Bartholemew de Glanville (circa 1360) and translated by the Cornish cleric John Trevisa and published by Wynkyn de Worde in 1495: 'Salt maketh potage and other mete sauoury'. The earliest mention of a vessel in precious metal as a container for salt occurs in a contemporary inventory of 1439, '36 ij Salers of gold (probably silver-gilt) whereof yt oon ys a man and yt other a woman, holding ye Salers in her hondes'.

By courtesy of the Worshipful Company of Goldsmiths.

Henry VIII Hourglass Salt, silver-gilt: of sexafoil outline on a plain flanged base. The alternate lobes of stem and bowl are chased with scrolling flowers and foliage. The knop has pierced Gothic tracery divided by miniature butresses with gargoyle monsters and pinnacles above.

Maker: A Crescent enclosing a mullet, London, 1516.

6½″ in height.

Weight: 16 ozs. 3 dwts.

Goldsmiths' Company Collection.

The belief was long held that the expression 'above (and 'below') the salt' held some truth, namely, that the salt-cellar on the table served to 'divide the lord and his nobler guests from the inferior guests and menials'. Jackson and other writers after him, discounted this surmise, but some primary sources indicate otherwise. The famous late 15th Century primer for the table manners of the young, the *'Babees Bok'* circa 1495 gives the following instruction 'for to serve a Lord': 'The boteler or panter shalle sette the seler in the myddys of the tabull accordyng to the place where the principall soveran shalle sitte, and sette his brede iuste couched unto the salt-selar', in other words, the host sat adjacent to the salt-cellar which was obviously a place of honour. If the host and his guests occupied such special positions, the place 'above the salt' *was* considered superior to the lower.

The 16th Century dining table had fewer encumbrances than the modern 'place-setting': only such utensils and vessels as knives, spoons, tankards and salt-cellars stood upon it. A richly adorned Standing Salt would therefore not look out of place; it would stand near the principal diners and serve as both a conversation piece and an object of utility. It is conceivable that the state of the victuals in the 16th Century might not be over-fresh, and would demand copious salting to compensate for the loss of flavour or the reverse!

The diner would take a small portion of salt on his knife and place it on his 'trencher'—this was a square of wood upon which the food was carved, served and eaten. The earlier form of this platter was a thick slice of bread; this, after being soaked with the gravy and the juices from the meat, was also eaten or thrown into the alms-basket to be given to the poor. Each slice of meat or other comestible was then dipped into the salt and eaten.

The silver salt-cellar proper appears to have originated in the last quarter of the 15th Century. The earliest English salt-cellar for table use was

By courtesy of the Worshipful Company of Goldsmiths.
Henry VIII Standing Salt and cover: octagonal in form and silver gilt. The terminal formed as a figure of Hercules as a child holding a serpent with a human face and a shield.
Maker: A Sceptre, London, 1522.
9¾″ in height.
Weight: 22 ozs. 4 dwts.
Goldsmiths' Company Collection.

probably that intricate form known as the 'Gothic' type; Jackson defines the term at length: 'the 'Gothic' style applied to the mediaeval form of architecture which prevailed in Europe from the latter part of the twelfth century to the end of the fifteenth . . . for a period of about three hundred years, beginning in the thirteenth century, patens and other articles of plate were ornamented with various geometrical forms such as the quatrefoil and the sexfoil, with plain and enriched spandrills (the space between the shoulder and the surrounding moulding of an arch), obviously inspired by the window tracery of churches dating from the twelfth century downwards'. These gothic saltcellars are of the 'hour-glass' shape, that is to say, the top and base are conical, and both of the same diameter, but the centre is 'taken in at the waist' so to speak, and usually enriched with a collar or 'knot' bearing applied foliage or occasionally with a 'boss' depicting animals.

The interesting thing about these and all the other Standing Salts is the size of the 'salt-bowl', which is usually of circular form and fits into the top of the vessel. This bowl is quite small by comparison with the otherwise massive

From the Munro Collection in the Henry E. Huntington Library and Art Gallery, San Marino, California, USA.
James I silver-gilt Standing Bell Salt: the sides matt-chased and engraved with rose and carnation floral motifs and on three ball feet engraved with birds' claws. The pierced ball terminal was used as a pepper caster. By the London maker TS in a Monogram, 1603. This type is fully discussed on page 63. Height: 8½".

body of the article; it is shallow and would not have contained a great deal of salt. The Standing Salts underwent a number of evolutionary changes from the mid-15th Century downwards: the earliest noted specimens stem from the 1460's and take the form of the gothic 'hour-glass' variety described above. The next development is the 'pedestal' form, ('because', says Jackson, 'of its resemblance to the pedestal of a column') the body of which was a cylindrical 'drum', the lid surmounted by a cast figure-terminal, usually a warrior or a boy, the base on a 'skirted' spreading foot, the whole enriched with elaborately repoussé floral motifs. These examples date from the 1550's. The following two decades saw the introduction of the 'rectangular pedestal' variety, which comprised a large box-like vessel mounted on four cast sphinx or claw and ball feet, the lid also surmounted by a cast 'warrior' terminal.

At this point, in the last decade of the 16th Century, a new form of Standing Salt made its appearance: that is to say, it was not altogether new, but the majority of 'Bell Salts' which remain extant stem from the 1590's. That tireless researcher, the late Dr. Norman Penzer, who always endeavoured to approach a subject from the beginning, found references to bell-salts in the Royal Inventories of Henry VIII and the early days of Queen Elizabeth's reign. He quoted A. Jefferies Collins's 'Jewels and Plate of Queen Elizabeth I' Brit. Mus., 1955: No. 979: 'Item two Saultes guilt belle fation with a Couer poiz xxxiij oz. iii quarters'. That there are no mid-16th Century examples extant may be due to damage or destruction.

As opposed to the cylindrical or rectangular vessels, the bell-salts were small pieces, not designed as were their larger brothers to impress as 'centre-pieces', but of pure utility; they generally stood about 9″ high. These newly introduced salt-cellars were shaped as 'bells' of inverted form, the base forming the 'mouth' of the bell, the upper section crowned with a pierced ball finial; they were constructed of three sections: the base, which had its own salt-bowl atop the cylinder, the middle section which narrowed considerably, but had yet another salt-bowl as its terminal, and the pierced ball finial which contained and dispensed pepper. The vessel was mounted on three ball feet, and the enrichment normally consisted of engraved floral and foliate motifs on a matt-chased ground; many bell-salts were silver-gilt. About two dozen specimens are known to remain extant, and the latest noted example was dated 1617.

Still another variation on the 'standing Salt' theme made its debut in the early 17th Century. This was of the 'Covered Salt' variety and known as the 'architectural' type, being in the form of a tetrastyle shrine, that is, an edifice with four pillars supporting a ceiling. These fine 'centrepiece' salts had an additional centre column to give added stability and were supported on four spherical or cast 'fabulous animal' feet at each corner of the base. The salt-bowl was in the centre of the top and was covered by a domed lid which was usually surmounted by a cast 'warrior' terminal.

The point to remember is that all these magnificent salt vessels were merely structural receptacles made to house the salt-bowl, which maintained its simple shallow 'dipped' form through all the evolutionary cycles, but was generally hidden from view under the lid. The last of these 'standing' varieties conformed with another decorative concept introduced in the closing years of the 16th Century—the famous 'Steeple-cup' group—the symbolism of which, like the steeple of architecture in churches, points to heaven and perpetuity. The early Stuart diner was thus edified by two powerful symbols— the white salt, signifying purity ,and the pointing steeple, recalling eternity— as he ate.

With the advent of the 1630's, the salt-cellar lost its stepped base, and taking its form from foreign influences, chiefly French and Dutch styles, assumed the famous 'Scroll' motif. The salt-bowl was now uncovered, and the vessel emerged as a 'spool-shaped' body, the base slightly larger in diameter than the top, (almost recalling the early gothic 'hour-glass' specimens) and approximately 4″ or 5″ high.

The distinctive feature of these simplified salt-containers was the presence near the salt-bowl around the rim, of three or four cast scroll-terminal arms or brackets, the purpose of which was conjectural and subject to all sorts of speculation until Penzer noted a Dutch still-life painting by Pieter de Ring (1615–1660) depicting a scroll-salt supporting a dish on its brackets. It becomes obvious that the 'spool-shape' of the vessel would absorb heat and act in much the same manner as the 18th Century Irish 'Potato Ring' of very similar shape, could prevent the heated dish from spoiling the patination of a fine table.

With the middle of the 17th Century came the shallow circular, triangular or quatrefoil shaped 'Trencher-salt' which was simply a development of the earlier salt-bowl but without the encompassing trappings. The shallow 'dip' alone remained, but the borders and mouldings were often severely plain. These trencher-salts were to see the century out, but acquired a rectangular shape and continued in use until the mid 1730's (see illustrations). The

reign of George II saw the introduction of cast circular salt-cellars often enriched with rocaille ornament and on three 'lions' masks' terminal feet, or quite plain, with shell terminals at the union of the body and the feet, which were of the 'hoof' variety. The interiors were now washed with gold, as it became fashionable to leave the salt in the vessel; the early salt-cellars were not gilt and thus the salt was removed after every meal. The final developments included circular inverted-dome vessels on cast collet bases, the sides of which are enriched with acanthus foliate motifs rising from the base, dating from about 1720 and concluding circa 1749, the oval salt-cellar on four hoof feet, with gadroon rims, which appeared circa 1750, an extension of which theme was the use of pierced ornament with beaded rims and on four claw and ball feet. The advent of the 'Adam Period' contributed boat-shaped vessels for salt, often with voluting cast terminals and ring handles.

Top
Pair George III shaped octagonal Salt-cellars: of the type known as 'Bat-wing' for the resemblance to the nocturnal animal. With reeded rims and on shaped reeded bases. By Hester Bateman, London, 1788. 4½" by 2½". Weight: 3 ozs.

Centre right
By courtesy of the Worshipful Company of Goldsmiths.
George III circular Salt-cellar: enriched with cast swags of foliage and with massive 'lions' mask' terminals at 'paw' feet. Silver-gilt and with gadroon and shell border.
Maker: Paul Storr, London, 1814.
2½" in height.
Goldsmiths' Company Collection.

Centre left
George II octagonal Trencher Salt: of rectangular form with moulded border and shallow salt-bowl. By Edward Wood, London, 1735. One of a pair. 3⅛" by 2½". Weight: 2 ozs. 15 dwts.

Bottom
George II octagonal Trencher Salt: of sturdy gauge. By the well-known Guernsey maker Guillaume Henry Crown, 'above in a shaped shield', circa 1740–50. 'Richard H. Mayne's superb account in *Old Channel Islands Silver, its makers and marks*, published by Print Holdings & Investments, Ltd, Jersey, C.L. 1969, cites many important makers and marks.

Pepper is one of the oldest spices known to man: its origins are obscure, but the great historian Edward Gibbon (1737–1794) states in his *'Decline and Fall of the Roman Empire'* that pepper was a favourite ingredient of the most expensive Roman cookery. References to this digestive stimulant, anti-flatulent condiment, are found as early as 1309 in the Guildhall Records where the name of 'Ralph le Balancer, Pepperer' appears in the Hustings Rolls for that year. The designation 'Pepperer' was later to become 'Grocer', indeed, the Grocers' Company was originally described as 'Twenty-two persons, carrying on the business of pepperers in Soper's Lane, Cheapside'. In 1345, the pepperers and spicers amalgamated and were known as the Fraternity of St. Anthony.

The plant *Piper Nigrum,* or black pepper, is a climbing shrub indigenous to the East Indies, that is, applied in the widest sense, to that region embracing both the whole of India and the Malay Archipelago. It is mentioned in early English herbals: an account of circa 1400 states: 'Pepre growez in maner of wilde wynes be syde the treesse of the forest, for to be suppowlled by tham', and continues: 'There is iij maner of peper all vpon o tree, Long Peper, blak peper and white peper . . . the long peper cometh first'.

By courtesy of the Worshipful Company of Goldsmiths.
William III Lighthouse Caster: the cylindrical body on fine fluted base enriched with *dancette* border, the superbly pierced top enriched with amorini and foliate motifs. The caster here shown open to reveal deep sleeve and fine marks on side.
Maker: Pierre Harrache, London, 1699.
8⅞″ in height.
Weight: 17 ozs. 15 dwts.
Goldsmith's Company Collection.

The first mention of a silver vessel for pepper occurs in an inventory of 1546: 'A peper box, weying vj oz, iij quarters', but, of course, the pierced ball terminal of the early 17th Century bell-salt also served as a primitive caster. The actual mention of the caster as a vessel in its own right is well-known: it occurs in an advertisement in the London Gazette for 1676 in which the advertiser asks for information about 'A Sugar Castar, A Pepper Caster, A Mustard Pot'. There has been a good deal of conjecture on the difference between the pepper caster and the vessel which contained crushed sugar, namely, the sugar caster; as far as may be ascertained, both were homogeneous. In fact, even the famous so-called 'Spicebox' of the charming but very rare 'Escallop-shell' type, usually found at the beginning of the 17th Century, appears in an account, contemporary to 1639 as a 'Scollup Sugar Boxe', while an inventory of 1620 lists a 'Sugar Boxe' and 'one sugar boxe spoone', thereby revealing both a secondary function for the former, and the explanation of the method of casting sugar before a vessel was specially wrought to contain it in the latter.

Left

George I octagonal Pepper Caster: of heavy gauge and with octagonal baluster terminal. By Benjamin Blakely, London, 1719. Engraved with a contemporary Coat-of-Arms. 5½″ (including terminal). Weight: 5 ozs.

Right

George I small 'shouldered' Pepper Caster: the top geometrically pierced and surmounted by baluster terminal. Maker's mark only struck in base: William Fleming, London, circa 1725. Articles bearing only the maker's mark were probably refashioned from another article, and thus escaped the attention of the assay-office. 3¼″ (including terminal). Weight: 2 ozs.

The 'Caster' as a vessel originated in mid-17th Century France: the famous 'Puiforcat Collection' now in the Louvre, contains a caster of the 'Lighthouse' variety, that is, of tall cylindrical form and with a 'bayonet-fitting' on the domed pierced lid. The 'bayonet' refers to a then novel method of fastening whereby the rim atop the body has a collar broken in two places to admit the two lugs soldered on the lid, which, when twisted in a sideways motion, locks both parts into position. The French specimen was made at Amiens in 1650, a good twenty years before the English lighthouse casters made their appearance, and resembles the latter in every way, even in the 'cut-card' applied enrichment, which consisted of acanthus motif foliage soldered on the body of the vessel.

Left

William IV pair 'Kitchen Peppers': engraved 'Pepper' and 'Salt'. By J. McKay, Edinburgh, 1832. This is a typical Scottish form, a specimen made in Glasgow, 1763 was exhibited at the 'Loan Collection' of Scottish Silver at the Empire Exhibition, Glasgow, 1938. 2½″ by 1½″ in diameter. Weight: 3 ozs. 10 dwts.

Right

George III 'vase-shaped' Pepperette: of very heavy gauge, with 'faceted-motif' on lower body, on circular beaded base and with light gadroon rim on the rising dome lid, which is simply pierced. By Hester Bateman, London, 1787. 3″ by 1½″ in diameter. Weight: 2 ozs. Silver-gilt.

The earliest English caster noted was dated 1669, but differed slightly from the later specimens in that it possessed an unpierced lid, known as the 'blind' type; some later variations had silver collars inside the lid, which could be removed at will, or be permitted to remain and thus restrict the flow. These would appear to have been intended to contain dry mustard: Commander How, in a pre-war advertisement, illustrated what he termed a 'Condiment Pot' together with a small oval-bowled trefid-terminal spoon, stated to have been found inside the vessel and bearing the same maker's mark as the larger article. This was none other than a blind caster by Francis Garthorne, London circa 1680, and Penzer subsequently confirmed this impression.

The evolution of style of the English casters was as follows: the lighthouse variety gave way to pear-shaped vessels encircled with a strengthening rib on the lower part of the body. These, in turn, developed into octagonal containers of the most superb quality and weight but still retaining the 'pear-shape', The succeeding specimens embodied the octagonal line, but achieved a 'moulded' shoulder, this evolved into a 'reversed pear-shape' in which the upper portion continued to have the same incurve, but the lower part became bulbous, tapering down to the conical circular foot. This latter variety sometimes had a light cable gadroon motif on the shoulder. The final development in this group was the 'stemmed' type of the 'vase-shaped' form which retained most of the features of the earlier specimens, but, being of the latter years of the 18th Century, lost some of the quality of the hand-made articles, through being constructed from factory-made units. The lids were simply pierced in the second half of the century, but occasionally consisted of 'swirled flutes' and shaped domical lids.

With the coming of the 'Adam Period', a new type of pepper-caster made its appearance: it was quite small, and of the 'vase-shape', or better, 'urn-shape' variety, with a pull-off domed pierced lid and pierced in the body with vertical, broken horizontal and 'star and diaper' motifs; obviously, this charming little vessel could not contain pepper without a glass liner, and thus the delightful little blue Bristol liners were made from a plaster casting. Some glass liners still bear the impression of the original mould on the sides of the glass. The type is particularly associated with the work of such excellent exponents of the 'Adam Motif' as the Hennells and Hester Bateman.

The Mustard Plant is a member of the genus *Brassica,* and the black or brown mustard is known as *Brassica Nigra.* It has been known in history from very ancient times both as a condiment and a medicinal substance, having been used, in the latter capacity by Hippocrates (circa 460 B.C). The method of grinding the seeds is indicated in the following quotation from a verse of the Scottish poet William Dunbar (circa 1460–circa 1520) in the tale of '*The Freiris of Berwik*' (written circa 1550) 'He was sa ferce he fell owttour the sek, And brak his heid vpoun ane *mustarde stane* (mustard stone). John Wycliffe's reservations on the value of certain religious writings (circa 1380) are well-known, but of such charm that they could bear repetition: 'These lettris mai do good for to covre mostard pottis, but not thus to wynne men blis'; he was referring to the contemporary practice of sealing the small jars containing crushed mustard seeds steeped in vinegar with scraps of parchment cut from useless or discarded manuscripts.

The earliest mustard pot of true vessel form noted—not the blind casters of the 1680's—was dated London 1714: it was exhibited at the Park Lane Exhibition in 1929 and is described in the catalogue as 'a George I silver-gilt Cruet, with three octagonal casters, Mustard Pot and Spoon, and two glass bottles. Maker: William Faudery, London, 1714'. They were loaned by the Duke of Portland. The existence of the mustard pot as a type has already been referred to above, in the extract from the London Gazette of 1676. The early 18th Century specimens appear to have been inspired by Dutch specimens of ovoid form; the famous pair of massive 'barrel-shaped' mustard pots sold at Christie's in 1953 were outstanding examples of the Huguenot craft, having been made by Jacob Margas (who entered his mark at Goldsmiths' Hall in 1706) in 1724.

The most attractive type of mustard pot was the plain 'drum' variety illustrated: it had a cylindrical body, a flat or very slightly domed lid, a

George III 'Lighthouse' Caster: with reeded border and plain pierced top. By John Emes, London, 1803. This is a development of the late 17th Century vessels of the same name, but the article resembles a feeding bottle rather than a 'lighthouse'. 4½″ by 2″ in diameter at base. Weight: 3 ozs.

Opposite Left
George III domed lid Mustard Pot: the body finely pierced and enriched with swags of foliage. Plain 'S-shaped' handle and pierced shell thumbpiece. By John Deacon, London, 1776. 2½″ by 2¾″.

George III vase-shaped Mustard Pot: Grecian in conception, the foot is formed as a centrally placed lion's paw on a circular base. The handle, terminal and the rim are enriched with acanthus foliage. The interior is silver-gilt. By Emes and Barnard, London, 1809. $3\frac{1}{4}''$ by $2\frac{3}{4}''$ in diameter. Weight: 6 ozs.

George III 'Drum' Mustard Pot: the sides vertically pierced, and with 'openwork' scrolling thumbpiece and 'S-shaped' handle. Beaded rim and border and with contemporary blue Bristol glass liner. By Hester Bateman, London, 1776. $2\frac{1}{2}''$ by $2\frac{1}{2}''$ in diameter.

George III 'Drum' Mustard Pot: the perfectly plain body with scrolling 'S-shaped' handle and scrolling thumbpiece on lid. By Andrew Fogelberg, London, 1768. This is an early specimen of the type. Various researches have failed to reveal more about Fogelberg than is already known, namely, that he was an Anglo-Swede who worked in London from about 1770. Paul Storr was apprenticed to him in 1785. A full discussion about Fogelberg appears in Penzer's excellent study of the life and work of Paul Storr, published in 1954 under the title: '*Paul Storr—the Last of the Goldsmiths*'. $2\frac{3}{8}''$ by $2\frac{3}{4}''$.

pierced thumbpiece, and usually, a plain S-shaped handle; the earliest specimen noted was dated 1763. A pleasant variation consisted of a cylindrical body entirely pierced with quatrefoils or flowerheads, these dating from about 1767. The early 'drums' had completely closed-in flat bases, the later developments of this style received openwork circular bases, usually found on pierced pots, so that the removal of the blue glass liner could be facilitated by pushing it from below. One charming variety occasionally encountered is the 'vase-shaped' type, generally pierced and bright-cut, on a 'trumpet-shaped' base and with a 'hand-raised' rising-dome lid surmounted by an urn finial. These delightful articles have blue glass liners and beaded S-shaped handles. They are invariably of the 1785–90 period, and many are from Hester Bateman's *atelier*.

With the arrival of the 19th Century, oval examples of sturdier gauge metal usually enriched with 'half-fluting' on the lower section of the body and domed lids became fashionable. Some specimens of these possessed elaborate bright-cut motifs consisting of swags of floral festoons; others boasted embossed lids topped by ball-terminals. The second quarter of the century saw a coarsening of style, but, in keeping with other articles, some silversmiths, chiefly the great craftsmen—Storr, Benjamin Smith and the Emes and Barnard partnership—produced some superlative mustard vessels.

From the collection of H. A. Cooper, Esq.

Top

Queen Anne large octagonal caster: with appliqué cut-card work formed as acanthus foliage on a matt-chased ground. The top pierced with geometrical motifs and surmounted by heavy octagonal baluster finial. By William Fawdery, London, 1710. (6¾″ by 2¾″, weight: 10 ozs.).

Pair George II circular salt-cellars: the sides enriched with appliqué 'cut-card' work (strips of silver cut, shaped and soldered on surface of vessel) depicting scrolling floral diaper (diamond type) motifs. The high collet foot with cast acanthus foliage and heavy gadroon rim to top. Heavily gilt in bowls to preserve metal against corrosion from salt. By Jacob Marsh, London, 1746. Engraved in bowl with contemporary crest. (3¼″ in diameter by 2¼″ high. Weight: 16 ozs.).

Bottom

George I taperstick: on sexagonal sunken centre base, and similar baluster column capital. By Joseph Bird, London, 1722. Engraved with contemporary crest. (4⅝″ by 3¼″ at base, weight: 4 ozs. 2 dwts).

Pair Queen Anne cast 'sunken centre' stepped octagonal base candlesticks. By Pierre Platel, London, 1708. Engraved with contemporary Coat-of-Arms. Platel, who entered his first mark in 1699, was one of the important Huguenot craftsmen whose designs influenced the creations of the early eighteenth century: Paul de Lamerie was apprenticed to him in 1703. (7½″ high by 4½″ at base, weight: 32 ozs).

This page

George III rectangular Mustard Pot: of heavy gauge. On shaped foot with reeded border and plain 'loop' handle. The domed lid surmounted by rectangular baluster terminal. With contemporary 'Greyhound' crest. By William Abdy, London, 1807. 3″ by 2¾″.

Tea is a beverage which is widely drunk all over the world, and it is not surprising, therefore, that the vessels connected with it should be so varied. It has ancient origins, and, as is so often the case, myth and folklore is bound up with fact, and the Chinese mythology is a particularly rich one: tea is believed to have stemmed from China, although there are schools of thought which have attempted to ascribe the plant to Assam. The origin of the Tea-plant is attributed to the piety of a Celestial Being, one Darma (circa 519 A.D); the story of the 'Eyebrows of Darma' is well-known, but it bears telling yet once again.

This particular version of the fable is taken from 'A Dissertation upon Tea' by Thomas Short, M.D., (1690–1772), published in 1730. 'Darma was a most austere man, who, from an aim at perfect holiness resolved to deny himself all rest, sleep and relaxation of body, and consecrate his mind, day and night, without intermission, to God. After he had watched many years, one day

being weary and overfasted, he unluckily dropped asleep; awakening the next morning full of sorrow for breaking his solemn vow, he cut off both his eyebrows, the instruments of his crime, and with indignation threw them on the ground; returning the next day to the same place, behold! out of the eyebrows were grown two beautiful Tea-shrubs'.

It is remarkable that although tea was popular among the Chinese at the time of Marco Polo's visit (1275–92) this fact is not mentioned in his otherwise meticulously detailed record of contemporary Chinese customs and culture. It is fortunate, therefore, that early Chinese sources do mention tea as a beverage, and one scholar, Lu Yu (780 A.D) actually cites a recipe which almost duplicates the processes of tea-making in the 20th Century: 'To make tea as a drink, roast the cake until reddish in colour, pound it in tiny pieces, put them in a chinaware pot, pour boiling water over them, and add onion, ginger and orange'. Later on, only salt was used as a flavouring.

The first mention of tea in European literature occurs in a book by the

This page

George III oval Teapot and Stand: of the finest proportions. With beaded rim and similar enrichment on base. The rising domed lid with wooden baluster terminal. The straight spout in line with the top of the lid, the handle similarly placed.
The Stand enriched with beaded rim. On four 'claw and ball' feet. By Hester Bateman, London, 1783. Teapot: 6″ by 4½″ Stand: 7″ by 5½″. Weight: 18 ozs.

16th Century Italian traveller Giambattista Ramusio (1485–1557) in which he tells of a Persian merchant-traveller whom he met in Venice, who told him about 'Chai Catai', that is, Chinese tea; it was good, he said, for various ailments. This could be construed as a possible proof that the early Chinese employed tea as a medicine as well as a beverage. The Stuarts, incidentally, believed that tea had the following virtues: 'It is good for gout, gravel in the kidneys, if you drink it after meals, it takes away all indigestions and crudities of the stomach'.

The earliest mention of tea in England is believed to have occurred in a letter written in 1615 by a Mr. Wickham, an officer of the East Indies Company to a brother-officer in Firando, Japan, asking him for a 'pot of the best sort of *chaw*', and in the accounts prepared by the recipient, Mr. Eaton, there appears the following item: 'three silver porringers to drink chaw in'. Although tea is thus noted as having been introduced during the reign of James I little more was heard of it until the Restoration. When, in 1660, the government imposed a duty of eight pence per gallon on made-up tea as dispensed in the coffee-houses, this tax was understandably highly unpopular—they had had enough taxation under the reign of Charles I—and many protests were uttered. In 1669 the English East India Company imported 143½ pounds from Java, and, gradually, very large quantities were imported.

So bewitched were the credulous Englishmen of the late 17th Century with the beneficial properties of tea, that almost no price was too high for them. The prices of tea were exceptionally high: it has been noted that there was more fluctuation in its price than in any other article of food. In 1704,

73

black tea varied in price between 12 to 16 shillings per pound. In 1707 (which appears to have been an exceptionally dear year) between 16 and 32 shillings per pound. These fluctuation arose not only from difference in age, but from the fact that it was quite usual for old leaves to be re-dried and used again in the cheaper sorts. Indeed, there is a very curious advertisement in *The Tatler* for August 26th, 1710: 'Bohea Tea made of the same materials that foreign Bohea is made of, sixteen shillings a pound. Sold by R. Fary, only, at the Bell, Grace Church Street, Druggist. Note: The natural Peko Tea will remain after infusion, of a light gray colour. All other Bohea Tea tho' there be white in it, will change colour and is artificial'.

Various interesting tea-taking ceremonies have been noted by contemporary historians. In Edinburgh, for instance, the Scottish ladies did not consider it correct to return a cup for refilling until all were emptied, so it came about that the spoons were numbered to ensure that each guest recovered back her own cup. An amusing sequel to this custom appears in a print published in 1835 depicting a tea-party in which the caption is as follows: 'A Frenchman, not aware of the custom (of leaving his spoon in the cup) constantly returned his cup without the spoon in it—which being immediately replenished by the Lady of the house, he thought it a point of politeness to drink the contents which he continued to do, to the great surprise of the company, until he perceived the Lady pouring out the fourteenth cup, when he rose in great agony and cried Ah! Madame excuse me I can take no more! . . .'

Yet another contemporary print by Thomas Rowlandson shows the great Doctor Samuel Johnson, surely the tea-drinker *par excellence* taking tea with the Boswells. The Doctor is depicted taking a lump of sugar from the bowl with a clumsy pair of tongs, while Boswell is obviously declaiming about something, and Mrs. Boswell looks on enraptured with the conversation and

From a private collection:
George III silver-gilt 'drum' Teapot: the body enriched with applique *putti* and *amorini* playing under a tree, chasing birds and holding garlands. The border embellished with band of 'ribbon and wreath' motif common to the Adam Period. The lower section of the body decorated with alternating matt-chasing and strap-work. The short spout with applique cast foliage, and with a similar foliate motif at boxwood handle. The pull-out lid also with bands of this enrichment, and rising domed 'laurel-motif' to the wooden ball terminal. On 'trumpet' base. Engraved with the Arms of the Douglas Family and the motto *Spero Meliora—I hope for better things* By William Pitts, London, 1783. This article was probably made to match a Sèvres tea-service. William Pitts was famous for the quality of his casting and as an inspired designer. 5″ by 4½″ in diameter. Weight: 18 ozs. 10 dwts.

clasps her hands in ecstasy, while a bored servant looks on in the background, yawning and scratching his head. The candle gutters low in the wall-sconce, and the hands of the clock point to ten minutes past midnight!

The earliest silver Teapot is in the Victoria and Albert Museum, and appears to be the only one of its type in existence: the body is formed as a tall tapering cylinder with a straight spout set high in the side, almost in line with the rim, under the conical cover. The handle is leather-covered, of small C-shaped form and is set at right angles to the body of the vessel. It greatly resembles the coffeepots of the same period, but there is no doubt as to its use, for it bears an inscription including the words 'This silver Teapot'; it was given by the East India Company to George Lord Berkeley in 1670.

There can be little doubt that the early teapots were made to resemble the Chinese porcelain pots, and this is natural in view of the oriental origins of tea; most teapots of the early 18th Century were formed as 'reversed pear-shapes', that is, the body was wider at the base than at the top. The attractive 'Bullet' variety illustrated appears as a globular vessel at about 1720; the early specimens were very heavy and usually fairly small, plain spherical articles, set on a circular ring foot. They had straight spouts often set in a line with the top of the lid. The slightly later versions, of the 1740 period, were still spherical, but with a tendency to narrow towards the base, and their younger brothers, the 'reversed pyriform' specimens, completely escaped from the usual pear-shape, by turning themselves upside down. Thus: the vessel was wider at the top than at the bottom. Another interesting variety was the 'Drum' type of teapot, first encountered circa 1770, this usually had a flush, or 'sunken' hinge and the spout was also set in a straight line with the top of the body. The charming oval 'compressed' variety usually associated with the Bateman Family commenced about 1780 and became gradually larger; those early 19th Century examples noted were generally

From a private South African collection.

George III oval 'flat-top' sunken-hinge Teapot: of exceptionally heavy gauge and engraved around rim and base with bands of bright-cut 'star-motifs' and swags of floral festoons around body. Engraved with contemporary monogram in oval cartouche surmounted by 'ribbon-motif'. With boxwood 'C-shaped' handle and tapering spout in line with lid. Boxwood terminal on lid. By William Vincent, London, 1775. 4½″ by 3½″. Weight: 14 ozs. This weight is far in excess of most teapots of the period.

rather cumbersome. The final evolvement consisted of the pleasant 'Cape' style, in which the top of the lid is protected by a kind of rising cowl. The advent of the second quarter of the 19th Century saw the introduction, or rather revival, (for it had appeared for some years in the mid-1730's) of the 'Melon-shaped' teapot. This form of enrichment consisted of fluted segmentation so that the vessel resembled a pumpkin.

THE VESSEL & THE INVESTOR

The vessel has been more affected by the continued upward trend in prices than any other item of English silver. As will be shown, domestic vessels of a good age, including tea, condiment and drinking vessels, have all appreciated beyond any foreseeable level. In order to explain this seemingly inexplicable phenomenon, it should be pointed out that for many years, English silver was the most under-valued of all the fine arts. Many of the remaining articles —paintings, furniture, antiquities, jewellery and books—had almost reached 'saturation point' by the time that silver began to attract the attentions of the world markets. A new wave of interest resulted in massive exports to hitherto untapped destinations, and this unaccustomed movement took the trade by storm; it was not long before stocks which had been accumulating for years began to dwindle. It might be safe to assert that there is more fine silver in Rome, Hamburg or São Paulo than there is in London.

From a private collection:
George III Beer Jug: of large size, on high collet foot. By Walter Brind, London, 1777. 7¼″ high by 4½″ diameter at widest point. Weight: 16 ozs. 17 dwts.

This revolution in marketing has also embraced the domestic scene where post-war prosperity subtly engaged the attention of middle-class investors whose better living conditions permitted investment for the future, and this trend further depleted available stocks. Yet a third factor could be the continued prosperity of legatees who might otherwise have sent articles bequeathed to them for auction, but whose satisfactory circumstances did not compel them to sell, and thus a supply which would normally circulate remained unavailable.

The greatest price appreciation has been in the important drinking vessels of the pre-Georgian era: a fine Charles II tankard which in 1957 might have cost up to £500, $1,400 is eagerly acquired for between £2,000, and £3,500, $5,600 and $9,800, but oddly enough, Queen Anne specimens may be bought for as little as £500, $1,400 rising to £1,500, $4,200 for fine specimens with exceptional enrichment. A George I example might obtain between £350 to £600, $980–1,680, but the greatest fluctuation is seen in George II specimens which for years could not be sold at all; a good George II tankard might have realised £50, $140 seven years ago, but today is a popular seller at £250 rising to £400, $700–1,120.

It is not thought that this popularity in drinking vessels has anything to do with an increase in drinking, in fact, many of the collector-investors who acquire them are remarkably abstemious; the reason may be connected with the 20th Century conception of 'home enrichment' whereby many people like to decorate their homes with relics of bygone days. While they have no objection to taking ale or wine at table from a fine Georgian mug or beaker, they would find the massive Carolean tankard with the heavy lid an embarrassing vessel to use, both in its great capacity which is out of keeping with modern drinking trends and in the heavy weight which would command the use of both hands, in a primitive fashion. Such items therefore are intended to serve as investments, though they may be incorporated in the furnishings of the home.

Mugs of the George I-II period which in 1960 sold for £125, $350 are priced at between £300 to £500, $840–1,400 or up to £750, $2,100 for exceptionally fine and heavy examples. A beaker dated 1680 retailed for between £75 and

Top right

George I saucepan: more familiarly known as a 'Brandy Saucepan': with everting rim and on 'skirted' base. By William Fleming, London, 1717. Maker's mark also struck on handle. There appears to be no definite provenance for the 'Brandy' ascription; these articles were probably used for mulling wine and ale. 3⅝" by 2⅜". Weight: 5 ozs.

Top left

George III small Saucepan: more commonly known as a 'pipkin', (usually a small earthenware pot). By Phipps, Robinson and Phipps, London, 1815. 2" in diameter by 1½".

Bottom

George III Saucepan: with everting rim and on high collet foot, the contemporary boxwood handle with 'heart-shaped' terminal at side. By Peter, Anne and William Bateman, London, 1800. 3⅝" in diameter by 3⅛". Weight: 6 ozs.

£150, $210–420 in 1957 and now realises £600 to £750, $1,680–2,100, George II beakers are in the £150–£250, $210–700 range, and beer-jugs of the George II-III period which sold for £250–£550, $700–1,540 in 1960 now reach £2,500, $7,000 for the former and £700, $1,960 for the latter, depending upon age, maker and condition.

Porringers were slow sellers in all but the rarest varieties for many years: a fine Commonwealth specimen sold for £250, $700 in 1957, and the same article would realise at least £1,000, $2,800 in 1967. A small 'punched ornament' specimen of the same period which sold for between £50 and £75, $140–210 ten years ago, might fetch between £350 and £500, $980–1,400 nowadays. The same is true of the Commonwealth wine taster of similar enrichment. A massive soup tureen which was difficult to dispose of for £300, $840 in 1960 has increased in value to £1,000, $2,800 rising to £1,250, $3,500 for George III specimens, but at least double for George II examples.

A more predictable price increase has affected the work of the great 'name' silversmiths—Paul de Lamerie, Hester Bateman and Paul Storr—which have been highly priced, many people thought *overpriced*, for many years. Such pessimists as the latter were undoubtedly wrong, and their rejection has cost them a great many comparative 'bargains'. Not only have prices for items by these silversmiths been consistently maintained, but some of them, notably the work of Paul de Lamerie, have risen to a point where they are now only available to the higher income brackets. The charming little Lamerie cream-jug, which is illustrated in one of the colour plates, cost its lucky but perspicacious owner far less than the £1,250, $3,500 which was obtained for a poorer specimen in a saleroom not long ago, and similar pieces have been noted which cost even more.

Articles from the workshop of Hester Bateman and her family were also considered to be highly priced over the past decade: the fine pear-shaped coffee-pot illustrated was sold for £340, $950 in 1957 and would fetch between £1,250 to £1,600, $3,500–4,500 today depending on condition. The superb pair of Hester Bateman sauce-tureens also illustrated, (perhaps the finest articles ever to emanate from her *atelier*) are in a class of their own, and would always have commanded a fine price. Similarly, articles like the excellently conceived Lamerie salver shown in another colour plate would have cost between £750 to £1,000, $2,100–2,800 five years ago, but its value today might extend to the region of £4,000, $11,200!

Paul Storr was a 'great' silversmith in almost every definition of the term: he produced opulent masterpieces of the finest quality, massive weight and superlative enrichment, and it is not surprising, therefore, that his *chefs-d'oeuvre* are excellently received. It used to be calculated that Lamerie articles cost five times as much as comparable George II items, Bateman pieces three times as much and Storr items four times. Today, Lamerie and Storr are almost equally popular, and their articles achieve impressive prices wherever these appear, in the metropolitan saleroom, in antique shops, or from provincial sources.

Of the smaller vessels, notable increases have been recorded in pepper and sugar casters of all the varieties whether of the lighthouse, octagonal or 'shouldered' types. Single casters of good quality of Queen Anne origin which used to produce between £100 and £175, $280–490, now realise between £250 to £650, $700–1,820 whereas a set of three Queen Anne casters which sold for £400 eight years ago, now retails at about £750 rising to £1,000, $2,100–2,800.

Salt-cellars have appreciated from about £50, $140 for a pair of oval Hester Bateman specimens in 1960 to between £175 to £220, $490 to $615 for the same in 1967. A pair of good George II trencher salts cost approximately £60 to £80, $170–225 in 1960 and now realise between £200 and £400, $560–1,120 if in fine state. Mustard pots have also shown a marked rise: a fine 'drum-mustard' sold for about £45, $125 in 1959 and now averages between £120 and £180, $335–500 and a Hester Bateman example (which sold for £50, $140 ten years ago) realised £290, $810 at auction recently. Even a plain George IV late 'drum' mustard pot will fetch between £100 and £150, $280–420.

Teapots of early type were always comparatively expensive, and a fine George II 'bullet' specimen might sell in 1967 for upwards of £2,000, $5,600

Top left

George II Scottish Slop Bowl: of bombé shape, on three trefoil and paw feet, with cast shaped rim. By Alexander Forbes, Aberdeen, circa 1735–40. Engraved with contemporary initials. Marked with Maker's Mark and Town Mark. The 'slop-bowl' was used for emptying the dregs of cups at table. 4⅛″ by 3⅛″ in diameter. Weight: 7 ozs.

Top right

Old Sheffield Plate Slop Bowl: with everting 'vine-leaf' border and on high collet foot. Engraved with contemporary crest. Circa 1810. Silver-gilt interior. 7″ in diameter.

Centre left

George III 'bat-wing' Sugar Basket: of heavy gauge, with pierced and bright-cut 'star-motif' enrichment. The border and shaped foot with thread-edge'. With contemporary blue Bristol glass liner. By Hester Bateman, London, 1789. Fully marked in foot and with lion passant on handle. 5¾″ by 4½″. Weight: 6 ozs.

Centre right

George IV circular Soup Tureen: of massive weight. The body enriched with heavily applied 'vine and grape' motifs, and spreading acanthus foliage springing from the base and rising to the body. With 'egg and tongue' border and foliate border on the collet foot. The lid enriched with matt-chased and cast ivy-leaf motifs, and possessing a castellated rim. The handle formed as intertwining oak branches. Engraved with the Arms of Blakemore. By John Bridge, London, 1827. With fully marked silver liner which possesses shell-terminal lifting handles. 12″ in diameter. Height: including handle: 13″. Weight: 207 ozs.

Soup Tureens are commonly believed to be named for the great French Marshal Turenne (1611–1675) but in fact are nothing more than earthenware dishes, i.e., 'terrineus' the Latin for 'made of earth'. An account of 1706 defines the tureen as 'An Earthenware Pan'.

Bottom left

George III large oval Soup Tureen: formed as 'ogee' body with divided thread and foliate enriched 'harp-shaped' handles and on four cast acanthus motif feet. The rim with heavy gadroon border and the fluted domed lid with cast tendril handle. By William Fountain, London, 1804. Engraved with contemporary Coat-of-Arms and crests. 12″ by 8½″. Weight: 110 ozs.

Bottom right

George III Sugar Basket: with covered-in 'self-handle', on oval base. By Hannah Northcote, London, 1801. 5½″. Weight: 5 ozs. 10 dwts.

George II heavy gauge Pint Mug: of 'ogee' form and on circular collet foot. Engraved with contemporary scrolling cartouche. By Joseph Allen & Co, London, 1732. 4½" by 3⅜" in diameter at top. Weight: 12 ozs.

Centre

George III Argyle: the oviform body with curving spout and on reeded step-base. The rising domed lid similarly reeded, and with ball terminal. With conical 'hot-water' compartment inside vessel, surmounted by pull-off lid and ball terminal. By Hester Bateman, London, 1787. The Argyle is first encountered in the third quarter of the 18th Century, and the legend is related that it was named for the vessel invented by John, 4th Duke of Argyll, who was a member of the Campbell Family of Mamore and who died in 1770. It is thought that he disliked cold gravy and devised the hollow hot-water 'jacket' to counteract this anomaly. The early 19th Century *Cook's Oracle* by Kitchiner stated 'We have in the English kitch our Argyll for gravy'. 6½" by 3½". Weight: 12 ozs.

Top right

From the collection of John R. Rayment, Esq.

George III cylindrical Tea-caddy: with vine-motif bands around body and 'egg and tongue' border and lift-off lid. By John Angel, London, 1812. 4¾" by 3½" in diameter. Weight: 14 ozs. This type is uncommon.

Bottom left

From a private Canadian collection.

George III Tea-caddy: of plain 'compressed oval' shape, the rising domed lid surmounted by ivory vase-shaped terminal. Enriched with band of 'beading' on base. With contemporary lock. By Hester Bateman, London, 1782. 5" by 3½". Weight: 11 ozs.

Bottom right

George III small oval Tea-caddy: with lift-off 'thimble-type' lid. Delicately bright-cut and engraved with foliate festoons and with contemporary crest. By Thomas Halford, London, 1807. 3½" by 2½". Weight: 3 ozs. 10 dwts.

Reading from left to right
George II three-legged Cream-jug: the bulbous body enriched at the terminals to the feet with chased fluting, and with chased floral cartouche on front. With double scroll handle and shaped rim. By Phillips Garden, London, 1756. 3″. Weight: 2 ozs. 10 dwts.

George III 'pyriform' Cream-jug: with beaded foot and rim. By William Sumner, London, 1780. 4¾″. Weight: 2 ozs. 10 dwts.

George III 'helmet-shaped' Cream-jug: on square base, with 'punched-bead' enrichment on rim, and with plain 'loop' handle. Bright-cut with swags of foliage. By Peter and Anne Bateman, London, 1793. 4″. Weight: 3 ozs.

George III 'pyriform' Cream-jug: with gadrooned rim and foot. Double scroll handle. By Hester Bateman, London, 1775. 4″. Weight: 3 ozs. 10 dwts.

George II 'Frog' Cream-jug: with cast oviform body supported on three 'hoof' feet, and rare 'balance' terminal on base. London, 1732. Maker's mark illegible. 3½″. Weight: 6 ozs.

George II 'Pitcher' Cream-jug: the plain body of sturdy gauge, on circular collet foot and with 'dewdrop' spout and 'S-shaped' handle. By Edward Wood, London, 1740. 3″. Weight: 2 ozs. 15 dwts.

Cream, or rather milk, jugs (cream was not taken with tea until the late 18th Century) originated early in the century, but do not appear in any quantity until the second decade. There have been a few pre-1720 specimens, mostly of the octagonal variety: a magnificent example was illustrated in an article in *Country Life* (March 1st, 1902) 'How to choose Old Silver: IV', and was exceptionally fine; the octagonal panelled body stood on a shallow ring foot, and the neck and lid were reinforced by a moulded rim. The lip had a 'dewdrop' terminal and the handle was of the high 'double-scroll' type. The vessel was dated 1706 but no other details were given.

From a private collection:
George II plain 'frog' Cream-jug: the massive 'hand-raised' body with finely conceived shaped rim, and on three 'hoof' feet. Double scroll handle. Completely unmarked, circa 1735. This fine jug is possibly from the workshop of John Pollock, as he made some excellent specimens of very similar form. Some of the finest cream-jugs were unmarked: a probable explanation is that they were recast from an existing article. 3½″. Weight: 5 ozs. 17 dwts.

and a 'pear-shaped' Queen Anne vessel of quality might top even this eminently satisfactory figure by at least another £1,000, $2,800 at a conservative estimate. Tea caddies were never greatly popular items, as there is little use for them in a modern world, especially sets of three, and prices are more reasonable in keeping with this dislike. Single caddies are better sellers and there are quite a few collectors of this type of vessel. A fine domed lid example will sell for between £220 to £275, $615–770 for an ordinary example and £300 to £450, $840–1,260 for a Hester Bateman specimen. Lamerie caddies, of course, are another matter, and prices can run well into four figures. Even the argyle for hot gravy, which was not particularly sought after in former years, is now quite a rarity and commands an excellent price.

The less useful objects such as the brandy saucepan and the goblet sell for respectable sums: up to £250, $700 for the former if of the George II-III periods, and £200 to £400, $560–1,120 for the latter if of exceptional quality and with fine enrichment. Cream-jugs of all kinds, both the 'pitcher' variety and the 'helmet' type obtain good prices. The former might fetch up to £400, $1,120 and the latter to £150, $420 for an ordinary specimen or £200 to £250, $560–700 for one by Hester Bateman.

As has been mentioned in another context, investor-collectors need have no great fear of spurious articles if they use a little common sense and/or employ the services of a reliable dealer. It might, however, prove useful at this stage, to advise them of the existence of a practice which, though not against the law, could nevertheless affect the subsequent price. Until quite recently, when public interest became so widespread that it no longer mattered whether an article was contemporarily enriched or not, it was the habit of some misguided dealers to send articles bearing 'out-of-period' enrichment to the silversmith to have the embossing removed—or 'de-chasing'—as it was called, and a great many fine articles of otherwise impeccable form were irretrievably ruined. The work tended to destroy the purity of line of the vessel and to weaken its gauge.

This type of restoration took the form of hammering the embossing flat

George III Coffee-pot: of tall pyriform shape, on high collet foot, and beaded on rim and foot. With scrolling spout, and domed lid surmounted by beaded 'urn' terminal. By Hester Bateman, London, 1785. Engraved with the Arms of the Castle Family of Suffolk. Fully marked in base and with maker's mark and lion passant in lid. 12" including terminal. Weight: 28 ozs.

Samuel Johnson, in his great *Dictionary* quotes the following reference to coffee by Francis Bacon: 'They have in Turkey a drink called coffee, made of a berry of the same name, as black as soot, and of a strong scent, but not aromatical, which they take, beaten into powder, as hot as they can drink it. This drink comforteth the brain and heart and helpeth digestion.'

George III Coffee-pot: of pyriform shape, formed as a full-bellied vessel of generous size, on circular foot and with beaded spout, base and lid. By James King, London, 1786. Bright-cut and engraved with swags of foliage. 11¾". Weight: 30 ozs.

From the collection of Mrs. David Lawrence.
George III Hotwater Jug: of shaped 'vase' form, and on high shaped 'trumpet' foot. Bright-cut and engraved with foliate motifs at neck and on foot. By Samuel Hennell, London, 1792. 12¼" in height. Weight: 21 ozs. 10 dwts.

and then attempting to disguise the work by re-polishing. Not only was the original patination removed, but the remnants of the many hundreds of tiny 'nicks' which remained even after the motifs had been eradicated disfigured the article. To the uninitiated observer, these imperfections are often mistaken for the minute 'pitting' which is the result of genuine 'wear and tear' over many centuries, but the knowledgeable buyer, looking at the surface of the silver with a magnifying glass, can easily detect the previous surface with its remaining vestiges of enrichment. There is, however, a simple test which will soon reveal whether there has been 'de-chasing' or not: often the restorer could not be bothered to remove the handle of the mug, tankard or cream-jug he was working on, and worked round it, thus leaving signs of deep embossing in places which he thought would not show. A careful scrutiny of these points should uncover any traces of restoration or attention.

What of the future? Can the present trends continue to rise and will progress in values be maintained? On careful consideration, it is felt that prices of the important articles will remain high, perhaps static for a long time, but unless new markets become available, it is probable that 'saturation point' is gradually approaching. The increase will continue, however, in articles which have not hitherto achieved great public interest. Queen Anne tankards, George III beakers, and wine jugs, hot-water jugs, salvers and trays, baskets of all kinds—sweetmeat, bread and cake—tea vases and cruets have still not appreciated sufficiently and could rise greatly in value. Victorian articles by the better makers George Fox, Emes and Barnard and Richard Hennell, to name but a few, could also attract interest. Hester Bateman articles still have a good potential, and Storr items of the smaller variety can show reasonable appreciation.

THE BOX

It may be claimed with some certainty that boxes are among the most useful and attractive objects known to man. The staggering number of these articles extant, the bewildering variety of uses to which they have been put, and the serious attention which they appear to have merited in literature, must surely compel a deep and penetrating examination of their story. It is not the intention of this survey to embrace *all* types of containers—caskets, trinket boxes and the like—but when the group begins to embrace receptacles made in precious metals, much wider implications are involved and a detailed evaluation of the box *per se* becomes essential.

The early history of the simple container with the pull-off or sometimes hinged lid which has come to be known as the 'box' is nebulous within the framework of antiquity: certainly, small chests, surely the forerunners of the box, have been discovered in ancient Egyptian tombs, originating as far back as 2000 B.C., and it is very probable that those coarse vessels—pots, amphorae, and bottles—which continually come to light in archaeological finds, were *homo sapiens'* pitiful attempts to construct some protective container for his primitive 'treasures'.

It is not, however, so much with the primeval origins of the container that students of the box are concerned, as with its development and style within the past millenium, both as an ecclesiastical object and latterly as a simple protective container. The term 'box' would seem to derive from the Latin 'buxum', literally, boxwood—the wood of the box-tree—*B. Semper Virens,* a highly workable vegetable material combining the qualities of pliability and strength. The bush was introduced into Britain by the Romans, but was known throughout Europe, and subsequently found great favour both as a medium for religious carvings, and for a wide variety of domestic items; spoons, ladies' combs, instrument cases and the like. But it was the ecclesiastical function which gained it most fame. There are also certain authorities who believe the root of the word to originate from the Greek word 'πυξίς'—a pyx—namely, the circular shallow box which has, from mediaeval times, served to accommodate the consecrated Host in the Christian communion service.

Indeed, it is as such that the word receives its earliest mention in English mediaeval literature. Robert of Gloucester, the famous monkish chronicler of the 13th Century, writing in the vernacular in 1297, refers to it both as a box and, (by implication) a pyx: *'the box that heng ouer the weued. Mid godes fless and is blod'.* Later references to the box occur, amongst others, in the works of the Alsatian typographer, bookseller, and pupil and successor to William Caxton, Wynkyn de Worde who, in 1531, mentions *inter alia* the 'swete oyntment was closed and shutte in the boxe', and of course, Shakespearean references abound.

Presumably the early boxes were made of the yellow boxwood or other similar forms of treen, but even allowing for the popularity of the material, there must have been disadvantages: with the exception of articles intended for church use, where sacred ritual demanded reverent care, articles of domestic utility, such as have been described above, were subject to misuse, damage and general 'wear and tear'. It became obvious that more permanent media were both necessary and desirable.

The turning point arrived with the advent of The Renaissance. An era of magnificence was heralded: gems and precious metals speedily replaced the humbler articles in treen and base metals. The treen box (or by this time it might have changed to ivory, ebony or horn) lost its purely utilitarian aspect and was transmuted into a glittering, sturdy and beautiful *objet d'art*. It was not that the wealthy Tudor courtiers and their ladies or the powerful European merchants objected to the possession of ostentatious jewels or precious *bibelots*, but that, perhaps, it simply did not occur to them to have about them these 'well considered trifles'.

Towards the end of the third quarter of the 16th Century an event occurred which was, had they but known it, to have far-reaching consequences for the pleasure-loving and slightly gullible populace of the Elizabethan era—more, for the whole of posterity, wherever indeed civilised humanity assembled—this was, of course, the introduction of the tobacco plant into Europe.

Charles II oval box: the lid with wrought iron spring fastener on the inside, opened by pressing the button outside. With contemporary mantelled Coat-of-Arms. Maker: EL in shaped shield (Jackson, page 125, line 19), circa 1660–65. Marked with the maker's mark only in lid. Hinged-lid specimens are very uncommon. (3¾″ by 2¾″).

The actual history of *N. Tabacum*, how it came to England, and who is believed to have brought it there, is too well known to require repetition. Far more absorbing is the fact that the folk-lore surrounding the 'divine weed' is among the most prolific of all quasi-scientific material. Hundreds, if not thousands of books have been written on the subject, and many of these give a fascinating insight into those peculiar 'political' situations which could even influence the design of the most paltry articles—a mere container for tobacco among them—during a period when a life could be forfeit for nothing more than a hasty word or an imagined slight.

There are many types of boxes, and all will receive due attention in this survey, but as the tobacco box is the first good example of a 'personal' as opposed to a 'utilitarian' container this article claims first place.

The contemporary mood of the English nation at this critical stage of its development has been lightly touched upon above: in order that the fine distinction between 'utility' and 'personal preference' be clearly understood it is necessary to analyse how an unimportant event could be affected by superstition and personal animosities—powerful weapons when wielded by a vacillating monarch—at a time when the 'Divine Right of Kings' (soon, tragically, to end fatally) was still regarded as sacrosanct.

The tobacco plant was brought to Europe in 1558, and by the end of the 16th Century was firmly entrenched throughout England. It was an age of 'scientists'—untrained enthusiasts whose untapped leisure led them into all sorts of odd, not to say dangerous experiments. When a new trend or fashion was announced, it was accepted with an almost hysterical zeal. Thus, when tobacco 'smoaking' became known, the ardent 'tobacconist'—the term applied originally to the smoker not the retailer—would implore his supplier for some 'good stinging geare', probably referring to strong tobacco (it was a matter of some pride as to who could outlast the other in this new game) and, perhaps in those early days of primitive tobacco-curing methods, his wish might be gratified beyond his dreams!

The really devout smoker would sport a large case of several 'Winchester Clays'—long-stemmed pipes, (it has been suggested that the additional length was necessary if the gallant was not to singe his beard when lighting his 'chimney' with a pair of 'ember-tongs' containing a piece of wood plucked from the fire). The very earnest dandies would carry about with them small silver porringers into which they 'would measure the exact amount of saliva which, through their correct use of tobacco, they were able to expectorate during the day'. This, and other such delightful 'occupations' were indulged in either at a convivial alehouse or within the precincts of St. Paul's Cathedral—it was the custom to use the Cathedral for social rendezvous — where many 'smoakers' gathered, there to 'spit private' as it was called.

Silver 'smoakers' utensils' such as ember-tongs—which resembled a pair of fire-tongs—and tobacco boxes of this period have not apparently survived, but a long-stemmed silver pipe claimed to be of James I provenance has been noted: this article was unmarked, but was very similar to the clay pipes contemporary to the era. If silver tobacco boxes (or 'cases' to be more correct) ever did exist, it is probable that they were adaptations of Renaissance caskets, as they needed the capacity to accommodate about a pound in weight. It may be imagined, therefore, that all this 'geare' must have appreciably encumbered the Jacobean gallant as he sped through the streets to join his friends, as pockets were almost unknown in English costume until the third quarter of the 17th Century—such few as did exist were very small pouches at the back of the doublet—and personal items: pomanders, hawking whistles and purses were generally carried either at the waist in a needlework pouch, or hung about the neck on a golden chain.

George III Tobacco Box: an out-of-period copy by Hester Bateman, London, 1780. The lid bright-cut and engraved with 'wriggle-motif' and with contemporary monogram. The base inscribed 'William Hall, Folkston'. This owner was the mayor of Folkestone in 1780. Fully marked inside box and with maker's mark and lion passant inside lid. Pull-off lid.
(4″ by 2⅜″).

Smoking in the privacy of one's own home, would not have been to the taste of the convivial Elizabethans: pleasures were made to be shared; presumably other 'refreshments' too, were 'on tap', and all in all, the English citizens of the late 1590's began to take this new panacea for 'all ills' (as many quacks hastened to describe it) for granted. It must not be imagined, however, that the 'smoakers' had things all their own way: in the same manner as they so quickly convinced themselves that tobacco was a bountiful stimulant, there were other 'scientists' who believed, and what is much more important, convinced King James the First (who had lately acceded to the throne) that catastrophic results would occur if the 'weed' were nationally accepted.

It was at this juncture that those 'personal animosities' referred to above manifested themselves. James's motives against tobacco—'the custome lothsome to the eye'—appear to have sprung from a variety of prejudices, the most cogent of which was that the tobacco trade was largely in the hands of his Spanish enemies, the most illogical, his own naive medical superstitions about the 'drug'. Bearing in mind that James's own personal habits were not particularly beyond reproach, it must be assumed that this pseudo-virtuous attitude was aimed (as has been suggested by historians) at vilifying the reputation of Sir Walter Raleigh—who was reputed to have brought the 'weed' back with him from Virginia—at the instigation of Raleigh's old adversary, Robert Cecil, first Earl of Salisbury.

86

Although at first glance, there appears little connection between the oft-quoted 'Counterblaste' of King James, published in 1604, and the tobacco box, there was a very definite link, nevertheless. Whatever the origin of the plant, no matter who was responsible for its introduction into England, notwithstanding all the agitations against it, tobacco was in general use all over the country until the king placed a crippling tax of six shillings and tenpence per pound (*it had been twopence*) upon it.

Whether James was genuinely seeking to eradicate tobacco smoking or cunningly striving to increase his exchequer is immaterial: what is important, is that the ridiculous tax, and the persecutions which followed in its wake, had the effect of driving smoking 'under the counter', and the inevitable smuggling commenced. The use, therefore, of the 'smokers' equipage' described above ceased abruptly—in public, at any rate—and such 'whiffing' as was done took place in the back-parlour of some sympathetic inn-keeper where a group of friends would gather to 'enjoy a pipe together', or, worst of all for the gregarious Stuarts, within the safety of one's own home. It is for this reason, perhaps, more than any other, that the connecting links between the reigns of Queen Elizabeth I and (if 'reign' is the correct word) Oliver Cromwell were severed. Few 'smokers' utensils' of English make of the intervening period, namely, the reigns of both James I and his more tolerant but devoted son Charles I remain extant.

The solitary exceptions would appear to be the James I period silver pipe and one single oval tobacco box dated 1643, (the latter was not available for examination but *was* seen by an eminent authority many years ago). The Commonwealth regime—otherwise so puritanical towards 'worldly pleasures'—regarding smoking if not with favour, at least with tolerance; indeed, the first known tobacco boxes of any appreciable number stem from the early years of Cromwell's Protectorate.

What was described as a 'Cromwellian tobacco box, date 1652, maker GS with arrow between', (*vide* Jackson *English goldsmiths and their marks,* page 126, line 19) engraved Arms and name 'John Wreilub' was exhibited at what was probably the last great Loan Exhibition to be held under private auspices—that of Sir Philip Sassoon in June 1929—when no fewer than eight hundred supremely important pieces of English Plate were shown. Many were subsequently dispersed to national collections overseas, never to be seen together again.

The box is No. 535 in the illustrated catalogue, and when carefully examined under a powerful glass, the half-tone plate discloses that this particular specimen is much deeper than any of its somewhat later contemporaries, being about two inches in depth. Moreover, it has the unusual feature, at this early date—when most boxes had unadorned lids—of a 'stepped lid'; that is to say, there was a raised cartouche of oval form within the ellipse of the lid. This type of enrichment is not normally encountered until the first decade of the 18th Century.

Another Commonwealth specimen is illustrated in Jackson's *Illustrated History of English Plate,* where it appears as figure 1187 on page 907. This is dated 1655 and is by the maker whose mark was IS in Monogram, of whom Cripps (11th edition, 1926, page 441) states, 'this maker's mark is found on much plate', and indeed, it is found over a long period: Jackson records it at 1673, and Yvonne Hackenbroch's superb evaluation of Judge Irwin Untermayer's Silver contains a silver-gilt mug bearing the same mark dated 1693. Bearing in mind that it is first encountered in 1655, this may have been a 'father-son' business, and many such long-lasting partnerships occur within the realms of silversmithing.

This latter tobacco box, dated 1655, could be termed the true forerunner of all the oval tobacco boxes, as it possessed most of their features: a slightly domed pull-off lid, gently incurving or 'moulded' sides, the top and bottom rims enriched with that twisted-wire ornament known as 'cable-gadroon'. The closely fitting lid bore the Arms of the Wayte Family of the Isle of Wight.

It is noteworthy that the earliest specimens were constructed with both sections, top and bottom, of equal proportions. Thus, the actual capacity of the box could be controlled, as the 'bezel' or rim of the top was the same depth as the base, and if a greater amount of tobacco was placed inside, this merely raised the lid to accommodate the greater amount. This measure might have been necessary in view of the coarser quality of the early tobacco. The later boxes have a fairly deep base but a shallower domed lid. Generally, sizes were in the region of 3¾″ long by 3″ wide by 1¼″ deep.

One aspect which appears to have received no mention by contemporary historians (probably because it simply did not occur to them that one day people might want to know the answer) is the ever-vexing question whether the so-called 'tobacco box' was for smokers' tobacco or grated snuff. It should be noted that there is ample provenance for Queen Anne and later specimens, but none at all for the period under discussion, namely, the Commonwealth and the two reigns which followed it.

The confusion really stems from the existence of the so-called 'snuff-rasps', which are found in richly carved boxwood or elaborately enriched Limoges enamel, and which appear to originate from this period. There is no question of the provenance of 'snuff'—it has early origins—but whereas contemporary literature has revealed, as has been stated, that tobacco boxes existed as far back as 1643, little, if anything, is said about 'snuffboxes'. Another 'false scent' has been the introduction of the 'carotte' theory; a specially prepared tube of tobacco shaped like the familiar vegetable, originating from France (which was the main exporter) was used in conjunction with the 'snuff-rasps'. It has been suggested that this object reposed in the early 'tobacco boxes'. The possibilities are endless, and, on the surface of it, inexplicable.

The answer to the enigma might possibly lie in a fragment of information contained in an Elizabethan account of the contents of a 'smokers' equipage' where there is mention of 'a maple trencher for *shredding* the tobacco'. The italicised word may have an important bearing upon the subject, as it appears to exclude any process of rendering the tobacco into snuff, when 'rasping' would be a much better description of a finely milled powder. Indeed,

Charles II 'Boscobel Oak' snuffbox: the lid and base of oak, mounted with cut-out silver engraved plaque. Depicting the scene in Boscobel Wood as Charles II sat in the tree: a cherub offers him three crowns (symbolic of the Three Kingdoms) while at the base of the tree two armed riders search. The motto 'Sacra Jovi Quercus' completes the composition.
(3″ by 2½″ by ⅝″ deep.)

Dr. Johnson cites a splendid Baconian quotation to support his definition of 'shredding'—a small piece cut off—'gold' grown somewhat churlish by recovering, is made more pliant by throwing in *shreds* of tanned leather'. The term is thus shown to refer to what, in our own day, might be called 'sliced tobacco'.

The second solution is really much simpler: not possessing pockets (as has been stated earlier) the seventeenth century gallant, should he wish to take snuff, would have to carry the container in his hand. Since the early boxes (with the one exception described below) had pull-off lids, the would-be 'snuffer' would have to take the lid off with one hand and take a pinch of snuff with the other, all the time fumbling around until he could replace the lid, and endeavouring to refrain from sneezing until he could do so! This is obviously why all so-called 'snuffboxes' have hinged lids, to make 'one handed' operation possible.

From the collection of Maurice Newbold, Esq.

Left, Top - Bottom

George I large oval silver-mounted snuffbox: the container is formed of a terrapin-shell, and the lid engraved with the Arms of the Butchers' Company and inscribed 'Joseph Oliver Butcher at Ash in Kent 1721'. The above was recorded in the parish register at the adjoining parish of Hatley as a yeoman farmer and died circa 1741. The article is unmarked, and as the 'exemption' for articles weighing less than half an ounce had not yet been introduced, and in any case, the lid weighs considerably more, it is probable that it was made to commission from an existing piece, melted down and refashioned. The excellence of the engraving points to it having been done in London and not by a country silversmith.
(4½″ by 3⅛″).

Queen Anne flat 'powder horn' type snuffbox: with silver ferrule, which is not, however, removable. The horn lid mounted with silver plate contemporarily scratched with the owner's name 'John Dune 1709' and with castellated rim. The 'powder horn' is a typically Scottish motif and a whole series is known which bear various mottos pertaining to bravery: 'a man his mynd should never sett upon the thing hee canne nott gett' or 'a man of words and not of deeds is lyk a garden full of weeds'.
(4½″ by 2″).

George IV baby teething stick: formed as silver-gilt cast floral and acanthus leaf finial set with coral 'pacifier'. The ancients ascribed great powers to this marine animal substance: it is chiefly carbonate of lime secreted in the tissues of certain polyps, and the Romans hung branches of coral on children to preserve them from danger. Coral 'gum sticks' were held to cool a babe's aching gums, as well as acting as a 'dummy'. By Charles Rawlings, London, 1820.
(3¾″ in length).

Charles II silver-mounted boar's tusk: formed as a powder horn, the tip with silver ferrule, the mouth with stopper forming seal. Scratch-engraved with foliate motifs and later owner's name 'Robert Reid 1745'. Circa 1680.
(4″ in length).

Right, Top - Bottom

George II 'vase-shape' snuffmull: of Scottish origin, the ivory body supported by struts of silver and with similar decoration on lid. The date '1784' is probably not contemporary to the box, having been scratched when the owner acquired it. With three-lugged hinge and silver base. Circa 1750.
(2¼″ by 2⅛″)

Charles II large oval spicebox: scratch-engraved with foliate motifs on lid and with floral acanthus motifs on base. Set with cornelian in cartouche on lid and similar gems at 'pinch-sides'. 'Snap' fastener. By DS Crowned, London circa 1690.
(3⅜″ by 1⅝″).

Queen Anne oval snuffbox: the lid cast with portrait of the Queen in full Garter Robes, copied from the portrait by Sir Godfrey Kneller shortly after her accession in 1702. Of shallow content and with seven-lugged hinge. Maker's mark only: AH crown above, pellet below, circa 1702.
(2¾″ by 2½″).

Joseph Oliver
Butcher at Ash in Kent 1721

TMP
1734

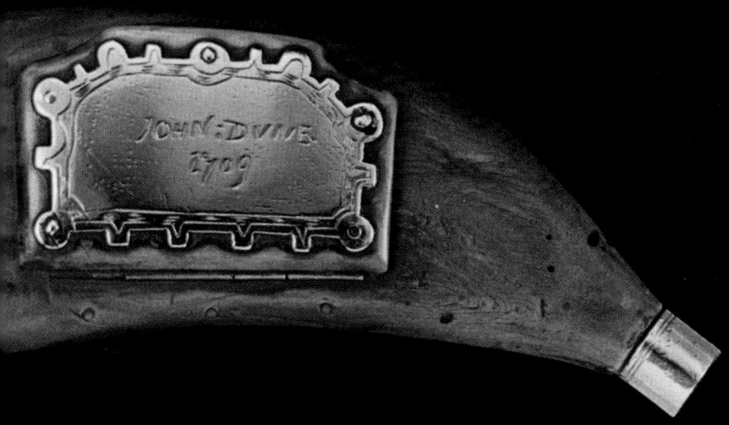

JOHN DUVE
1709

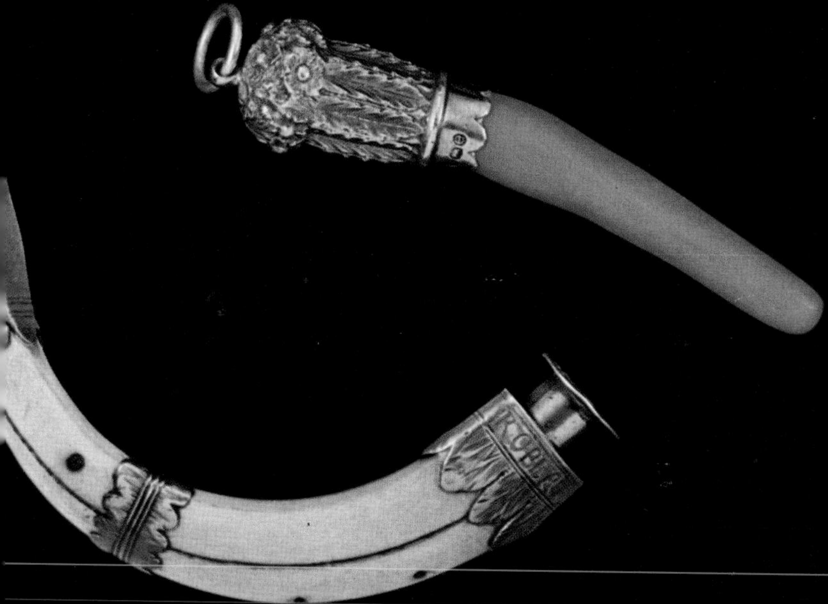

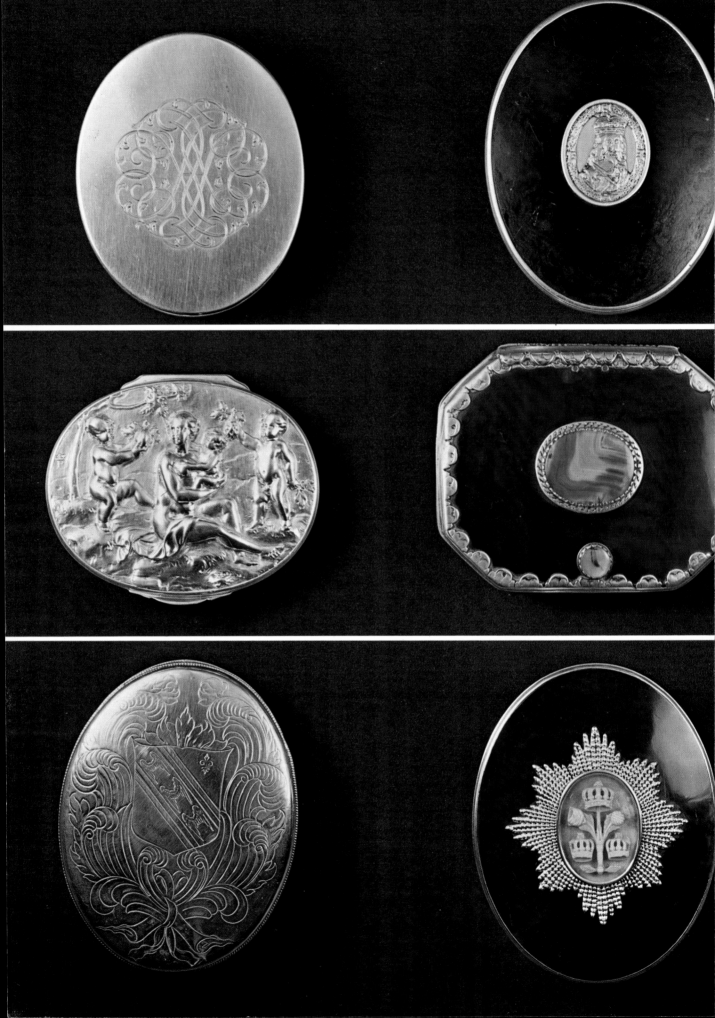

The smoker had no such problem: he needed a table to set out his 'equipment', and therefore a pull-off lid gave him no trouble. The one exception to the rule of pull-off lids is a curious oval tobacco box which has a hinged lid: the type, in fact, greatly resembles the modern 'pinch-sides' tobacco boxes, where the lid flies open when the sides are squeezed. This early oval container dates from circa 1660–65, and differs from the later types—where 'fastening' is effected by means of a 'snap'—in that there is a most elaborately sprung wrought-iron spring inside the lid which connects to the outside 'button-snap'; thus, by moving the outside button, the box is opened. This is a great rarity.

Such boxes, then, which possess hinged lids, were intended as snuffboxes. Specimens possessing pull-off lids were either tobacco boxes, or, if a smaller size, patchboxes or toilet boxes. A full description of these will be found later in this chapter.

In passing, it is interesting to observe that King James's antipathy towards tobacco was reflected in the almost sycophantic silence with which those sensitive contemporary chroniclers, the Jacobean dramatists, treated the subject. Nowhere, for instance, in the Bard's works is there anything but an oblique reference to the 'weed'. Thus, the well-known public image of such convivial fellows as Sir Andrew Aguecheek and Sir Toby Belch in *Twelfth Night* flourishing their long tobacco pipes is purely apocryphal, and must have been depicted later by artists ignorant of Jacobean politics.

Even the much quoted passage from Henry IV, I, iii, in which the choleric Hotspur derides 'the certain lord, perfumed like a milliner'; in the following terms:

> 'twixt his finger and thumb he held
> A pouncet-box, which ever and anon
> He gave his nose, and took't away again;
> Who therewith angry, when it next came there
> Took it in snuff'

does not, in fact, refer to tobacco snuff, but to one of the medicated aromatic powders popular with dandies and fops of the day.

Another version of the 'Boscobel Oak' theme: the lid being inlaid with panel of oak and inset with the Coronation Medal of Charles II by Thomas Simon, and four finely engraved plaques composed of scrolling reversed cyphers and acanthus foliage set in each corner. The inside of the lid possesses an ivory miniature of St. Francis of Assisi bearing a child in a wheat-sheaf on his back—possibly an allusion to the incident in the Boscobel Oak—unmarked, circa 1680.

(3″ by 2¼″ by ½″).

George I oval domed lid snuffbox: with beaded border and similar enrichment on 'lift-up' flap. The lid and surround finely engraved with 'Hogarth-type' motifs and scrolling foliate cartouche. By James Smith, London, circa 1725 (maker's mark only). (3½″ by 2¼″).

Large Old Sheffield Plate snuffbox: of rectangular form with panel bearing mythological scene in high relief set in lid, the sides repoussé with scrolling foliage. Circa 1750. These early Old Sheffield Plate boxes are among the earliest of all articles in this medium; Thomas Boulsover is known to have experimented with their design and production. (3½″ by 2½″).

George III circular snuffbox: with sliding lid, which when revolved, opens to reveal space for the insertion of two fingers for 'a pinch of snuff'. With contemporary crest and motto: 'Tria Juncta In Uno', which refers to the family crest of 'three hands joined'. By A. J. Strachan, London, 1800. (2¾″ by 1″ deep).

George III 'cast-top' snuffbox: the lid
enriched with 'shepherd amidst pastoral
scene' motif, and with cast vine-leaf and
reeded borders. By Lawrence & Co.,
Birmingham, 1817.
  (2¾″ by 1⅞″).

George IV 'cartouche-shaped' snuffbox:
silver-gilt and decorated with Romanesque
foliate cast motifs on a matted ground. The
centre of the lid bears a pastoral scene in
the Louis Quinze manner: the shepherdess
with her flock, the shepherd with his dog
and pipe. The base is enriched with a sphere
of concentric engine-turning. By John
Bridge, London, 1822.
  (3½″ by 2½″ by ⅞″ deep, weight: 6 ozs.
10 dwts.)

George III 'snail' snuffbox: the lid finely
engraved with 'starfish' and other marine
animals, the base simulating the shape of
the snail. By Matthew Linwood, Birmingham, 1804.
  (2½″ by 1⅞″).

George III silver-gilt rectangular snuff-box: with oval corners and enriched overall with 'swan on lake' motif, the sides with 'matt-chasing' (obtained by 'pitting' the surface with a very thin punch) and bright-cut engraving. By James Beebe, London, 1806.
($3\frac{1}{4}$" by $1\frac{3}{4}$").

George III engine-turned snuff-box: of rare 'rhomboid' shape, that is, an oblique equilateral parallelogram, which appears in outline to resemble a military tank. By RB, London, 1817.
($2\frac{5}{8}$" by 2").

George IV engine-turned snuff-box: with cast 'racing scene' subject in centre of lid, and with reeded sides. By Thomas Shaw, Birmingham, 1825.
(3" by $1\frac{3}{4}$").

Finally, the 'smoking habits' of the Elizabethan 'tobacconists' were mentioned earlier, but curious Stuart developments (heralded in the 16th Century) included one which was deliberately omitted at that juncture, as possibly appearing to over-emphasise what might be termed in our own more hygienic age 'a filthy habit'. As an alternative to smoking, perhaps due to over-indulging, the exquisite socialites chewed 'plug' tobacco and spat into silver basins. A contemporary engraving reveals these as greatly resembling those well-favoured 'sweetmeat dishes' of the light repoussé type, normally associated with the work of the silversmith William Maundy. One wonders if this lowly function was the real use to which these fragile little shallow dishes were put . . .

The ornamentation of tobacco boxes, and, for that matter, of most other 'personal boxes' (as the whole series under discussion might be classified) echoed the enrichment applied to other contemporary plate. Some boxes possessed lids which compared with the fluted and half-fluted dishes and cups of the late Charles II—early William and Mary period. Others, taking advantage of the flat surfaces, sported elaborate heraldic motifs, often of exaggerated form, and yet others had sly rebuses, referring in pictorial form to the name of the owner (a fine example is shown on page 90 where the name 'Wingfield' is depicted as the heraldic device of wings on a field). Sometimes subtle intertwining cyphers were used, the complexity of which must have taxed the ingenuity of the talented engravers on plate, and given great pleasure to the puzzle-loving Stuarts, both from the view of ownership and the riddle of trying to penetrate the identity of the discerning connoisseur who commissioned them.

The primary function of these enigmatic cyphers and complex Coats-of-Arms, however, was to render identification possible should the article be found in the possession of an apprehended highwayman or pickpocket. The practice of thus applying identifying designs on plate may account for the existence today of many items bearing quite fictional Coats-of-Arms and inscriptions, for which there is no heraldic provenance whatsoever: a man invented a crest even if he was not entitled to the use of one.

This, at least, is the charitable view to take, otherwise our Stuart forebears would have to be equated with our Victorian ancestors who were fond of the same solecism. In passing, one particular instance comes to mind: a fine George III tankard bearing a most detailed description of a deed of bravery at sea, citing full names and dates, was submitted to the scrutiny of the National Maritime Museum at Greenwich. Unfortunately, there was not a mention anywhere in the very complete naval records of the vessel named, nor indeed of the occasion itself. In fact, there was not one iota of truth in the whole tale—there never had been a certain Captain 'X'—and on careful re-examination, the mode of the engraving was found to be mid-Victorian!

As the seventeenth century drew to its close, certain innovations were introduced to 'box-lid' enrichment: one favourite motif was the inserted 'repoussé' plaque (the term refers to that method of silversmithing whereby the design is hammered from the back, to appear in high relief on the front); this might portray mythological scenes pertinent to contemporary *masques,* or delineation of The Holy Family or other similar ecclesiastical subjects. Sometimes these inserted plaques bear a maker's mark, the great majority, however, do not.

There are a variety of oval tobacco boxes which bear plaques of the 'tavern-scene' subject associated with the work of the great Flemish painter David Teniers the Younger—the group is known as 'The Topers'—and one is never quite certain whether the work of the plaque is contemporary or a Victorian electrotype plate copied from a genuine painting. It is sometimes difficult both for experts and dilettante collectors to decide whether an article is genuine or not. In this connection it is recalled that more than a decade ago a dealer purchased a pair of superb silver-gilt William and Mary toilet caskets; these, had they been of contemporary enrichment, should have possessed, at most, panels of engraved ornament. Instead, they sported great massive 'swag and festoon' motifs, and were considered by all who examined them to be Victorian chased, that is, the ornament was applied in the Victorian era. It was then held that plain surfaces were out of keeping with the

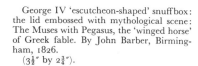

George IV 'escutcheon-shaped' snuffbox: the lid embossed with mythological scene: The Muses with Pegasus, the 'winged horse' of Greek fable. By John Barber, Birmingham, 1826.
($3\frac{1}{2}''$ by $2\frac{3}{4}''$).

general trend of decoration and a great number of really fine pieces were thus irretrievably ruined.

To return to the caskets: large items of this type, being intended to contain perfumeries and the like, were often fully lined inside with silver-gilt panels, and it is not always possible to determine whether the 'swagging' is repoussé right through the side-panels. A discerning collector, realising this, took a chance and purchased the caskets. Working with great care, he succeeded in prizing away a corner of one of the panels, and a band of glorious seventeenth century engraving was revealed! It is pleasant to recall that for once, Victorian vandalism did not mar a work of art, and that the collector was able to acquire for very little what was worth a great deal.

The above story is told neither to denigrate the reputation of the dealers nor to laud the perspicacity of the collector. It simply illustrates the difficulty facing the dogmatist: if there is a lesson to be learned from this instance it is that, to adapt the old adage 'too much learning can be a dangerous thing'; there is peril in being too dogmatic about everything—one has to rely on intuition as much as on knowledge—and experts, especially writers, must be very careful not to state categorically that 'such-and-such *must* be so-and-so'. One can only present documentary evidence, or, on rare occasions, purely logical deduction, and leave the reader to make his own decision.

William IV 'engine-turned' snuffbox: with heavy encrusted borders and rare 'incused corners' which are also 'engine-turned'. Circular malachite plaque in centre of lid surrounded by collar of foliate engraving. By Edward Edwards, London, 1831.
(3½" by 2¼").

No analysis of 'box-lid' decoration could be complete without a detailed account of the wonderfully engraved tobacco box which appears on the front cover. The article itself is of the usual pull-off lid type, with a slightly domed lid, and top and bottom 'cable-gadroon' enrichment. It is a sturdy piece, being four ounces, two pennyweights in weight, and the lid is of deliberately heavier gauge to take the depth of the engraving. The craftsman who made the box, was the eminent 'elder statesman' of the London Huguenot silversmiths' colony, Pierre Harrache, Senior, and the article is dated 1686. The size is comparable with other boxes of the period, being 3½" long by 2¾" wide by ⅞" deep. This is identified as 'acid-etching' which is described on page 103 of *Silver Boxes*.

The subject of the portrait is William Sancroft (1617–1693) Archbishop of Canterbury to both Charles II and James II. Writing of Sancroft, a wise historian epitomised his character thus: 'He behaved with singular prudence and integrity in the difficult and critical times in which he lived; and it was reckoned very happy for the church of England, in the furious attacks made upon it in the latter years of King Charles and the whole reign of King James II, that so steady a pilot was at the helm.'

Sancroft's stand against James's allegiance to Catholicism eventually resulted in the notorious 'Trial of the Seven Bishops'. In April 1687, James II published a Declaration of Indulgence, exempting Catholics and Dissenters from penal statutes; in April of the following year, he issued a proclamation to force the clergy and bishops to read the Declaration from their pulpits. Sancroft and six of his bishops declined, and were indicted for libel, sent to The Tower and subsequently acquitted by a jury to much popular acclaim. James eventually lost his throne, and Sancroft, in his turn, was deprived of office when he refused to take the oath of allegiance to William and Mary on their accession.

The Primate is depicted on the box in skull-cap and rochet (the surplice-like vestment used by bishops). The mien is dignified yet humble; it is obviously a portrait commissioned by a friend, as it is robbed of the stern severity which appears in the original 'portrait from life' by the great 17th Century engraver David Loggan (1636–1692) dated 1680. It should be explained that most engraved ornament on boxes and other plate was taken from existing designs, the engraver of the actual article merely copying the work of the original artist. Using subtlety of line, the engraver could reduce any defects of character, such as haughtiness, and introduce nobler emotions: compassion, humility and gentleness. This the unnamed engraver has done in full measure, as the original engraved portrait in the British Museum differs only slightly from the engraving on the box, but enough to make Sancroft appear approachable instead of imperious.

As with most engraved ornament of the period, the portrait on the box is unsigned. Such facility of craftsmanship was obviously taken for granted at the time, and thus the name of the engraver is conjectural. Not so the quality of the workmanship, clarity of line, economy of detail and dexterity with the 'graving tool'. When it is recalled that the box originated in the *atelier* of the Huguenot, Pierre Harrache, the name of Simon Gribelin springs to mind: he is known to have worked for Harrache at the time the box was made, namely, the late 1680's, having also lately come to England as a refugee from religious persecution. It is not the purpose of this panegyric to seek to prove Gribelin's direct association with this box, yet the temptation is almost irresistible in view of the quality of the workmanship.

Simon Gribelin himself engraved the subject of 'The Seven Bishops' as a group portrait, with the bust of Sancroft surmounting his Brothers. The engraving appears as No. 89 in his famous book of engravings in the British Museum *Livre d'Estampes de Sim. Gribelin, fait Relié à Londres* 1722. Here, Sancroft is depicted as an ageing, sunken-cheeked old man, not at all the dignified prelate of Loggan's day; the change is quite understandable in view of the Royal persecutions which he must have endured.

It is hard to see who else could have undertaken the task of engraving the portrait on the box; Hogarth could have done it, but he was not even born until 1697 and presumably was not skilled enough until the mid 1720's. Certainly the craftsmanship must be considered the apotheosis of English engraving of the late 17th Century.

The oval tobacco boxes of Queen Anne's day, as well as the George I period were mostly functional containers of heavy gauge, and being of the Britannia Standard, much brighter in colour. For the most part, they were completely plain, with here and there a mantelled Coat-of Arms in a scrolling cartouche. It is at this period that the 'stepped lid' is first encountered in any great variety. There were many box-makers, but one of the most prolific was the London silversmith Edward Cornock who appears to have specialised in boxes and salvers. Two other makers whose boxes appear fairly regularly, but whose marks have not been identified were 'HB a demi-lion above', circa 1725, and 'GO crown above' dated (on one specimen) 1718. The latter mark does not appear in Jackson at this date, but might be a variation of the mark of John Goode entered in 1700.

The oval tobacco box seems to have gone out of fashion towards the middle of the 18th Century, but specimens dated 1740 and 1748 have been noted, and of course, out-of-period copies (the fine Hester Bateman box is an outstanding example) are known throughout the century—probably because snuff-taking had by then become popular throughout Europe, and England shared in this trend. A small word of caution is indicated at this stage: a knowledgeable collector might spot 'at a glance' that the marks on one of innumerable 'commemorative items'—modern copies of early spoons, forks, and tobacco boxes—produced for such occasions as the Silver Jubilee of King George V and Queen Mary in 1935 and The Coronation of Queen Elizabeth II in 1953, were of the Britannia Standard, but with modern date-letters. A beginner might not: he would see the coveted seated female figure of Britannia and the lion's head erased and leap to the conclusion that the item was an early piece.

As was mentioned earlier in this survey, gentlemen's clothing seldom contained pockets until about 1670, and this may account for the lack of any pocket container which can be dated accurately as being of this period. Such pockets as did exist were inconveniently placed out of reach and this would undoubtedly discourage use for anything but the most essential items. The absence of contemporary snuffboxes might also stem from this. Such snuff containers as are noted generally bear a maker's mark traceable to circa 1680–90. These emerge as shallow rectangular cut-corner boxes with hinged lids; there might be three, five or seven lugs to the hinge and all possess a fastener of the 'snap' type, or very occasionally, a sprung iron fastener of the 'button' type, described above in relation to the rare oval tobacco box, circa 1660–65.

A series of 'repousse-top' snuffboxes by the famous Birmingham silversmith Nathaniel Mills.

Victorian large table-size snuffbox: subject: Windsor Castle, in high relief, in cast foliate border, the base finely 'engine-turned', the sides with foliate motifs. Birmingham, 1844.
($3\frac{1}{2}''$ by $2\frac{1}{4}''$).

Warwick Castle: in shallow relief. Birmingham, 1838.
($3\frac{1}{2}''$ by $2\frac{1}{4}''$).

Buckingham Palace: with the Marble Arch in front (it was removed to the present site in 1850) and ornamental pool with swans. Birmingham, 1846.
($3\frac{1}{2}''$ by $2\frac{1}{4}''$).

Durham Cathedral: in deep relief. Birmingham, 1840.
($3\frac{1}{2}''$ by $2\frac{1}{4}''$).

At about this time, a new type of embellishment was introduced, probably from Dutch designs. It is known as 'scratch-engraving' and consists of lightly incised engraving informally applied with no apparent attempt at symmetry or balance. The motifs usually depict prancing amorini or cherubs or contemporary landscape views of rural scenes—churches, houses and inns—and some boxes bear amatory mottos such as 'true lovers are in unity, their true affections united be' engraved around the front and back of the article,

Stuart 'amatory' locket: of heart-shape with repoussé 'pierced heart on an anchor between two forget-me-nots' theme. The message is: 'I hope you will not forget my love'. The back engraved 'a small requitall', i.e., a penance for hurt. Unmarked, circa 1650.
($\frac{7}{8}$″ by $\frac{1}{8}$″ deep).

or motifs of the 'hearts pierced' or 'hearts aflame' theme. Whether, in fact, these little boxes were 'lovers' tokens or merely expressing the idiom of the day is not known.

While on the subject of 'amatory' themes, a charming little heart-shaped locket, strictly a box, since it is composed of a pull-out lid and a base, is illustrated here. It is quite tiny, being no more than $\frac{3}{4}$″ in size, and has lost its suspensory ring (it was worn around the neck) and the lid is repoussé with a pierced heart on an anchor (symbolising hope) and two 'forget-me-nots' on either side. The base is contemporarily engraved 'A small requitall' and the date is circa 1650.

As the 17th Century drew to its close, a new type of box appeared: the silver-mounted specimen. That is to say, the sides and sometimes the inner lining were of silver, but the lids and bases were of 'allied materials', that is, horn, tortoiseshell or occasionally treen. The size of the container grew, the shape frequently recalled the oval form of the earlier tobacco box, but being hinged, there could be no mistaking the one for the other.

From a private collection.

George III large rectangular shallow vinaigrette: the lid superlatively engraved with commemorative portrait of Admiral Lord Nelson, his sleeve pinned to his chest, and set in a frame containing the immortal motto: 'England expects every man will do his duty'. By Matthew Linwood, Birmingham, 1806. The grille vertical with cast view of 'The Victory' and the words: 'Trafalgar Oct 21, 1805'. Engraved on base with Linwood's characteristic 'sunburst' motif. (see page 113)
($1\frac{3}{8}$″ by 1″ by $\frac{1}{4}$″ deep).

Charles I memorial locket: heart-shaped: with 'incised' diagonal background and applied oval plaque of cast form depicting King Charles's bust. The back engraved with 'pierced heart' motif. Unmarked, circa 1650. With suspensory loop. Royalist supporters wore these little memorial boxes around their necks on a chain.

($\frac{3}{4}$" by $\frac{1}{8}$" deep).

Centre

Ivory Plaque depicting Greek mythological scene: Diana and Actaeon. He spied on her in her bath, and was turned into a stag, whereupon his own hounds devoured him.

Circa 1670, a fine example of 'scratch-engraving'.

Right

Charles II 'drum-shaped' comfit or sweetmeat box: with semi-spherical 'scratch-engraved' lid, five lugged hinge and with 'snap' fastener. Maker's mark only inside box: M crowned, circa 1670.

($1\frac{1}{2}$" in diameter by $\frac{7}{8}$" deep).

Left

From the collection of Maurice Newbold, Esq.

Restoration thanksgiving locket: heart-shaped, the obverse die-stamped with portrait of King Charles II, the reverse with image of Queen Catherine of Braganza. Scratched owner's initials and with suspensory ring. Unmarked, circa 1660.

($\frac{7}{8}$" by $\frac{1}{8}$" deep).

There are so many different types of silver-mounted snuffboxes extant that it is difficult to select typical examples. Perhaps the most celebrated subject is that type of shallow rectangular box known as the 'Boscobel Oak' variety. This specimen—of which there are few known examples, few, that is, by comparison with the great mass of other memorial boxes, of the Nelson, Wellington and Napoleon species—is generally found with oaken panels forming the base and lid of the box and with a pinned-on cut-out plaque bearing contemporary engraving.

The theme is that tragic event in English history when Charles II, newly vanquished at the Battle of Worcester, fled from the Roundhead soldiers into the precincts of Boscobel House, Shropshire, in September 1651. The sixth day of that month found him concealed within an old oak tree in Boscobel Wood, about twenty-five miles from Worcester. The king is depicted in the branches of the oak; to his right, a cherub offers him three crowns—symbolic of the Three Kingdoms to which he had succeeded in 1649—while around the base of the tree two armed riders prowl. The oak surmounts the Latin motto, 'Sacra Jovi Quercus', which is taken to refer to incidents in the king's early life, when he was in the habit of taking a billet of wood to bed with him. For this juvenile habit it was considered at the time that 'when he came to reign, he would either be like Jupiter's log, for everybody to ride and contemn, or that he would rather choose to command his people with a club, than rule with a sword'.

The identity of the actual engraver who first applied the 'Boscobel' design to the lids of the boxes cannot be ascertained, but an early 'broadsheet' dated the first year of the Restoration, 1660, has a scene remarkably like the one on the box, but without the motto or the two riders. Both the great Prague etcher Wenzel Hollar (1607–1677) and Charles's Sarjeant Painter, Robert Streeter, portrayed Boscobel House and the Whiteladies Priory in which the forest containing the Royal Oak stood, but these were general views of the subject. The theme is even found engraved on mother-of-pearl boxes, similar in every way to their silver counterparts.

To claim that all the 'Boscobel Oak' boxes were made from genuine relics of King Charles's tree is a little like believing that all the religious reliquaries extant contain saintly bones! Nevertheless, the famous diarist, John Evelyn, writing in 1678 stated that he had heard of the Boscobel Oak being destroyed by people who hacked off the bark and boughs as souvenirs. Later accounts indicate that a brick wall was erected around the stump to try to protect the tree, but by 1734 nothing remained.

Among other favourite media for snuffboxes was the tortoiseshell container. The use of plates taken from the carapace of turtles originated from ancient Egypt, and moulded articles made from the substance were popular in Roman times. The vogue for articles made in tortoiseshell appears to have reached England during the early Stuart era, but subsequently the material was popularised through the work of yet another Huguenot craftsman, John Obrisset the Younger.

The only clear facts which can be established about Obrisset, are that he was born in Dieppe circa 1666 and died in England after 1728. He worked in both horn and tortoiseshell, producing mostly boxes, medallions and plaques based on the designs of earlier as well as contemporary craftsmen and medallists. Thus, the celebrated 'signed' oval snuffboxes bearing the portraits of Charles I were copied from the posthumous medal by John Roettiers, dated circa 1670, and the famous series of oval boxes—of which a few silver specimens have been noted, one appears here and is by the maker whose mark 'AH crown above, pellet below' is dated by Jackson as circa 1700—with the bust of Queen Anne in full Garter robes were based on designs by John Croker, who in turn copied Sir Godfrey Kneller's portrait of the Queen painted shortly after her accession in 1702.

With the advent of the 18th Century, many silver-mounted articles were introduced, among them exotic sea-shells such as cowries and conus-shells, and the carapaces of various marine animals such as small turtles and terrapin, and these possessed finely engraved close fitting lids. The illustration shows a specimen of this type, although the mount alone is shown. The interior of this box was lined with lead, which has now, sadly, disintegrated. It was obviously intended for table use, as it would be too bulky to carry in the pocket, and, in any case, when not in use, would have to be placed face down, as the shape would cause the box to tumble over.

The George II period was the most prolific of all for snuffboxes and indeed boxes of all kinds, but to enumerate all the various types would require a book unto itself—in fact, many have been written—but there are a few outstanding examples which must be carefully examined. Readers are probably familiar with the shell-shaped or rectangular containers of the George I—II period, as well as with the heavy gauge 'bombé' and 'cartouche-shaped' cast and wrought specimens, which reflect the rococo taste, so this latter group will not be analysed; they are merely containers embodying foreign influences, particularly French and German, and beyond an aura of beautiful opulence, they are not of great interest.

It ought to be stated at this stage, that the contemporary trend towards massive cast silverwork—so much sought after in the twentieth century—was not then received with enthusiasm by all sections of the community. English silver had, until the arrival of the Huguenots, been of delicate, even primitive form, and the isolationists, believing that the foreigners would deprive their own craftsmen of work, attempted to limit the franchise. This was, of course, not acceptable, and the Huguenot school, Platel, Harrache, Willaume, Lamerie and many others began to flood the country with their magnificent, if cumbersome plate.

It should be remembered that the householder of the 1730's or 40's knew nothing of 'colour' or 'patination', the joy of acquiring antique silver. The thought of 'collecting' older plate never entered his head; for him plate was simply utilitarian, to be melted down if faulty, to be sold if superfluous, candlesticks to light his rooms, dishes to hold his meat, spoons to sup his soup. Silver had no value beyond the actual metal content plus a few shillings for the work. The curious phenomenon of the Huguenot preoccupation with massive articles has been carefully examined, and a parallel situation uncovered.

During the Gurkha War in Nepal circa 1814, it was noticed that the English settlers were ordering great quantities of enormous tea services and gigantic trays: the weight was of such magnitude that the combined tea service and tray would have been almost impossible to lift even if empty. These items were either produced locally or sent out from England. The answer, of course, is quite simple: these were no utilitarian vessels, but subtly disguised forms of instant currency, to be melted down and used as money should the need for sudden flight ever arise. More sophisticated moderns might carry a few diamonds or some rare postage stamps for such an eventuality.

Similarly, the Huguenots, being recently harried by religious persecutions, noting the hostility of the natives, sought to express their fears through the medium of heavy silverware. It is gratifying to recall that such extreme measures were never needed, and the heavy gauge articles which were produced are admired throughout the civilised world. While it would be pure sophistry to pretend that *all* refugees are mindful of their obligations to their adopted country, it is safe to say that the Huguenots contributed far more both in the Arts and Commerce than they ever received.

The age of heavy cast-work on boxes had arrived. The favourite themes for 'box-lid' enrichment included subjects based on mythological incidents; one favoured motif was Helen and Paris with King Priam in the background, another, biblical aspects, such as Queen Esther's appeal to King Ahasuerus and his extending the sceptre of mercy towards her. Other themes included historical episodes, scenes from ancient Rome, simulations of battles, and, finally, and most enigmatic of all, a series of snuffboxes, dated the first quarter of the 19th Century, which depict adaptations of Dutch or French paintings. These include the famous series of 'The Pedlar' boxes, an example of which is illustrated. With only one exception (a specimen by Rawlings and Sumner dated 1838, probably copied to commission) all the other specimens bear the mark of the mysterious silversmith 'JL in a lobed indent'—that is, the maker's initials are conjoined in the centre and indented top and bottom of the shield, rather like Paul Storr's mark—who is identified by Jackson (page 231, line 8) as 'John Lacy or John Law (probably) 1841–2'.

The Register of Makers at Goldsmiths' Hall does not contain Lacy's or Law's mark, but it does list 'John Linnit', who first entered his mark on the

25th of April, 1815 when it appeared in a plain rectangle, and whose second mark, entered on the 31st of January 1824 assumed the familiar 'lobed' form. As the punches for London hall-marks are changed on the 29th of May each year, articles made in 1823 would continue to receive the date-letter for that year until the 29th of May, and all the repoussé-top snuffboxes noted bearing the 'Pedlar Motif' appear to emanate from this date or a few years thereafter.

It is often asked 'what's in a name; what difference whether the maker was John Lacy or John Linnit?'. But of course, it makes a great deal of difference if, as Jackson states, the mark of the former was not entered until 1841. Firstly, Linnit's name is in the Register at Goldsmiths' Hall, and Jackson's ascription is conjectural, and, secondly, the date '1823' might have an important bearing upon the choice of subject for the 'box-lid' motif, whereas the date '1841' might not.

It should be stated at this juncture, that were it not for a happy coincidence, any theory behind the motive of selection of this particular theme 'The Wine and Spirit Pedlar' would have been doomed to failure. After a massive research the name of the original artist—the subject is quite obviously a detail from a painting—and the *genre,* that is, the type of painting, are still not known. As may be seen, the pedlar proffers his wares from a tray about his shoulders; on the tray are various flasks and bottles. He is clad in elegant early eighteenth century costume with a cockaded tricorn hat. The background is a familiar exterior scene with figures around a well, others peering out of a door and another leaning on a barrel. The name which springs immediately to mind is that of the great French artist Antoine Watteau (1684–1721) who specialised in mock-pastoral subjects, and who founded a new school which rebelled against the decaying classicism of the Louis XIV period. Again, nothing approaching the 'Pedlar' theme has been discovered.

The coincidence referred to above, was the discovery in a famous London dealers' of another snuffbox by John Linnit also dated 1823 or 1824 which had as *its* subject a plaque repoussé with the grotesque figure of a 'toper' holding a jug and dagger and wearing a feathered hat. By pure chance, it was discovered that the original theme had been executed by the famous Dutch painter of the early seventeenth century Gerrit Van Honthorst (born Utrecht 1590, died 1656) and was known as 'The Man with the Hambone'—what was thought to be a dagger was in fact, a hambone—(a fine etching of this is in the Royal Collections at Windsor) and the picture is dated circa 1620.

It becomes immediately obvious that Linnit, seeking a new theme to place on 'box-lids' searched for centenaries or bi-centenaries of interesting paintings of the 'Dutch Droll' type: thus, if the 'Man with the Hambone' was painted circa 1620, and the 'Wine and Spirit Pedlar' (if of the Watteau school) was painted circa 1720, it is conceivable that Linnit lit upon the idea of issuing a series of snuffboxes with this 'centenary theme' upon the lids. That Linnit was influenced by current events is shown by the famous frontispiece by Seymour of the first edition of Charles Dickens' 'The Pickwick Papers', the subject being 'Mr. Pickwick addresses the Club'. The first edition and the box were both issued in 1837.

Also shown is a very fine cut-corner Table snuffbox of small size: this is by John Linnit and his partner William Atkinson, dated 1811. Again, Jackson does not identify this partnership, merely stating the mark to be $\frac{\text{IL.}}{\text{WA}}$ Linnit's last mark was recorded at Goldsmiths' Hall in 1848 when he was working at 44 Berners Street, off Oxford Street. In his earlier years he was entered in the Register as a 'small worker', later as a 'gold worker'. He seemed to specialise in out-of-the-ordinary articles—a fine silver-gilt inkwell formed as the Round Tower of Windsor Castle appears elsewhere in this work—and several fine caddy-spoons dated 1816–19 have been noted. The quality of his work was excellent. Not for him the coarse containers of the early Victorian era: a box from his workshop weighed upwards of five ounces, and was most superlatively enriched.

There is one more 'box-lid' theme which deserves mention: rectangular snuffboxes are sometimes encountered with the repoussé motifs always worn away, but which are designated 'Mazepa boxes'. The motif is first discovered circa 1760, but has been noted as late as 1838. The story of the origin of the theme is an interesting one. Ivan Mazepa-Koledinsky (1644–1709) was a Russian nobleman who was educated at the court of the Polish king John

Casimir. An intrigue with a married Polish lady nearly cost him his life, when, on discovering Mazepa with his wife, the enraged husband tied him to a wild horse and sent him naked into the savage steppe. His subsequent escape (he found refuge with a cossack band and eventually became their leader) brought him to the notice of Peter the Great who honoured him and sat him at his own table. In the latter years of his life, Mazepa, fearing that Peter's current favourite, Menshikov, would supplant him, turned traitor and joined forces with Charles XII of Sweden in that monarch's campaign against Peter. When the war failed, Mazepa fled to Turkey, where he died in 1709. The condition of the 'Mazepa boxes' noted has always been very bad and it was not possible to see how the English designers coped with the 'nudity' theme, but, perhaps, as many of the boxes were made well before the Victorian era, this feature did not cause offence at the time.

Having so exhaustively examined the subject of tobacco and snuffboxes, it is possible, at last, to proceed to other types of 'special purpose' containers, which are, nevertheless, still within the enormously wide group; in order to keep to a form of chronological precedence, it is necessary to consider three small groups, namely, patchboxes, toilet boxes and spice boxes.

Charles II small oval patchbox: with 'light cable-gadroon' rims on lid and base. This enrichment is obtained by twisting a silver wire; the thickness of the wire dictates the coarseness of the 'cable'. The pull-off lid engraved with seated figure of 'Justice'. Maker's mark only: IK, pellet below in shaped shield (see Jackson, page 134, line 1) circa 1670.
($\frac{3}{4}''$ by $\frac{5}{8}''$).

William and Mary circular patchbox: the top engraved with 'Tudor Rose' motif. By WW, pellets above, mullet below, circa 1690–5. (see Jackson page 484, line 20).
(1'' in diameter by $\frac{1}{2}''$ deep).

The first fully hall-marked patchbox noted was dated London 1669, but the vogue of wearing patches or 'court plasters' as they were known, is at least thirty years older. The story of how the first patch came to be used is interesting: there is a tradition that a court beauty stuck a little patch of black leather on her face to hide a disfiguring mole and found the effect so satisfactory that she continued to wear it. As with all trends of fashion, excesses soon manifested themselves: the ornament became so popular that the ladies of the court, first in France, then in England, began to out-do one another in the fanciful and often grotesque designs which they stuck on their faces. An excellent illustration of this queer fashion appears here where the lady has not only applied spots, stars and crescents, but also a coach and pair; this sketch is circa 1650. It is recorded that other fantastic motifs were applied to the face: fully masted sailing ships, and even a massive chateau!

The famous English dramatists Beaumont and Fletcher wrote '*The Elder Brother*', a play, circa 1614, but first acted circa 1635. Act III, scene ii declaims the following:

'Your black patches you wear variously,
Some cut like stars, some in half-moons,
some lozenges'.

The popularity of the fashion and excesses was shown in a Bill entered in Parliament on the 7th of June 1650 by the Puritans for the suppression of 'the vice of painting and wearing black patches and immodest dress in women', which was surprisingly dropped after the first reading. An early mention in literature of the patchbox *per se* occurs in a stanza by Alexander Pope:

'this morning omens seem'd to tell
thrice from my trembling hand the patchbox fell'.

In the eighteenth century the Whig ladies wore the patches on the right cheek, the Tories on the left.

In practice, the patchbox is a sturdy container about one and a half inches in diameter by half an inch deep. The hall-mark is usually struck inside the base, and the maker's mark inside the lid. The later specimens became rectangular or elliptical, but these also contained tiny mirrors inside the lids, and are more usually found in gold. The early patchboxes were simply enriched: there might be a roughly scratched 'Tudor Rose' motif on both lid and base; slightly later specimens, dating from the 1690's are flimsier in gauge, but might have become more 'box-like' in appearance. The early patchboxes were evidently 'raised from the flat', that is, hammered up from one flat piece of silver, whereas the later examples were made by soldering circular rims or 'bezels' to flat circular discs, which might thus project slightly. These of course, accommodated the normal type of patch; what kind of container was required to house the 'coach and four' type is beyond imagination. . . .

The earliest toilet box noted was dated circa 1630 and appeared in an exhibition in aid of the Red Cross in 1915. It was stated in the catalogue to be of plain moulded octagonal form with a hinged lid and 'button' snap, dated 1630, but the type is more reminiscent of the 1670's. The magnificent toilet services emanating from the William and Mary period all contain toilet boxes which were used to contain orris-root for cleaning the teeth, almond-paste for the complexion, powder, rouge and lipsalve.

The most enigmatic container in this group is the spicebox: in type it greatly resembles the oval sunken-hinge tobacco box described above as of the 1660–65 period, except that it is opened by pinching the oval plates soldered onto the sides of the box, which thus permits the 'snap' of the lid to be sprung. The enrichment is of the 'amorini and cherubs' variety scratch-engraved on the lid, and scrolling floral motifs similarly engraved on the base; occasional mottos declaring love and fidelity are also encountered. The purpose of this box is not strictly documented: it can only be assumed that grated nutmeg or cloves were carried in it to be added to mulled ale or punch; nutmeg graters were already in use at the time that these little containers made their appearance, namely, circa 1685–90, and it is probable that the former were used in conjunction with the latter. Sizes varied: some were about $1\frac{1}{4}''$ long by $1''$ wide by $\frac{5}{8}''$ deep, others (a fine example decorated in the centre of the lid with a cornelian is illustrated) were much larger, being upwards of $1\frac{3}{4}''$ long.

It now becomes necessary to turn from the study of the box as a container for tobacco and snuff, and approach the subject from a completely different angle: prophylaxis, that is, the use of perfumes and spices to remove the risk of contagion from disease or disagreeable odours. This facet introduces both the pomander and the vinaigrette, the first being the early prototype of the second. The early pomanders originated as spherical objects, imitating the ancient practice of rolling a paste of aromatic substances into a ball and threading it on to a necklet which might be worn on the person.

Charles II small circular spicebox: shallow container, the pull-off lid pierced with simple geometric motif, and surrounding 'Tudor Rose' motif and with light 'cable-gadroon' borders. Maker's mark struck thrice only: TI in square punch, circa 1660–70.
($\frac{7}{8}''$ in diameter by $\frac{3}{8}''$ deep).

The practice of the use of aromatics and perfumes as prophylactics is very old indeed, and is recorded as far back as 1800 B.C., in an ancient Egyptian formula given in the '*Papyrus Ebers*', where it is called 'The Sacred Perfume of Kyphi' and is recommended for perfuming or fumigating the house or clothing for sanitary purposes. The compound consisted of various herbs including Myrrh, Frankincense, Cyprus Wood, and Mastic. The use of such perfumes was continued right through the ancient civilisations: Greece, Rome, the early Hebrews, India and Burma all subscribed to the theory of prophylaxis through perfumes.

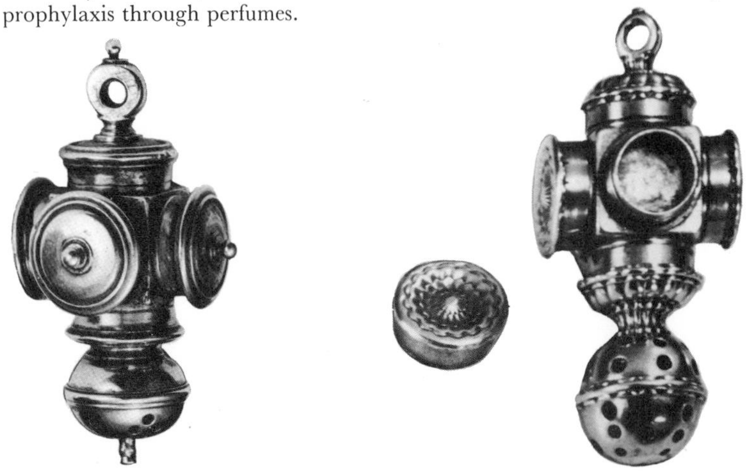

Left
Charles I 'cruciform' pomander: fully described in text. Unmarked, circa 1630.
(2″ by 1″).

Right
Charles I 'cruciform' pomander: of similar form to the above, but with 'guilloche' or 'engine-turned' enrichment on the caps of the perfume cells. Unmarked, circa 1630.
(1¾″ by ¾″).

The pomander as such, that is, the little box-like container with pierced lid, was known to the early period of the Roman Empire, when Roman matrons vied with each other in the beauty of the little silver or gold boxes enriched with enamels or precious stones, which they carried next to the skin and were pierced where they came into contact with the body. Whether there is any foundation for the belief that the pomander arrived in England from France is conjectural, but the theory undoubtedly arose from the combination of two French words 'pomme'—an apple—and 'ambre'—ambergris, a frequent ingredient—thus both the shape and the purpose of the article are

Opposite
From the collection of John R. Rayment, Esq.

Top
Victorian cast and chased 'thistle' vinaigrette: with 'arabesque' motif pierced grille. By Edward H. Stockwell, London, 1876. This maker evidently specialised in cast floral objects as several variations have been noted; one such was a silver-mounted scent-bottle with the stopper formed as a thistle and another formed as a rose.
(4″ in length by 1⅜″ at widest point, weight: 4 ozs).

Victorian cast 'rose' vinaigrette: the cover comprising hinged petal, the grille being concealed in the top of the bud. By Edward H. Stockwell, London, 1888.
(4¾″ in length, by 1½″ in diameter at widest point).

Victorian oval vinaigrette: with ribbed sides and engine-turned enrichment on base. Deep repoussé top, subject: The Martyrs' Memorial at Oxford with the church of St. Mary Magdalen in the background. By Nathaniel Mills, Birmingham, 1847. The 'Martyrs' were Nicholas Ridley, Bishop of London, Hugh Latimer, late Bishop of Worcester and Thomas Cranmer, Archbishop of Canterbury in Henry VIII's time. On the death of Edward VI in 1553, Ridley and Cranmer were involved in the attempt to place Lady Jane Grey upon the throne of England; Latimer offended Queen Mary who charged him with heresy. All three were sent to the Bocardo or common prison in Oxford in March 1554: Latimer and Ridley were burnt at the stake in Broad Street on the 16th of October 1555, when the former greeted Ridley with the immortal words: 'Be of good comfort, Master Ridley, and play the man; we shall this day light such a candle by God's grace in England as I trust shall never be put out'. Cranmer died at the same spot in March 1556. The Memorial was erected in 1841 in St. Giles High Street to a design by Sir George Gilbert Scott, the famous Victorian architect who adapted the column from the late 13th Century crosses in honour of Queen Eleanor.
(1⅞″ by 1⅜″).

George III 'snuffbox cum vinaigrette': the vinaigrette contained in side of box, which is of the cut-corner variety and enriched with 'abstract' motifs. Foliate grille. By Samuel Pemberton, Birmingham, 1807.
(2¼″ by 1⅛″).

Centre
Elizabeth I 'segmented apple' pomander: of octafoil type, the central section with four spice compartments protected by small rectangular hinged doors. Bell-shaped finial surmounted by suspensory loop. Circa 1600. Unmarked.
(2″ by 1″ in diameter).

Elizabeth I sexagonal 'segmented apple' pomander: silver-gilt and engraved with contemporary figures in costume of the time; the base containing an unguent spreader and forming intaglio seal. The spice-compartments with sliding lids, and engraved with foliate motifs. With suspensory loop. Circa 1600. Unmarked.
(1½″ by 1″).

James I octafoil 'segmented apple' pomander: engraved with arabesque motifs, the spice-compartments with sliding lids. Unmarked, circa 1620. With shaped finial and suspensory loop, and on collet foot.
(2″ by 1½″).

Bottom
From the collection of Dr. David Lawrence.
Pair George III 'boat-shaped' sauce-tureens: of oval form, on similar beaded feet and with rising domed lids surmounted by urn finials; the 'harp-shaped' handles, the rims and the finials are all with bead enrichment. Beautifully bright-cut and engraved with swags of floral festoons on the bodies and 'festoon and tassel' motifs on the lids. By Hester Bateman, London, 1785. The art of 'hand-raising' from the flat silver plate is never more evident than in these 'rising domed' lids.
(9″ overall by 4″ wide, weight: 38 ozs. 10 dwts).

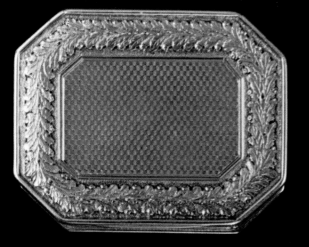
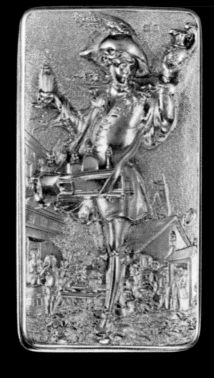

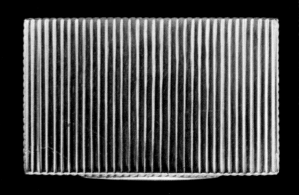

Top

George III cut-corner rectangular small table snuffbox: silver-gilt, and with engine-turned panel in centre surrounded by green gold cast oak-leaf ornament within gold rim. Engine-turned on sides and base. By John Linnit and William Atkinson, London, 1811. (3″ by 2⅜″ by 1″ deep).

George IV repoussé-top snuffbox: subject: 'The Wine and Spirit Pedlar'. By John Linnit, London, 1823. Vertical sideways opening, otherwise plain. This specimen is fully discussed on page 103. (4″ by 2″ by 1″ deep).

Centre

George III silver-gilt shallow elliptical patchbox: finely bright-cut and enriched with foliate motifs. By Phipps and Robinson, London, circa 1790, maker's mark only. (3½″ by 1¼″ by ¼″ deep).

Charles II oval spicebox: scratch-engraved on lid with cherub holding a heart and motto 'Un seul me sufit'—'one heart alone', and on base with acanthus foliage. By Thomas Tucker or Thomas Townley, London, circa 1690 (the mark is TT crowned in a shaped shield). (1⅝″ by 1¼″).

George IV silver-gilt 'ribbed' rectangular snuffbox: of plain form and with simple thumbpiece. By Nathaniel Mills, Birmingham, 1827. The 'ribbing' has been soldered onto the lid and sides. (3″ by 1¾″).

Bottom

Victorian silver-gilt rectangular snuffbox: the cast lid in shallow relief depicting 'Mr. Pickwick addressing the Club', from the original print by Seymour forming the frontispiece of 'The Pickwick Papers' published the year the box was made, 1837. By John Linnit, 1837. The base engraved with foliate motifs. (3½″ by 2¼″, weight: 6 ozs. 10 dwts).

George III silver-gilt 'satyr's mask' snuffbox: high repoussé and with ruby eyes. The base set with moss-agate panel and flatchased with vine motifs. Marked only with lions passant on lid and side. Circa 1770. This type is exceptionally rare. (2¾″ by 1¾″).

adequately described. The word as it is now known 'pomander' appeared in the late 16th and early 17th Centuries.

The association with the article and Cardinal Wolsey is too well-known to require mention. In fact, all the Tudors loved perfumes: Stephen Hawes, the Poet to Henry VII in his 'Passtyme of Pleasure' 1509, has it thus:

'The rose was knotted with pomaunders right swetly,
Encencing out the yll odours misty'.

The noted English diplomat and politician Sir Nicholas Throgmorton, a celebrated courtier of Queen Elizabeth's day, and father-in-law of Sir Walter Raleigh, wrote in 1562 to his friend the English ambassador in Madrid asking him to buy him a pair of gloves perfumed with orange flowers, and another scented with jasmine, the one for his wife, the other for himself.

The early English silver pomanders of the 'segmented-apple' type, that is of spherical form and with segmented compartments, date from the 1580–1600 period. The segments are usually eight in number, the lower parts of which are hinged to the circular base, and are held together at the top by means of a circular cap with a screw which goes into a central pillar of octagonal form. The segments, or *loculi*, each held a separate perfumed substance: those illustrated here are unusual inasmuch as the specimen on the right does not have the normal slide-out lids to the segments, but four little doors in the centre column marked with the Latin names. Three perfumes are identifiable: 'Nerdi' is spikenard, 'Carvi' is carroway, 'Macis' is Mace, but the fourth 'Cocco' (unless it is 'cassia'—cinnamon) cannot be traced.

The centre example is of sexfoil type and is engraved on the outside surface with characters in contemporary costume. The base screws off to reveal an unguent spreader, and the flat bottom is formed as an intaglio seal. The type on the left is a typical octafoil pomander with slide-out lids to the *loculi*. Another rare type is the 'cruciform' variation which is illustrated which Jackson's *History of English Plate* illustrates as figure 1221 and describes as follows: 'formed as a die with circular cap screwed over a shallow perfume cell on each of its four sides; the finial is screwed to the top and covers a central perfume cell, which is connected by a small orifice with the globular sprinkler beneath it, and may have been used as a syringe for discharging liquid scent upon a curious or amorous admirer'. The date is circa 1630, and the size is usually 2″ by 1″ across. The mode of enrichment is an early form of 'guilloche' or what is known in England as 'engine-turning', whereby the groove is gouged out in a concentric motion.

Finally, the pomander evolved into the famous 'vinaigrette' which now reverted to the 'box-form' of the other containers in the wider group. The catalogue of the Stuart Exhibition held at the New Gallery London in 1889 cites a great many relics of Charles I, and item No. 1038 reads: 'Ivory carved head (the top of a walking cane) which belonged to Charles I and was used by him during his confinement in Carisbroke Castle. The top is pierced to be used as a vinaigrette. The staff with this head was presented by the king to Mr. Thomas Cooke, who was at the time Master Gunner at the Castle'. Since Charles I escaped to Carisbroke in the Isle of Wight in November 1647, this must constitute a very early mention of the vinaigrette as such, although Jackson's 'History' illustrates (figure 1223) 'a physician's walking-stick' with a pierced top forming a vinaigrette, and dated circa 1613, presumably because that is the date engraved upon it.

An early type of aromatic container comprised a shallow circular box with a tightly fitting pull-off lid and a primitively pierced pull-out 'grille'—the pierced foil which prevented the caustic acid forming the vinegar constituent from splashing onto the skin—unmarked except for a maker's mark dated circa 1700. Towards the end of the 17th Century, the fear of contagion lessened somewhat owing to improved methods of sanitation, and the use of 'prophylaxis' waned slightly. It returned towards the middle of the 18th Century when the ladies reverted to tightly fitting costume and towering, elaborate coiffure. This trend, coupled with laxity in personal hygiene, made the use of restoratives imperative.

The perfumes employed in the manufacture of aromatic vinegars were usually made up from the following ingredients: clove, nutmeg, cinnamon, blended with rose, bergamot and lemon. A specimen of this solution, made to order by a modern pharmacist, emerged as a pungent, pervasive odour, well equipped to rouse and revive many a stout matron who was too tightly laced or overcome by some of the more unsavoury smells of the streets of the day. The recipe cited was not the only one used; many others, containing 'fragrant quince, wormwood, rue, mint, angelica root and camphor' to name but one, were universally popular.

The 'Vinegar of the Four Thieves' is well-known. The legend is related that when a plague was raging in Marseilles and Toulouse circa 1720, four thieves went about plundering the dead and dying, and people wondered why they never took the disease; but they were ultimately brought to justice, and were offered pardons if they would reveal the secret of their prophylactic. Their immunity was said to be due to a vinegar mixed with certain aromatic essential oils. The story is told by the Abbaye Le Montey. In passing, it might be noted that our Georgian forebears must have had complexions of steel! The following is a quotation from an early Hanoverian recipe for a beautiful complexion: 'The Vinegar of the Four Thieves is antipestilential, and is used successfully as a preservative against contagious disorders. *The hands and face are washed with it every day;* the room fumigated with it, as also are the cloaths, in order to secure the person from infection'.

The end of the 18th Century saw the introduction of the small rectangular boxes with closely fitting hinged lids and hinged grilles. The interiors were heavily gilt to prevent the astringent acid from eating into the metal; at first, grilles were simply pierced with plain punched holes or primitive geometric motifs, but as the nineteenth century commenced, the industrious silversmiths, feeling that public interest had jaded, decided to introduce new shapes. The rectangle was forgotten: a whole series of intriguing, delightful articles emerged from the workshops. So many superlative examples are illustrated in this volume, that it is not considered necessary to enter upon a deep analysis of the vinaigrettes as a whole, but the types might be grouped as follows:

(a) Shapes.
(b) Commemorative.
(c) Cast-top.
(d) Engraved-top.
(e) Repoussé-top.
(f) Allied materials.

The group embracing 'shapes' is exceptionally well covered. The following is a list of those specimens noted, but there are undoubtedly many others as yet undiscovered: Acorns, balloons, bags and reticules, books (in all sizes), baskets of flowers, bellows, balls, birds (the body of shaped horn, the head of silver), bottles (the neck contains the perforated grille), crowns (made to celebrate the Coronation of George IV in 1820), cannon, cows, champagne bottles, cornucopia, fish (both of articulated and 'box-form'), fishermen's creels, hearts, Maltese Crosses, padlocks, roses, shells, strawberries, sunflowers, snails, scarabs, ships' lanterns, thistles, turtles and watches. The list seems endless. The period covered is from circa 1790 to 1875.

George III 'snail': oval shaped body, engraved with 'stipple-enrichment' and finely conceived 'eagle' on base. Superb 'leaf' grille. By Matthew Linwood, Birmingham, 1803. There appears to be no reason for the 'eagle' ornament; it is probably purely ornamental.
(1⅜″ by 1″).

George IV large 'book': the covers engraved with scrolling foliate motifs, the spine heavily ribbed. By Joseph Willmore, Birmingham, 1820.
(2⅛″ by 1⅜″).

George III 'articulated fish': engraved with bright-cut ornament simulating scales and fins. The lid is formed of the head, which is hinged, and the tiny pierced grille also possesses a lion passant. By Joseph Willmore, Birmingham, 1817. Fully marked on the tail.
(3½″ by ¾″).

George III 'acorn': the top matt-chased and with suspensory loop, the base with acorn terminal, silver-gilt. By Phipps and Robinson, London, 1816.
(2″ by 1″ in diameter).

George IV 'basket of flowers': the finely repoussé lid formed as hinged basket-top with basketweave rim and handle and similar enrichment on sides. By Thomas Shaw, Birmingham, 1820.
(1″ by ⅝″ by ½″).

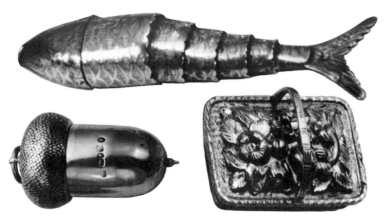

George III 'padlock': engraved with bright-cut foliate motifs and 'keyhole' in centre. By Lawrence & Co., Birmingham, 1818.
  (1¼" by 1⅜").

George IV 'bag': with twisted wire handles, engraved all over with 'basket-weave' motif. By John Barber, Birmingham, 1820.
  (1" by ¾").

George IV 'concentric ball': with pull-out filigree grille. By Wardell and Kempston, Birmingham, 1820.
  (1" in diameter).

William IV 'sunflower': the circular body repoussé in floral motif and finely chased petals, the short wire stem with cast leaf. By Joseph Willmore, Birmingham, 1830. Marked on 'bezel' or rim of grille. This is one of the rarest of all the 'shape' vinaigrettes.
  (1½" by 1" in diameter).

George IV 'heart-shaped': silver-gilt and of sturdy gauge, bright-cut all over with floral motifs with cast suspensory loop. By Lawrence & Co., Birmingham, 1823.
  (1¼" square).

Victorian cast silver-gilt 'rose-spray': the vinaigrette contained in the back, with suspensory ring and chain. Unmarked, circa 1860–70.
  (2½" by 1").

George IV 'crown': repoussé and chased. Silver-gilt, made to celebrate the Coronation of King George IV in 1820. By Joseph Willmore, Birmingham.
  (1" by ¾").

George IV 'Maltese Cross': superbly bright-cut in 'raying' motif, and shaped as cruciform, with 'watch-type' handle. By Joseph Willmore, Birmingham, 1820. (1″ square).

Victorian 'bird': a very rare subject beautifully constructed from a piece of staghorn, and with cast and matt-chased bird's head and claws on broken-branch base. By H. W. Dee, London, 1870. (3¾″).

Victorian 'bellows': the shaped sides alternating in bands of 'engine-turning' and floral engraving. By Daniel Pettifer, Birmingham, 1857. (2⅝″ by 1⅛″).

Victorian 'ship's lantern': the grille masked by the sideways hinged lid, set with foiled glass dome, with three colour 'light': green, red and white, changeable at will; the fluted top with suspensory loop. By H. W. Dee, London, 1873. (1¼″ by ⅝″ in diameter).

Victorian 'strawberry': matt-chased and repoussé, the body simulating the fruit, and with foliage on base. By Hilliard & Thomasson, Birmingham, 1860. This is another rare type. (1½″ by 1¼″).

Victorian 'cannon': the top forms the perfume bottle, the breech contains a vinaigrette. By Thomas Johnson, London, 1873. (2¾″).

Victory Grille. From a Nelson Vinaigrette. By Matthew Linwood, Birmingham, 1806.

George III oval cast-top: subject: Admiral Lord Collingwood, Nelson's great friend and contemporary. Silver-gilt, the sides reeded. The grille depicting the figure of Britannia with a lion couchant at her feet, under a cypress tree. By Moses Westwood & William Nichols & Co., Birmingham, 1809.
(1¼″ by 1⅛″).

George III rectangular cut-corner: the lid containing an enamelled portrait of a Player declaiming on a stage. This might be a contemporary study of John Kemble (1757–1823). By Thomas Shaw, Birmingham, 1799.
(1¼″ by 1″).

CAST TOP
George III 'man with dog': silver-gilt, the sides cast with 'oak wreath' motif, the base with matt-chased ground. The grille is the typical filigree of Matthew Linwood, Birmingham, 1811.
(1⅛″ by 1″).

George IV 'mandarin with a mandolin': depicted on a desert island. Silver-gilt and set in vine-leaf border, with 'herringbone motif' on sides. By Thomas Willmore, Birmingham, 1821.
(1¾″ by 1⅜″).

The 'Commemorative Group' is small, mostly celebrating naval heroes, such as Admiral Lord Nelson, of which two types have been noted. The larger superbly engraved portrait on a stipple-ground (the whole surmounted by the immortal 'Signal of the Day') which is illustrated is unusual for its size and the fact that the lid is engraved sideways, and the smaller type, which bears the same portrait but the lid is vertically engraved. The grilles of both are the same: the cast and pierced 'Victory Grille', depicting the Admiral's flag-ship and the date '21st Oct. 1805'. There is also a cast-top portrait of Nelson's life-long friend and fellow commander, Admiral Lord Collingwood; this is very rare, and the grille is cast and pierced with the figure of Britannia, a couchant lion at her feet, under a cypress tree. It is remarkable that as yet no commemorative vinaigrette to the Victor of Waterloo, the Duke of Wellington, or indeed any reference to the illustrious battle has been noted, although the subject occurs quite often on snuffboxes.

The 'Cast-top Group' includes such rarities as 'Little Boy Blue' of the nursery rhyme, shown with his sheep and amid a rural setting; a fine 'Chinoiserie Revival' subject, 'The Chinaman on a desert island playing a mandolin'; the charming 'Man and his Dog' theme which embraces two scenes; the man having his dinner while the dog looks on, and the man exercising the dog; 'Game Birds' —pheasants and grouse; 'Racing Scenes'— illustrating various field sports; 'Hunting Scenes', sometimes showing the hunters jumping over hedges, occasionally showing the beagles, very rarely depicting the hunted fox; boxes with the French motto 'L'Amitie'—to friendship.

The 'Engraved-tops' and the 'Repoussé-tops' share the same subjects, mostly English Castles, Cathedrals and Country Houses, too numerous to mention. Many will be found illustrated within this chapter, the rarest are those of Wells Cathedral, Buckingham Palace (before the Marble Arch was removed in 1851), Gloucester Cathedral, Brighton Pavilion, The Houses of Parliament at Westminster, and The Tower of London. The period covered is circa 1830 to 1865.

Vinaigrettes made in 'allied materials' such as glass, ivory, treen, all silver-mounted, are very attractive, but emanate from the late Victorian era.

It is interesting to speculate on the origin of the repoussé Castle, Cathedral and Country House variety, as being wholly pictorial and amounting in topic to the 'present from Margate' theme, by which is meant, the desire to commemorate a visit to a famous location by the purchase of an article bearing a view of the spot. This undoubtedly sprang from the rise of the railway system all over England during the early 1830's, when the bad communications suddenly vanished, and the Briton realised that the whole country (or much of it) was spread before him, waiting to be conquered. The romantic novels contemporary to the period, or perhaps epoch would be the better word, with their mysterious 'properties' of rambling, romantic old castles, secret passages and vaults, also served to focus attention on buildings; the ever assiduous silversmiths obliged with views of famous public and private residences. Perhaps the rarest of all such views is the exceptionally fine Birmingham-made vinaigrette dated 1836 with the picture of the Great Hall of John O'Gaunt at Kenilworth Castle: this is possessed of an extraordinary 'three-dimensional' effect, and is of the finest conception.

ENGRAVED TOP

From the Collection of H. A. Cooper, Esq.

George III rectangular: 'fishing scene': with heavy gadrooned rim—the term refers to inverted fluting—by Matthew Linwood, Birmingham, 1810.
(1⅞″ by 1¼″).

Victorian 'York Minster': shaped rectangular, set in scrolling cartouche. By Nathaniel Mills, Birmingham, 1850.
(1½″ by 1¼″).

Victorian 'Crystal Palace': shaped rectangular, the base engraved with scrolling foliage. By Nathaniel Mills, Birmingham 1851. (The year of the Great Exhibition which was housed in the Crystal Palace).
(1½″ by 1¼″).

Victorian 'the view from Osborne House, Isle of Wight': Queen Victoria's Marine Residence, showing the vista towards the 'Needles'. Shaped and set in scrolling cartouche, the base engraved with foliate motifs. By Nathaniel Mills, Birmingham, 1846.
(1¾″ by 1¼″).

Victorian 'Norwich Cathedral': the base and sides engraved with foliate motifs. By Nathaniel Mills, Birmingham, 1849.
(1½″ by 1⅛″).

Nothing has so far been said about the makers. Most vinaigrettes originated from Birmingham, but many were made in London, where the weight and gauge were heavier, but the styles were chiefly staid. The Birmingham silversmiths were adventurous and could be counted on to produce imaginative designs. The rarest assay-office marks encountered are those of Scotland and Ireland. In fact, only two Dublin-made vinaigrettes have ever been noted: one of very poor quality with a primitive hinged grille, and one fine specimen. [Since this was written a superb plain cut-corner rectangular specimen of George III's time has been noted.]

There were hundreds of Birmingham makers. The twelve leading box-makers were: Joseph Taylor, Joseph Willmore, Samuel Pemberton, John

Shaw, Wardell and Kempston, Ledsam, Vale and Wheeler, Francis Clark, John Lawrence, Hilliard and Thomasson, Taylor and Perry, Matthew Linwood and Nathaniel Mills. Their vinaigrettes while of excellent quality and workmanship, were primarily utilitarian; only the last two craftsmen rose above the ranks in their superlative productions, showing both imagination and inventiveness beyond all else.

To sum up: the English vinaigrette spanned a period of some eighty years. In that time, much ingenuity and craftsmanship was expended in the creation of beautiful *objets d'art* which survive to delight the collector of the 20th Century as much as they must have intrigued their owners of the late 18th Century and early and mid 19th Centuries.

REPOUSSE TOP

William IV 'John O'Gaunt's Great Hall at Kenilworth Castle': a large three-dimensional view of the subject, excellently conceived. By RJ, Birmingham, 1836. (2¼″ by 1⅜″).

William IV 'Kenilworth Castle': struck in shallow relief, with reeded borders and engine-turning on base. By Francis Clark, Birmingham, 1836. (1½″ by 1¼″).

Victorian 'St. Paul's Cathedral': struck in high relief, with encrusted border and engine-turning on sides and base. By Joseph Willmore, Birmingham, 1842. (1¾″ by 1¼″).

Victorian 'Windsor Castle from the West': High relief showing the Round Tower in three dimensional effect, a rare aspect of the subject. By Nathaniel Mills, Birmingham, 1844. (1½″ by 1″).

Victorian 'The Royal Exchange': the rim of floral casting, the base engine-turned. By Francis Marrion, Birmingham, 1844. The Royal Exchange in its present form was erected in 1843. (1½″ by 1″).

Victorian 'Gloucester Cathedral': struck in high relief, with engine-turned sides and base. By Nathaniel Mills, Birmingham, 1844. This is a rare subject, and has been confused with Wells. (1½″ by 1″).

Victorian 'Lincoln Cathedral': shaped rectangular, with foliate motifs at corners. By Nathaniel Mills, Birmingham, 1845. (1½″ by 1⅜″).

Victorian 'Scotch Pebble': formed as ovoid elliptical container, double-ended for vinaigrettes, the grilles pierced with 'star' motif, and delicately engraved overall with foliate motifs. The domed lids of rock crystal. With 'finger-ring' suspensory loop on chain. Unmarked, circa 1860. (2¾").

William & Mary crystal and silver-mounted perfume bottle cum vinaigrette: with pomander fitted in ball finial. The contemporarily scratch-engraved boss lifts out of centre to form a vinaigrette, there being no grille at this early date. Unmarked, circa 1700. (3½").

VINAIGRETTE GRILLES

Musical Grille: in a London specimen by William Eley, 1815.

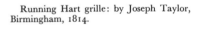

Running Hart grille: by Joseph Taylor, Birmingham, 1814.

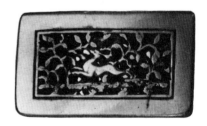

Before this lengthy analysis of the Box in all its forms can be brought to a close, two more aspects remain to be considered: the nutmeg grater and a miscellaneous group embracing such ephemera as counter-boxes, thread-boxes, and 'Memorial Boxes'.

The 'ephemera' may be dispatched first. The most poignant moments in British history are those associated with the Martyr King Charles I and his lamented death in 1649. His devoted subjects mourned his passing and waited with impatience for the Restoration of his son: a series of tiny heart-shaped boxes with pull-out lids commemorate the King by a portrait in the shape of a miniscule plaque applied to the face of the box (an example is illustrated) and the celebration of the accession of Charles II and his queen Catherine of Braganza is shown, a slightly larger example. Both these little boxes are very flimsy, but are excellently made. They date from circa 1650 and 1660.

The sport-loving Stuarts played many games in which the use of 'counters' took the place of money, and many such medallions are encountered; the specimens which are illustrated here are later in date, being of King

George I's reign, showing the king's bust to the right, with the royal initials on either side. The thin counters are contained in a tubular box, strengthened by 'ribs' around the centre, and the maker was Thomas Kedder, whose work embraces a whole series of small pieces, chiefly nutmeg graters, also of tubular form.

George I counter box: of shortened tubular form, with 'ribbed' strengthener around body, bearing a repoussé bust of George I on the lid and the same motif on all the seventeen counters contained therein. Circa 1714, probably a Coronation souvenir, by Thomas Kedder, London.
(1⅛″ in diameter by 1½″ high).

George III 'gaming counter' box: formed as shallow container, the pull-off lid engraved with Roman numerals from I to X, and moveable 'hand'. Central floral bright-cut motif. By Joseph Taylor, Birmingham, 1798.
(1⅛″ in diameter by ¼″ deep).

The 'thread-boxes' were very attractively made in the shape of Tudor Roses, or occasionally of plain circular form; their enrichment consisted of scratch-engraved foliate motifs and they originate from circa 1660.

The English Nutmeg Grater, in keeping with the other 'personal boxes' was restricted to use at a table, owing to the absence (already mentioned) of pockets until circa 1670. If the need for grated nutmeg or any other spice arose before that time, it must have been rasped on a steel grater, probably a snuff-rasp. The nutmeg itself originated from the Indies; the earliest recorded reference to *Nux Moschata* occurs in an epic poem by Petrus D'Ebulo, written in 1195, describing the entry into Rome by the Emperor Henry VI, on the occasion of his Coronation in 1191. As the Emperor entered the city,

William & Mary 'teardrop': the lid and base with five-lugged hinges. Simply engraved with scratch-engraved 'Tulip-motif'. By John Allbright, circa 1695.
(1⅝″ by 1⅛″).

From the collection of Richard Kingston, Esq.:
James II 'teardrop': engraved with 'tulip' motif and contemporary initials. The lid and base possess three-lugged hinges, and a coarsely punched silver grater. By CR, London, 1686. (See Jackson, page 144, line 11).
(1½″ by 1⅛″ by ¾″ deep.)

Charles II thread-box: shaped as Tudor Rose, and contemporarily scratch-engraved. By WT, London, circa 1680. With sliding lid.
(1″ in diameter).

the streets were sprinkled with nutmeg, as a fumigation against the plague.

The early nutmeg graters were either of 'heart-shaped' or 'teardrop' form, being of small size, but large enough to contain a nutmeg inside the box, which had hinged lids, top and bottom, the one to permit access to the punched steel grater, the other to remove the grated spice. Another popular type was the tubular variety which had a pull-off circular lid, and a silver 'sleeve' grater inside, which was removed for use and replaced. Yet a third, but rarer nutmeg grater was the type illustrated on p. 118 which consisted of a primitively silver-mounted cowrie-shell of the stag-cowrie' variety; the silver grater was mounted by 'strapwork' bands to the body of the shell, and the grated spice was shaken from the interior through a little hole pierced at the apex of the container. This form dates from circa 1690, and is never marked; all that it may possess is the scratched initial of the first owner, but it has a great deal of charm.

With the advent of the 18th Century, the methods of silversmithing im-

proved, and it became fashionable to use 'egg-shaped', 'barrel and keg-shaped' and 'mace-shaped' specimens, the latter being made with the grater resembling an acorn, and the tubular handle containing a cork-screw. The term 'mace' was, in this instance, of a punning nature, embracing both the shape and the name: mace is another name for nutmeg. Other varieties resembled goblets, urns, walnuts, shoes, and strawberries. The enrichment echoed the normal scratch-engraved motifs common to other silver of the period in which the article was made, and bright-cut embellishment for the late 18th Century examples. Late Georgian, William IV and Victorian specimens possessed 'engine-turned' decoration, and at this point the container reverted to the box-form, with heavy gauge metal and steel graters. The underlids (for the removal of the grated spice) were of the 'hidden hinge' variety, and the workmanship was very good. The period spanned in the use and manufacture of nutmeg graters was circa 1650–1865, but the earliest fully marked specimens do not arrive before circa 1697.

This detailed evaluation of The History of the Box is thus brought to its final conclusion. One fact above all others has become abundantly clear: Man's inventiveness. He succeeded in transmuting a common container into a tremendously varied group of delightful, historical and fascinating *objets d'art* which remain to mystify and intrigue the modern collector. It would have given the Stuarts and Hanoverians great pleasure to view the mass-produced packaging media of the 20th Century, with all their advantages, and compare them with their own primitive hand-wrought receptacles: the one is thrown away with the kitchen refuse, the other is treasured.

For a much fuller account of boxes, see *Silver Boxes* (Jenkins, London, 1968).

THE BOX & THE INVESTOR

With the exception of all but the most important tobacco boxes and a few imposing snuff boxes, the market in English containers was becalmed for many years. Even the finest gold boxes were regarded with indifference. A well-known London dealer, advertising in 1934, offered what was described as 'a magnificent 22ct. gold George IV 1825 jewel casket'. This bore the cast and chased Arms of Earl Lauderdale on the lid and foliate scrolling enrichment of Greek classical ornament on the sides. It was 6¾″ long and weighed 23 ozs. 6 dwts. The advertisement importuned: '*Must be sold this month for cash, reduced from 550 Guineas to £275*' . . .($1,630 to $770).

A brief glance at conditions prevailing at the end of the second World War and for the decade after that, reveals a nadir, both in commerce and interest. There had been, it is true, a certain amount of trade in articles in precious metals, but although the commodities were easier to sell, they changed hands at the pre-war price. Interest was at a low ebb, as Europe in the years following the war was more concerned with reconstruction than with collecting, and the American markets, having been 'bombarded' with a supply of fine goods for many years, were blasé and lethargic. It was only when, in 1957 or so, the collecting public could put its mind to matters less stringent that a fight for survival, that interest began to blossom and prices to mount.

Even so, by comparison with current values, prices were ridiculously low. The snuffbox and the vinaigrette being articles of charm but (unless used to contain cigarettes or pills) of little practical use, were regarded as an interesting relic of bygone days, but little else. A fine 'castle-top' vinaigrette was sold for a maximum of £25, $70 and a George III table-sized snuffbox for around £75 to £100, $200–280. Victorian articles were despised—the mystique of the word 'Georgian' reigned supreme—and collectors often ignored poor workmanship and shoddy condition as long as this magical term was employed. The fallacy was based on a misconception of art-appreciation by an ill-informed public. The Victorian era saw the introduction of some ghastly monstrosities, but a closer examination of Georgian styles reveals similar lapses of taste, especially in the more grotesque rocaille confections of the mid-1740's. Every period has its hiatus in design, but there are also finely conceived articles: the Victorian boxes were no exception. The fine Linnit 'Pickwick Club' or the superlative Nathaniel Mills repoussé-top examples are proof enough of this facility of craftsmanship.

The box also had to suffer the indifference of the trade, presumably because the profits on even the massive pieces were so slight that it simply did not pay to bother with small articles. An ordinary rectangular vinaigrette sold for between £2 and £3, about $7. These sums, though having a far greater purchasing power than the comparable amount today, were still much underpriced for a good quality piece of antique silver.

The tobacco box is only now realising a reasonable price, having been relatively ignored by all but a few specialist collectors. When it is considered that a fine Commonwealth example has not only a fine patination but also the significance of having been produced at a turbulent period in the history of English democracy, or that a good quality Charles II specimen has a satisfyingly 'chunky' feel and excellent engraved ornament, the price is still not in keeping with the importance of the article. A fine tobacco box of the late 17th Century commands between £300 and £400, $850–1,250 for fully marked specimens and the fact that few examples in crisp condition survive assists the price even further. A partially marked box is somewhat less costly,

Victorian 'champagne bottle': a vinaigrette cum perfume bottle; the top formed as 'foiled' cork, the base containing the vinaigrette and with blue Bristol glass body. By Mordan & Co., London, 1869.
(4″).

realising between £200 and £250, $560–700 depending on age or the identity of the maker.

Boxes of the 'Archbishop Sancroft' type are quite a different matter again: the presence of such exceptional enrichment might result in a 'name your own price' situation, but a reasonable value to place upon such an article would be in the region of four figures. William and Mary, William III and Queen Anne boxes frequently achieve breathtaking splendour and this quality is recognised by a rise in price. A good Queen Anne box today should fetch between £175 to £250, $500–700, and George I examples, though not quite so popular, are also well priced.

George III snuffboxes tend to be somewhat ordinary and unless of the Linnit 'cut-corner' variety enriched with gold borders and impressive 'engine-turning', bring between £75 to £125, $200–340 but the Linnit type boxes are highly sought-after and command between £150 and £200, $400–560 each. Similarly, the Linnit 'Wine and Spirit Pedlar' boxes are in exquisite taste and of the finest quality workmanship and could bring between £300 and £450, $850–1,250 each, and the Linnit 'Commemorative Cycle' of whcih the 'Pickwick Club' is but one, should realise between £250 to £400, $700–1,100. Nathaniel Mills snuffboxes are well made with attractive views and are comparatively reasonable in price at between £150 and £250, $400–700 depending upon the rarity of the subject and depth of relief— the Windsor or Warwick Castle specimens in shallow relief are perhaps the most common—and the general condition.

A note of caution should be introduced: the rise in interest in Victorian snuffboxes attracted the attention of a group of unscrupulous workers in precious metals in the late fifties, and, working on the assumption that plain-top boxes were less interesting to collectors than the repoussé-top variety, they dismantled Victorian card-cases (which also bear repoussé views) and inserted these into the cast foliate borders. While it may be arguable that 'what the eye does not see, the heart does not grieve over', it is nevertheless advisable for the would-be investor to bear this anomaly in mind and examine all repoussé-top snuffboxes with care, looking for evidence of tampered-with or disturbed borders which could affect the selling-price should he wish to dispose of his collection at a later date. It should be emphasised that such scrutiny should be made only with the full consent of the owner, as otherwise needless antagonism would result. Most dealers, however, are only too happy to assist genuine customers and are duly respectful of erudition in a client.

A fine 'castle-top' vinaigrette today commands between £100 and £150, $280–400 in the better antique shops; a good 'engraved-top' realises between £40 and £65, $110–180, and any of the charming 'shapes'—reticules, snails, crowns, Maltese Crosses—to name but a few, between £50 and £100, $140–280, depending on condition, crispness of engraving, subject of grille, etc. The superb 'Nelson Commemorative' vinaigrettes, of which there are two types, the smaller vertical portrait selling at between £100 to £150, $280–400, and the larger horizontal portrait at between £150 and £250, $400–700. Nutmeg Graters are also on a rising market, and early tubular specimens are priced between £40 to £70, $110–200, and silver-mounted cowrie-shells between £75 and £100, $210–280. The barrel-shaped and 'opening-type' varieties fetch between £15 to £40, $40–120, the 'urn-shaped' specimens between £30 and £50, $85–140, and the rectangular 'engine-turned' examples between £40 and £75, $110–210.

Pomanders of Elizabethan origin and cruciform specimens of Carolean type can command between £300 to £500, $850–1,400 for the former, and £150 to £250, $400–700 for the latter. Silver-mounted boxes are also worthy of consideration and prices of these are still quite reasonable.

There are people, collectors and dealers alike, who dream of past days when it was possible to buy a fine vinaigrette for a few pounds, but these tend to forget one important fact: the low prices were only possible because there was little interest. If they bought cheaply, they also had to sell cheaply; one cannot have it both ways, today's values and yesterday's prices. One must consider which was the better prospect: full shelves and little interest, or a steady demand for fine articles and correspondingly high prices. Careful meditation would probably determine upon the latter.

George III unusual large table grater: formed as monumental column on square stepped base, the four corners as well as the lift-off centre form spice-containers. The ribbed column, which is surmounted by a minaret finial, contains a steel grater secured by means of a 'bayonet' fitting. Unmarked, circa 1800.
(7¾″ by 4″ square. Weight: 12 ozs.).

George III 'urn-shaped' nutmeg grater: the prepared powder fell into the domed lid, the circular base contained the grater. Delicately bright-cut with swags and foliage. By Cocks & Bettridge, Birmingham, 1802.
(1½″ by ¾″ in diameter).

THE SILVER TOY

It is an odd phenomenon that anything small, yet perfectly formed, be it a painting, piece of furniture, dainty porcelain figurine, or even a young babe, should excite admiration and tenderness, often denied to a mature person or fully sized object. Whether the protective or acquisitive instincts are involved, is a matter of some complexity, but one thing is certain: a great many people take pleasure in the 'little things in life'. The silver toy enjoys the same popularity, and would seem to have captured the interest of both the craftsmen and owners early in its existence.

For unlike the utilitarian articles of large size made in precious metal which many households possessed simply for use, many of the miniature pieces were made expressly for the edification of the young who, in their fantasy-play, would learn both prudence and domesticity which would serve them in good stead throughout their adult lives. The early toymakers, therefore, strove to imbue their creations with that air of 'realism' which would engage the interest of the youthful possessors, and, incidentally, in a subtle form of dissemination, help to create a new generation of potential customers.

The earliest silver toys would appear to have been martial subjects, such as soldiers, arms and cannon. The metal toy-soldier industry originated in Germany in the late 18th Century, but there is evidence that individually-designed and wrought 'warrior-toys' existed much earlier. In keeping with many other aspects of antiques, the history of old toys would have been lost, were it not for the existence of contemporary accounts citing these.

The exceptionally detailed Journal kept by Jean Héroard, Physician in charge of the infant Dauphin of France, who was to become Louis XIII, was started in 1601, when the prince was born, and ended with the death of the guardian in 1628. Héroard's account contains much fascinating material and gives a clear picture of the life of an early 17th Century princeling in the rumbustious environment of the French Court. He speaks of the delight which the little prince took in drilling and mustering his devoted servants for many happy hours each day. It was natural, therefore, that the Dauphin should be passionately interested in martial toys of all kinds, but in fact, the collection of silver toys in the Bourbon Family was begun by his grandmother, Jeanne d'Albret, Queen of Navarre, for his father Henry of Navarre (Henry IV). She acquired a 'doll's set of table plenishments sette with diamonds', and on the birth of Louis, the collection was further augmented.

In view of the Dauphin's passion for soldiering, the accent was on military themes: Héroard quotes from a letter which little Louis sent (probably written for him or dictated by him) to the King, then in combat with the Duc de Bouillon at Sedan in the north: 'I have been to the Arsenal, papa. M. de Rosney (Maximilien de Bethune, Duc de Sully) showed it to me full of beautiful arms, and many, many cannon, and he gave me some sweetmeats and a little silver cannon'. This was in 1606 when the prince was five years old. The future king tied this same little cannon to his pinafore with a garter in order not to lose it.

Tea and Chocolate Service on quatrefoil tray. By David Clayton, London, 1725. Comprising:

Rectangular tea-caddy: pull-out lid. 1½″ by 1″. Maker's mark only.

Covered sugar-bowl, the cover with rising dome and baluster terminal. 1½″ by 1⅜″ in diameter. Maker's mark only.

Covered 'Pitcher-cream-jug': pull-out lid. 1½″. Maker's mark only.

Pear-shaped teapot: 1¾″ by 1¼″. Maker's mark only.

Chocolate pot with 'moulinet': 2⅜″ by 1″ in diameter. Maker's mark and lion passant, and marked three times with maker's mark on moulinet.

Tea-kettle on stand. Height: 3″. Maker's mark on kettle, handles and stand.

Quatrefoil tray on four tall pillar legs. Plain shaped rim. 5″ by 4¾″. Maker's mark and two lions passant.

Pair of sunken base, baluster capital candlesticks and Standing Snuffer *en suite*: Size of candlesticks: 3″ by 1¾″ in diameter at base. Lion passant only. Size of Snuffer: Stand 2¼″ by 1¾″ diameter at base. Snuffer: 2¼″. Lion passant and maker's mark twice.

In his turn, Louis XIII passed the collection to his son, the Dauphin born in 1638. The military strain continued: a set of silver soldiers was designed by an eminent artist and wrought for the staggering sum of 10 million francs. When, in subsequent years, France was in urgent need of funds to finance her wars, these were melted down, to realise only 3 million!

With the possible exception of silver baby rattles (not strictly 'toys' within the meaning of the term) which were known in England in Elizabethan times and appear in many portraits of young children, there were few silver utensils before the last quarter of the 17th Century, and, as Charles Oman carefully points out, 'English silver toys are always utensils; there are no examples of the little silver coaches drawn by horses, soldiers, acrobats, etc., which were so popular in Holland'. There are a few solitary Commonwealth vessels—wine tasters, skillets, porringers and spoons and forks—but the general mood of anti-frivolity of the Puritans would have kept these down to a minimum.

The primary English silver toys were seemingly copied in painstaking fashion from the large originals: the most interesting examples of this passion for exactness can be seen here to brilliant advantage where the beautiful little side-handle pot dated 1709 most closely resembles the famous Berkeley Teapot in the Victoria and Albert Museum having a cylindrical tapering body, a conical lid surmounted by a ball terminal, and a somewhat puzzlingly low-set spout. The only vessels which normally have the spout set so low in the body are chocolate pots: the exact reason for this feature is unknown, but it might have been connected with the viscosity of the thick beverage, where a low spout might have facilitated the flow. This little pot is certainly not a chocolate vessel as it lacks the 'moulinet' or stirrer-rod which was set in an opening in the lid and the handle of which formed the terminal to the lid.

Often a toy article is one of the few surviving examples of its class: once again, this may be observed in the charming little bulbous tea-kettle on its own matching brazier stand; Queen Anne tea-kettles emanating from the first decade of the reign are exceptionally rare, in fact, one of the earliest known large specimens is dated 1713, yet this little vessel ante-dates this by four years, being by the London toymaker Isaac Malyn, 1709. Another interesting point is that the small items, often of extreme fragility—some pieces were paper-thin—were carefully handled and have

Queen Anne bulbous tea-kettle on brazier: By Isaac Malyn, London, 1709. The kettle with bulbous body, straight spout, curving down at end, plain 'D-shaped' handle, pull-off lid surmounted by baluster terminal. Fully marked *inside kettle* with maker's mark, date-letter and lion's head erased. Size: 1¾″ by 1½″ in diameter. The brazier with half-fluted base on three scroll feet with flat, shaped handle. Fully marked inside base with maker's mark, date-letter and lion's head erased. (2″ by 1¾″.)

Queen Anne conical side-handle pot for tea or coffee: with baluster-knop terminal, short spout set low on body and plain 'D-shaped' handle. By Isaac Malyn, London, 1709. (2½″ by 1″ in diameter.)

survived, while paradoxically the larger vessels which were of robust weight were either damaged or melted down, to be lost for ever. Similarly, a fully matching George I large-size teaset is quite exceptionally rare, but the group on p. 122 embraces not only the four normal components of the tea-service: teapot, covered cream-pitcher, covered sugar-bowl, and 'thimble-top' tea-caddy, but a tea-kettle on a stand and a chocolate pot as well as the quatrefoil salver on four pillar feet to prevent the heat of the vessels from ruining the surface of a fine table!

Some silver toys were astonishing *chefs d'oeuvre* in their own right. Many of the early examples were simply made of rolled and soldered plates of thin gauge, in keeping with the larger vessels of prototype form, but some, like the little globular teapots and kettles were 'hand-raised from the flat'. Where the silversmith had room to manoeuvre his hammers, this was a fairly simple process, albeit a skilled one; in the fashioning of a tiny vessel where the whole article might measure less than one inch in height, the smith had to call on all his virtuosity, and he invariably succeeded. When he failed, and there are a few clumsily made toys, this anomaly points to one cause—the price. It must be remembered that the cost of a little silver toy in the late 17th Century was negligible, but even so, there were fluctuations: where money was no object, the article possesses elegance and style, but where cost *was* a factor, perhaps only a few pence, the result was a poorly constructed, ugly little vessel. This does not, of course, detract from its value today, as 17th Century silver toys are greatly sought after, but it does help to explain the difference in quality which is sometimes encountered.

George I Set of six tea-cups and saucers and set of five wine mugs on quatrefoil tray, comprising: the tea-cups: ⅞″ in diameter, maker's mark only. Saucers: 1⅛″ in diameter, maker's mark only. Wine-cups: 1⅜″ by 1″ in diameter, maker's mark only. Quatrefoil tray with shaped border on four tall pillar feet. 4½″ by 4″. Maker's mark and lion passant. By David Clayton, London, circa 1725.

Diminutive articles which have been noted included a set of three casters of the heavy 'pear-shape' type, with delicately pierced tops surmounted by a baluster terminal, which were fully hall-marked and were by David Clayton, London, 1712. The two smaller specimens were 1″ high and represented the pepper and spice containers, and the large vessel was for sugar, and stood 1½″ high; all three were on oval ring bases. There was also a fine heavy little Queen Anne tankard with a flat lid and repoussé acanthus chasing on the base, in full imitation of the massive drinking vessels common to the late 17th Century; one of the nicest features of this last specimen was the contemporary sharkskin case made to fit, beautifully lined inside with the softest chamois leather.

Undoubtedly the most interesting of all specimens noted were two Charles II silver toys. The first was a 'fire-grate' by the maker 'GM with two crescents above and one below' whose identity is not clearly known, but who is generally believed to have been George Manjoy. The suite comprised the grate itself enriched with repoussé floral and foliate motifs, the kerb or fender, the pair of finely turned fire-dogs, the poker, the brush and shovel, the pair of fire-tongs and a griddle for fish. It was fully marked on all the pieces and dated London 1682. It may well be, as Charles Oman suggests, that fire-grates were not copied from existing silver grates, as there were none, but certainly the other Charles II toy was a faithful replica of a now almost extinct type of large standish or inkstand, and as such, worthy of description.

The standish as a type first occurs in 1480, but what form it took then is not known. This toy specimen was of the 'half-crescent' shape, with a deep well for quills running along the back, and compartments for sealing materials and ink in the centre. It, too, was decorated with repoussé foliate enrichment, and was so light in gauge that it buckled during cleaning. This was also by 'GM' but dated 1680, and was 2¼″ long by 1½″ wide.

From the collection of Dr. David Lawrence.

Opposite

George II circular salver: the scalloped border and the periphery of the surface 'flat-chased' with 'diaper and floral and shell' motifs, on three cast vine-leaf feet. The centre 'flat-chased' with contemporary cartouche containing a crest. By Paul de Lamerie, London, 1749. The term 'flat-chasing' refers to the method of embellishment whereby the surface of the article is given ornament by indenting it from above and channelling the motif without removing any actual silver.
(10¼″ in diameter, weight: 23 ozs. 1 dwt).

There appears to be little difference between the *Salver* and the *Waiter*, except that both are apparently used to describe a form of tray, the former being the larger variety, usually of octagonal or circular type, the use of which Thomas Blount (1618–1679) defines in his *Glossographia*, first published 1656:
'Salver (from 'Salvo'—to save) is a new fashioned peece of wrought plate, broad and flat, with a foot underneath, to save the Carpit or Cloathes from drops'. The term 'Waiter' occurs in the Will of Frances, Lady Colepeper, 1738: 'I give unto my said niece, my dumb waiter, and the rest of my waiters'. In furniture, this type originated towards the end of the 18th Century, and some very elegant examples were designed by Sheraton and his school, and were used to hold reserve plates and table silver during a meal.

George II 'bullet' teapot: the globular body on moulded cast collet foot. The 'sunken-hinge' lid surmounted by boxwood and silver ball finial, and the boxwood handle with scrolling terminal at union with body: the 'swan's neck' spout enriched with scrolls. The engraved ornament consists of 'diaper and shell' motifs on the shoulder and a fine contemporary Coat-of-Arms on the side. By Gabriel Sleath, London, 1733.
The term 'bullet' is derived from the diminutive of the French word 'boule', that is, a ball, and adequately describes the shape; there are a whole series of these teapots, and one very small type is known as a 'skittle-ball' specimen: it resembles the ball used in the game.
(4″ in diameter, weight: 13 ozs. 2 dwts).

The most numerous of the George I toys noted are by the maker whose mark was long thought to be a gothic 'AC', and was erroneously ascribed, first by Jackson then by Jones, to Augustine Courtauld, the eminent Huguenot craftsman. Both authorities believed that this mark was entered in Goldsmith's Hall in 1708 (it was known that he was admitted a Freeman of the Company in that year) but as Oman revealed, in a brilliant analysis, the mark was in fact that of David Clayton, who entered it on the sixth of July, 1720, and which had to be looked at *upside down* in order to make sense. Had Jackson's assumption been correct, Courtauld's mark entered in 1708

Left

George I brandy saucepan: with everting rim and on circular 'skirted' base. By David Clayton, London, circa 1725. Maker's mark and lion passant on base. Turned wood handle. (Illustration is, of course, enlarged.)
(1⅝″ by 1¼″.)

would have appeared as 'CO', in keeping with the rule that silversmiths were obliged to enter a mark with the first two letters of their surname during the period of the Britannia Standard.

Opposite

From a private collection.

Left

George III oval pierced blade fish slice: with foliate scrolling and 'fish motif' in centre. Short 'feather-edged Old English' type handle with shell terminal at blade. By Richard Mills, London, 1771. (10″ long by 4″ wide).

Centre

Pair George III cast wine labels: formed as a pair of eagles, supporting from their beaks the title label. Titles: Madeira and Claret. By Joseph Foster, London, 1818. A pair of these eagles are in the collection of the New York Historical Society and are also dated 1818. (3″ in length).

Right

George III superbly pierced triangular blade fish slice: pierced and engraved with naturalistic flower motifs, with 'feather-edged' rim and beaded cast pierced-top scroll handle. By Aldridge and Green, London, 1774. (11″ long, size of blade: 5½″ by 4″).

George II shaped oval salver: with moulded rim of the 'Chippendale' type, and flat-chased with scrolling foliate motifs, and with cartouche in centre with contemporary Coat-of-Arms. On four heavy scroll feet. By David Willaume, the Younger, London, 1743. This silversmith anglicised his name and is thus entered in Jackson as David Williams. (8½″ by 5½″, weight: 12 ozs).

George III unusually elongated triangular fish slice: the blade cast and pierced with 'flying fish' motifs and scrolling foliage. Long 'Old English' type handle with bright-cut enrichment. By George Smith, London, 1776. (14″ in length).

This page

Top

George II 'baluster-shaped' mug: with 'tucked-foot', ogee body and scroll handle. By Joseph Steward, London, circa 1739, struck maker's mark three times only. This was probably a 'traveller's sample'. 1¾″ by 1½″ in diameter.

Centre

George I Bed Warming-pan: simply pierced grille and with turned boxwood handle. Size: pan: 1⅝″ in diameter. Overall size: 6″. Maker's mark and lion passant. By David Clayton, circa 1725.

Bottom

George II 'Table Equipage': formed as 18 piece dinner service in sharkskin case: comprising: 6 three-prong forks with 'dew-drop' ornament on back, six 'pistol-handled' knives with similar enrichment on backs and six spoons with similar decoration. Sizes: forks: 1¾″. Spoons and knives: 1⅞″. Size of case: 2½″ wide by 2″ deep. Unmarked, English, circa 1735–40. (Illustration is, of course, enlarged.)

David Clayton's first mark was entered in 1697 and was 'C enclosing L', and even this was wrongly ascribed by Jackson to Jno. Clifton. Clayton entered his second mark in 1720, and it is this which is found on the great majority of early 18th Century miniature silver. It is interesting that so few of his pieces were fully marked, and often carry only the maker's mark and the lion passant; they can therefore be only tentatively ascribed to circa 1720, the shape of the lion passant and the form of its shield supplying the approximate date. While on the subject of marks, it is also noteworthy that some articles which bear only a maker's mark were intended to serve as 'travellers' samples' only, and were never for sale: the uncertainty of travel on the robber-infested roads, with highwaymen and footpads lurking in almost every bush, necessitated 'miniaturisation' of sample wares. There was less fear of attack if the traveller appeared to have no bulky luggage; he could put a whole range of his master's stock into his pockets.

Clayton was a skilled toymaker and could put his hand to almost anything—mugs, candlesticks, tankards, warming-pans, tea-services, wine cups—the list seems endless. Other toymakers working in the 18th Century included Joseph Daniel, circa 1714, Joseph Steward, circa 1739, the Royal Silversmith Thomas Heming, circa 1750–60 and Samuel Massey working circa 1790–1800. It is not known which silversmiths were exclusively toymakers in the true sense, as the term in the 18th Century embraced most 'small workers' who were known as 'toyworkers', meaning that they produced minor articles.

A late, but charming toy was noted, which at long last, departed from engrossing the child and assumed a secondary function: this was a William IV 'watering can' shaped as a globular teapot with a pierced 'flowerhead' terminal to the spout, the whole conceived in the foliate manner with a 'branch and tendril' handle. It was made by the Brothers Aldous in 1833. There are few Victorian toys, but they can be very fine; a heavy little 'slop-bowl' dated 1847 was noted, it was by Nathaniel Mills of Birmingham and thus broke with the tradition that toys were only of London origin. The finest toys, however, are those dainty little relics of a past and gracious age when a lucky child played with a magnificent equipage of tea vessels and a not-so-lucky child played with a flimsy little beaker no more than $\frac{3}{4}$″ high: both would have been amazed to see their apparently paltry playthings treasured and cherished by later generations.

George III 'can-shaped' cream-jug: with reeded rim and plain loop handle. By Samuel Massey, London, 1796. (Illustration is, of course, enlarged.)
($2\frac{1}{4}$″ by $1\frac{3}{4}$″. Fully marked.)

George I miniature 'bullet' teapot: the spherical body with straight faceted spout, the lift-out lid surmounted by boxwood terminal and on shallow collet base. By David Clayton, London, circa 1725. Maker's mark and lion passant on base and maker's mark only in lid. (Illustration is, of course, enlarged.)
($2\frac{3}{8}$″ by $2\frac{3}{4}$″ in diameter.)
(Weight: 2 ozs.)

128

RARITIES

The primary purpose of this chapter is to illustrate the virtuosity and inventiveness of the English silversmith during his long association with the Arts. It is a curious paradox that the penalty extracted for the privilege of personal experience limits the spectator's field of vision to his own particular surroundings and affects his judgement of wider contemporary events and influences. Thus, our early ancestors could hardly have been aware of the great facility and skill which their craftsmen exhibited, whereas their descendents have the opportunity to view the whole vista of artistic endeavour through the ages.

English patronage was always more reserved than the acclaim accorded to artist-craftsmen overseas, and the enthusiast who thrills to the magnificence of Paul de Lamerie's *chefs-d'oeuvre* would be surprised to learn that Lamerie's contempories received the plethora of heavily cast rococo-enriched articles with mixed feelings. Many pieces made by silversmiths, often working in cramped conditions, with rudimentary tools, limited knowledge of design and general illiteracy—Hester Bateman could not even sign her own name—surpass products of a more affluent era. It has to be admitted, however, that the best of today's craftsmen are in every way as good as their earlier predecessors, but their overall artistry, though much admired within their lifetime, will, in turn, be more venerated in centuries to come.

In order that the great mass of interesting objects produced over three centuries should be clearly defined, it is necessary to place them into categories. Most of the items illustrated may be grouped as follows:
- (*a*) Lighting Appliances;
- (*b*) Writing Implements;
- (*c*) Needlework Accessories;
- (*d*) Culinary and Table;
- (*e*) Personal.

Articles for lighting domestic apartments do not exist much before the beginning of the 17th Century; such examples as are extant are primarily of ecclesiastical origin. The earliest reference to a silver candlestick was made in the works of Aethelwold, Bishop of Winchester in 960 A.D. He listed 'II Sylure candelsticcan and II ouergylde', and Bartholemew de Glanville's encyclopaedia, mentioned earlier, cites, circa 1360 'Candelis and other priketis (pricket-candlesticks with a spike instead of a nozzle, common to church plate) both set on candelstikkus and chaundelers'.

The early candles were made of tallow or beeswax, and those from France were thought to be superior to the English variety, and Henry VI imported some from Paris for this reason. The early candlesticks were sometimes known as 'tapersticks': a source of 1546 gives both alternatives: 'Two candall or tapire styckes of Shylver', but in later years, the term signified the narrow candles used for melting sealing wax and many fine little Queen Anne silver tapersticks are known, in fact, these were miniature specimens of the larger domestic candlestick.

Jackson's *History of English Plate* illustrates a silver 'Socket-candlestick' (as opposed to the 'pricket' type) which possesses the baluster nozzle familiar in the later specimens, but stands on a triangular wire frame supported on three domed circular pedestals; this article was dated 1618. Jackson further illustrates the next type developed which was adapted from the pre-1600 base metal examples, with a 'socket-column' or capital, and a base formed as an 'inverted cup'. The waxpan of this type was half way up the capital to catch the drips. This was followed by the 'pillar-shaft' variety with flutes

Pair George III 'Piano Candlesticks': of unusually small size:

Maker: Matthew Boulton, Birmingham, 1800. The plain tapering capitals with reeded base, bright-cut and engraved with foliate motifs on base, and with acanthus foliage on nozzle. Very heavy gauge and mounted on wooden bases. Fully marked on both bases and nozzles.

7″ by 4″ in diameter.

running along the capital or on octagonal or shaped bases. Jackson shows a pair dated 1669, but an important work by Nocq and others, published in Paris, illustrates a pair very similar to these, although by the Clermont-Ferrant goldsmith Charles Vassadel circa 1660, so that these French examples ante-date the English specimens by at least nine years. It is therefore possible that this type arrived in England from France, as did many other styles.

The candlesticks of the early Restoration possessed no nozzles until circa 1675, but acquired stepped bases and fluted capitals. The late 17th Century saw the introduction of heavy gadroons and flutes on the bases, the waxpans (which had by then become 'bosses', that is, heavy knobs) and the nozzles. The cast candlesticks appeared in the early years of Queen Anne's reign and survived as a type through the reigns of all the three George's, finally disappearing in the mid-1770's when the 'loaded' specimens arrived.

The dainty little tapersticks—which were really miniature versions of the larger candlesticks—the waxjacks and the taperboxes were necessary items of domestic use. Their primary object was to serve as 'sealing tapers'. The method of sealing down a letter was somewhat erratic; wafers were made from flour and gum mixed with non-toxic colouring matter, usually Chinese red. They were sold at 100 for a penny and were first used in 1624. The wafers were not particularly efficient and were replaced late in the 17th Century by sealing wax. This required heating until in a melted state, and thus waxjacks were introduced. The earliest known waxjack, which was also the most beautiful to be encountered, was the superb Charles II specimen sold in 1961 as part of the famous Makower Collection. It was a large article, being 9¼″ high by 8¾″ long. The waxjack was believed to have been the gift of Charles II to Benjamin Fellows of the City of London and was of circa 1680 origin. It was formed (to quote the catalogue) as 'a taper roll coiled on a horizontal spindle with repoussé, chased and pierced circular floral and foliate end-plates. Surmounting the framework a snuffer-shaped fitting for holding the taper engraved with foliage, and with corded border and handles in the form of ravens, the securing screw with a winged cherub head'.

The later examples retained the 'taper roll' but placed it vertically. A more restrained type of taper-holder was the 'bougie' or taperbox which was of cylindrical form with a pierced top guarded by a sliding lid, and with a conical snuffer attached to the body on a small chain. The 'bougie' was

Pair Old Sheffield Plate 'Piano Candlesticks':
Maker: 'A Slipped Flower', Sheffield, circa 1785–90. On square 'stepped' bases, the corners reinforced with silver edges, the faceted capital supported on octagonal boss, and on four pillars. Reeded rims to nozzles. 6¼" by 3"

named after the town in Algeria from which the wax originated—Bougiah—and is also the French word for a candle. The earliest mention of a 'Bougie' was in 1755.

The snuffer was an essential part of the domestic accoutrement in an age when the thick, loosely plaited wicks required constant attention to keep the candle flame bright and steady. If it was not watched, the wick would curl until the end dipped into the hot wax on the top of the candle and caused the flame to flare. Snuffers, or candle-shears as they were originally known, were formed as 'close sesours' as one early account describes them, and were used 'to quenche the tapers and snoffe them'. The 1517 records of the church of St. Mary at Hill contain the following item: 'Paid for Snoffers of plate for to put owte the tapurs'. Only two pairs of 'scissor-snuffers' are believed to survive: one, known as 'Cardinal Bainbridge's Snuffers', is in the British Museum. Christopher Bainbridge was Archbishop of York in 1508 and Henry VIII's Ambassador to the Pope in 1509. The snuffers were probably a Royal gift on his accession as Cardinal in 1511, and bear the Royal Coat-of-Arms on one of the two enamelled medallions, the other bearing the owner's Arms. The snuffers are silver-gilt and have two limbs of equal length, and when closed, the pans appear heart-shaped. The handles have looped scrolls terminating in cast squirrels—the Cardinal's Arms contained this motif.

The second pair, in the Victoria and Albert Museum, was acquired in 1926 and bears the legend 'God Save the Kynge Edward wyth all his noble Covncel' and the Royal Arms of England. The head is trowel-shaped and divided down the centre. Edward ruled from 1547 to 1551. The illustration shows a William IV copy of these early snuffers, of very similar form, with caryatid figures on each of the handles and amorini crowning a classical female figure with a laurel wreath. They are by Edward Farrell, London, 1830, and were probably copied from a Renaissance pair.

The most attractive type of snuffers were the Standing variety. These were formed with a candlestick base and a short stem, with a receptacle for the snuffers which fitted vertically. The earlier examples also had a small chamberstick on a scrolled bracket. A good example of the early 18th Century Standing Snuffer may be seen in the 'Toy' specimen shown which is an exact copy of the larger variety.

There were many curious folk superstitions connected with candles and candle-wicks. If the wick guttered as it burned, so that the grease collected unevenly and gradually lengthened into a 'winding sheet', it was an ill omen for the person sitting opposite it. A bright spark, on the other hand, foretold the coming of strangers. If it was wished to determine the exact time of their arrival, the candlestick was knocked on the table while the names of the following days were repeated; should the sparks fall with the first knock, the persons were already on their way. A girl could call her lover to her by sticking two pins in a lighted candle and reciting a verse over it. In typical 'witch-hunting' style, a woman named Joanna Benet was accused in 1490

From the Elizabeth B. Miles Collection, Cleveland, Ohio, USA:
George II Snuffer Tray:
Maker: Paul de Lamerie, London, 1728. Shaped rectangular snuffer tray with decorative shell-leaf at either end, and waterleaf on handle. One of the more restrained works by this maker. Fine Britannia Standard marks.
8¼".
Weight: 9 ozs. 18 dwts.

of attempting to murder a man by naming a wax candle after him, using
sorcery upon it so that it was consumed, and he wasted away . . .

The chamberstick, or chamber-candlestick as it was known, appears to
have originated in the third quarter of the 17th Century, but specimens
before 1680 are very uncommon. One Hand Candlestick, one that is, with
a long flat handle and a circular waxpan with an everting rim, was dated
1686, and another noted was by Eli Bilton of Newcastle, circa 1690. This
fine little article was exhibited at the International Art Treasures Exhibition
at the Victoria and Albert Museum in 1962, where it was described in the
catalogue as a 'taperstick', possibly because the nozzle was very thin, but in
every other respect it was a chamberstick: having a flat circular 'disc' waxpan,
a charming handle formed as a bird's head and four tiny ball feet to lift it
off the table. A very interesting example of the 'travelling candlestick' variety,
that is to say, of 'collapsible' type for easy packing, was noted, in which the stem
folded into a square; the nozzle unscrewed and fitted—in a bayonet lock—
into the centre of the square thus formed. When it was reduced, it occupied
a space of no more than 2″, but when fully extended stood 5″ in height on a
tripod base. This quaint little article was by the untraced London maker
JJ, made in 1867. Another type appears in colour on page oo and is one of a
pair by Thomas Heming, the Royal Goldsmith, dated 1777. The unusual
George III example which is dated 1813 has a conical snuffer formed as the
handle, which unscrews to cover and snuff the taper, and a fourth was noted,
by the great Paul Storr, in which the nozzle screwed into the waxpan on a
cushioned ball and was surmounted by a triple-bracketed stem at which the
loop handle terminated in a tulip-motif. This was dated 1825.

Two types of candlesticks illustrated are of the pleasant medium known as
Old Sheffield Plate. While on the subject, it may be pertinent to discuss
some aspects of this material which are not generally appreciated. The
legend of the invention of Old Sheffield Plate is well-known: Thomas Boulsover discovered it as he was trying to repair a knife-handle and the metal
fused, sometime in the early 1740's. In reality, the medium had existed,that
is the process of plating over another surface, from very early times, and many
church vessels were plated with gold in a laborious manner. What Boulsover
achieved was a commercially profitable method whereby the silver was
successfully fused to the base metal. When it is remembered that an article
produced in, say, 1760 has a layer of heavy silver on it, the colour and patination ought to resemble that of a solid silver article of the same period, and it
is this factor, more than any other, that ought to reassure would-be investors
in this medium; if they can tell antique silver at a glance, and many collectors
learn to do this without looking at the hall-marks, they ought to experience
no great difficulty in detecting the genuine piece of Old Sheffield Plate and
discounting the spurious.

It should be realised that no amount of 'rubbing down to show the copper'
or modern 'silver borders' (to name but two greatly feared anomalies) can
reproduce that 'antique look' which an old article acquires with the years.
There are additional guides to assist the would-be purchaser, such as the fact
that early Old Sheffield pieces are seldom plated on the underneath, merely
tinned or even left bare. Articles made after circa 1785 possess 'rubbed-in'
silver shields laboriously applied by skilled workers to accept an engraved
crest or monogram—a process which few 'fakers' could even contemplate—
and visible when 'breathed upon' to show the outline. Invariably, also,
most investor-collectors can obtain the services of a reliable dealer and it
would not be to his advantage to sell modern reproductions.

Curiously, Old Sheffield Plate has always had many more admirers in
America than in Europe, and the American antiques journals carry interesting
advertisements, whereas English collectors tend to spurn this very charming
and attractive medium. It is safe to prognosticate that really fine quality
Old Sheffield Plate will show a marked rise in value over the next decade,
as it has been sadly undervalued since the end of the First World War.
Articles likely to rise will be domestic utensils such as wine coolers, teapots,
inkstands, trays, candlesticks, cruets, entrée dishes, and tea services.

To return to candlesticks: the illustration shows a pair of rare Ionic column
tapersticks on square gadrooned bases made in Old Sheffield Plate dated
circa 1760. Frederick Bradbury's beautifully produced classic on the subject

Pair early Old Sheffield Plate Tapersticks:
Circa 1760. On stepped gadrooned square bases, with fluted Ionic capitals, and square gadroon rim nozzles.
7″ by 3″.

George III 'Travelling' Candlestick:
London, 1813. No Maker's mark. Formed with conical snuffer which screws into the side to make handle.
3″ by 1¾″ in diameter.

Bottom left
George III Waxjack:
Makers: Phipps and Robinson, London, 1791. On circular reeded base and with scroll handle. The nozzle similarly formed, and with urn terminal.
6″
Weight: 4 ozs.

Bottom right
George III circular 'Bougie-box':
Maker: Hester Bateman, London, 1790. Of plain cylindrical form with pull-off lid and plain 'S-shaped' handle and conical snuffer. With reeded borders and handle.
3″ by 2½″ in diameter.
Weight: 3 ozs. Fully marked on base, around bezel of lid and with maker's mark and lion passant on snuffer.

George III Chamberstick:
Maker: John Schofield, circa 1780. Maker's mark and lion passant. With circular waxpan, gadroon rim border, and curling-back short reeded handle. The capital on faceted base.
3″ in diameter.
Weight: 5 ozs.

From a private Canadian collection:
George III Oil Chamberstick:
Maker: Matthew Boulton, Birmingham, 1818. Formed as everting waxpan with heavy gadroon border and shell terminal handle. The frosted glass globe mounted on an Old Sheffield Plate 'bayonet-fitted' stand.
5¼″ in diameter.
Height: including globe: 4¾″.
Weight: 6 ozs.

History of Old Sheffield Plate illustrates another three specimens dated between 1772 to 1834. It should be pointed out that owing to protests from the contemporary silversmiths, makers of Sheffield Plate were not permitted to place 'hall-marks' or makers' marks on their goods between 1773 and 1784, but Bradbury was an expert who could date an article by its type and style, and even the maker's identity was no mystery to him. Oddly enough, the third taperstick shown in Bradbury is a copy of the early George III shell-corner variety, although it was made in Sheffield by Kitchen, Walker and Curr in 1834.

The remaining Old Sheffield candlesticks illustrated are exceptionally unusual: they are formed as a pair of 'Temple' piano candlesticks, that is, of shortened type suitable for placing on a piano for illumination, with square stepped bases, the corners reinforced with silver edges, and the faceted capital supported on four pillars. The maker's mark struck inside the nozzle dates them as of circa 1785 but is not recorded, being a 'Slipped Flower'. They are quite small, no more than 6½″ in height, and are very beautifully proportioned. This type of 'pillared rotunda' is occasionally encountered in late Georgian silverware, and a fine rectangular inkstand by John Angel, London, 1821 exhibited at the International Art Treasures Exhibition in 1962 had Ionic pillars supporting a rectangular-based chamber-stick.

Writing implements form another wide group: the earliest type of inkpot, for instance, originated in China, which knew ink as far back as 2697 B.C. when it was probably a mixture of soot or charcoal mixed with gum. The Romans used sepia, the black pigment secreted by the cuttle-fish, as a writing fluid. The most common form of ink, however, was prepared from nut-galls, barks and green vitriol. Pens were rudimentary, and the term implies the use of a long feather or a quill from a bird. Pens in precious metal were known from early days, the English poet, William Langland (circa 1332–circa 1400) wrote in 1362 of 'the glose (gloss—explanation) was gloriousely writen with a gilte penne'; whether this was a gold-mounted pen or simply a gold-coloured quill is uncertain. The London Gazette of 1672 contained an advertisement regarding a 'pocket book covered with Vellum, with silver claspes and *silver pen* and severall writings in it', and a late 18th Century reference was by the celebrated teacher of shorthand, Samuel Taylor, who, in 1786 wrote his famous *'Essay intended to establish a Standard for a Universal System of Stenography'* which did more than any other to establish the art in England and abroad than any of its predecessors: 'For shorthand a common pen must be made with the nib finer than for other writing, with a small cleft, but I would recommend a steel or silver one that will write fine without blotting the curves of the letters'.

Because so few people could write, itinerant scriveners travelled about the country with their own writing equipment, but when writing became fashionable, and ink-standishes were generally adopted, they lost their employment. The early scribes used inkhorns, but the travelling inkpot was known from the middle of the 17th Century. The Queen Charlotte Silver Exhibition in 1929 contained a very interesting article described in the catalogue as a 'travelling inkpot' with pen, seal and knife, circa 1620. This resembled a tubular holy-water sprinkler, being formed as a holder, presumably containing the writing implements, surmounted by a spherical ink-compartment, and in turn surmounted by a 'cruciform pomander' of the type described elsewhere. Robert Boyle, the noted English natural philosopher, wrote in 1663 (in his *'Experimental History of Colours'*) 'I have found pens backed, when I had a while carried them in a silver ink-case'. Finally, the Museum of Science and Industry in Birmingham contains a whole collection of 'travelling pencases' formed as conical containers screwed to penholders, the nib inverting into the barrel when not in use. One such specimen noted was by Joseph Willmore dated 1810 which was 4½″ in length.

Most inkstands, or standishes as they were originally known, employed pure feather-quills for writing, and there was provision for these in the form of circular holders, either of sunken form or as tubular containers mounted on the frame. The earliest standish recorded occurs in the Wardrobe Accounts of Edward IV of 1480: '131 standishes with weights and scales iij' (as has been mentioned elsewhere). Standishes were not only provided with a place for the pen but also with a sand-box, and in the later specimens, with wafers and sealing wax as well as a bell to ring for the servant to take the missive.

The sand used for blotting the ink was chiefly fine black sand, and must not be confused with 'pounce' which was the resin of the sandarach tree, a

George III silver-gilt Quill Pen:
Maker: JJ, London, 1815.
6½″.
Weight: 1 oz.

George IV silver-gilt Inkwell:
Maker: John Linnit, London, 1824. Formed as the Round Tower of Windsor Castle. On spreading base, matt-chased to simulate grass, and with 'oak-wreath' border. Two pen-wells and lift-out ink well.
3¾″ in diameter by 3¾″.
Weight: 12 ozs.

George III Filigree Inkstand:
Circa 1800. Unmarked. Formed as rectangular standish, with compartment for pens and with two inkbottles. Shaped rim.
4½″ by 3″.
Weight: 2 ozs.

Charles I Quill-case:
Maker: WB in shaped shield, pellets below (not identified), London, circa 1640. Of trefoil-shape with sliding top which forms seal, engraved with contemporary initials. 2⅝″.

coniferous type found in the Atlas mountains of North Africa and first used for drying ink on the roughened surface of vellum. The root of this word originates from the Latin 'pumex'—pumice—which was used for securing a smooth surface on vellum.

The earliest silver inkstand illustrated by Jackson, (figure 1178) is a trefoil-shaped little article with an inkpot, sandcaster and small covered box (presumably for wafers) and two tubular pen-holders. The piece is dated 1630, and must constitute the earliest known writing equipage with the exception of the pre-Reformation standishes, of which all trace has been lost. The Binning Collection in the Royal Scottish Museum in Edinburgh contains a superb Commonwealth specimen, of rectangular form on four spreading square feet enriched with cast acanthus motifs, and with a beautifully conceived centre-motif, raised and pierced with 'the sun in glory', a crescent, and the Arms of Baillie of Jerviswood. It is by the London maker ES, 1652, and is surprisingly opulent for the Puritan period.

The charming little Charles II 'Toy' standish is mentioned elsewhere, and the larger variety of this must have closely resembled the superlative William and Mary example advertised by a famous London dealer in 1951, which was formed as a rectangular frame with a heavy gadroon rim and with similar motifs on the circular inkpot frames, the bottles in which were of crystal and the back shaped as a crescent with a massive gadroon baluster taperstick. It was by Pierre Harrache, London, 1690.

The early 18th Century saw the introduction of several fine shapes: the famous Assheton Bennett Collection in the Manchester City Art Gallery contains a breath-taking rectangular inkstand by Anthony Nelme, who, though not a Huguenot, worked in the French manner. As had been noted, the Huguenot pre-occupation was with massive silver, and this wonderful article is no exception. It is formed with a heavily moulded base and a drawer with a ring handle in the lower part, the upper having three receptacles, two for the ink and sand pots, the centre compartment for wafers. It has a shaped flat lid, much the same as the 'Treasury Inkstand' of the late 17th Century, which was also of 'casket' form.

Another Nelme Inkstand was exhibited at the 1929 Exhibition at 25 Park Lane, and was dated 1718. This had an octagonal inkpot with sunken 'quill-holders' and a surmounting taperstick. The George II specimens gradually acquired deep wells to hold the writing materials, and centre bells, often of beautiful proportions. These bells, if sold on their own, command very high prices. A George I bell ten years ago sold for about £250, $700 and fetches at least £1500, $4,200 today, and later examples are correspondingly high in price.

The early George III period saw the advent of rectangular standishes with similar pierced frames for the cut-glass inkbottles, and the approach of the Adam Period heralded delightfully pierced articles of classical form. The

Old Sheffield Plate rectangular Inkstand: Circa 1760.
With blue Bristol glass bottles, the rectangular base mounted on wood, the bottle containers of reeded wire. 6″ by 3″.

Left

From the Collection of John R. Rayment, Esq.
George III 'Dinghy' Snuffbox: Maker: William Pugh, Birmingham, 1806.
3½" by 1¼".

George III 'Star' Wine Label: Maker: William Abdy, London, circa 1785-90. (No date-letter.)
1½".

From the Collection of John R. Rayment, Esq.
Victorian Sweetmeat Basket: of light-weight repoussé silver, comprising five views of British Castles and Country Houses, and with swing handle. The subjects are taken from the dies which the maker, Nathaniel Mills, used to decorate the tops of snuffboxes and vinaigrettes, and are as follows: Windsor Castle in centre, the sides with Warwick Castle, Abbotsford House (home of Sir Walter Scott, lately deceased when the article was made) Newstead Abbey, (the ancestral home of Lord Byron from 1540, it was a monastery sold by Henry VIII to Sir John Byron known as 'Little Sir John with the Great Beard' for £800) and Kenilworth Castle. By Nathaniel Mills, Birmingham, 1838. On shallow ring foot and with shaped rim. 4½" in diameter by 2¼". Weight: 4 ozs.

George III Fish Slice:
Maker: Hester Bateman, London, 1786. Finely pierced blade of elliptical shape, pierced vertical motifs, and with stained green ivory handle set at an angle to blade. Engraved 'Gratitude' and contemporary initials.
12″.
Weight: 4ozs.
Much nonsense has been written about the green ivory handles—that the green colour was obtained by burial for long periods—in fact, the ivory is stained by a pigment process.

George III 'Pastille Burner':
Maker: Robert Garrard, London, 1812. Formed as small circular pan, on three ivory ball feet and with boxwood handle. The inside of the pan with cast-iron trivet upon which a small copper dish is placed, the pellet of perfume being ignited on this. With simply pierced grille and ball terminal handle.
3″ in diameter.
Weight: 4 ozs.

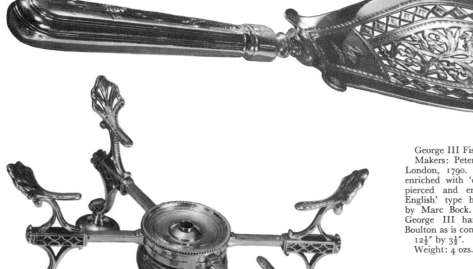

George III Fish Slice:
Makers: Peter and Jonathan Bateman, London, 1790. The finely pierced blade enriched with 'diaper-motifs' and florally pierced and enriched. The large 'Old English' type handle of 'thread-pattern' by Marc Bock. Bock made most of the George III handles, and not Matthew Boulton as is commonly supposed.
12½″ by 3½″.
Weight: 4 ozs.

George III Dish Cross:
Maker: Burridge Davenport, London, 1778. Of unusually small size, with beaded feet and lamp, and bright-cut and engraved stands, which do not slide up and down, as do the larger variety, probably owing to the small radius of the arms.
8″ by 4½″.
Weight: 15 ozs.

finest example noted was dated London, 1778 and was shaped as a proper boat, with cast 'Pan' terminals at either end of the upcurving ends, and superbly pierced sides and galleries. The base was formed of six pierced panels on 'bun-shaped' feet, and the 'upper-deck' contained no fewer than five vessels, two for ink and quills, two for pounce and sand, the centre box for wafers, surmounted by a domed cast terminal, a taperstick and a conical snuffer. This article was exhibited in the Daily Telegraph Exhibition of Antiques at Olympia in 1928.

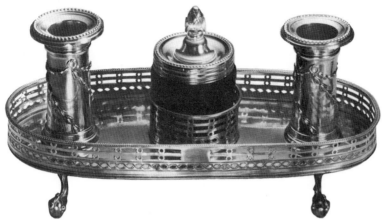

Three specimens illustrated in these pages merit detailed analysis: the oval Old Sheffield Inkstand-cum-Candleholder specimen is an unusual variety, even in Old Sheffield Plate where these charming pieces are much more common, perhaps because the makers felt they had to entice purchasers away from conventional silver articles; the user could thus be well lighted in his endeavours. The 'swirling festoon' motif on the candlesticks (they are too large to have been tapersticks) is pure Adam in conception, but the general construction points to a slightly later dating, circa 1785. The delightful 'Globe' inkstand is well enough known in silver, where most specimens noted are by John Robins of London, and one specimen even had the globe engraved as a 'Globe of the World'. Curiously, the type is also known in Meissen porcelain, and inkstands in this medium dated circa 1770 have been noted, one with a map of the world in Dutch painted on it.

Old Sheffield 'Globes' are uncommon; the present specimen is formed as a sphere with 'drop-down' sides which are released by pressing the spring-loaded terminal. The equipage included an inkpot, pouncepot, a square box for sealing-wax pellets, a quill-cutter, a quill-smoother, an ivory 'aide memoir' and a small, finely faceted seal. The globe had lions' head masks on

Old Sheffield Plate Globe Inkstand:
Circa 1800.
Formed as spherical container on four scrolling feet curving under, and with 'drop-down' sides which are released by pressing the spring-loaded terminal. The equipment comprising: Inkpot, pouncepot, square box for wafers or sealing-wax pellets, quill-cutter, quill smoother, ivory writing tablets and small finely faceted seal. All the bottles have reeded borders. The Globe enriched with swags of foliate motifs and lions' head masks on all four supporting straps.
9½″ including terminal by 5″ in diameter.
Size of bottles: 1¾″ by 1″.
In contemporary fitted leather case.

Victorian silver-gilt Inkstand:
Maker: George Fox, London, 1851.
Formed as finely cast rose-spray, the inkwell contained in the flowerhead.
6″.
Weight: 18 ozs.

all four supporting straps and stood 9½" high. Another attractive feature about this charming article was the contemporary fitted leather case. which hugged the globe almost like a second skin. It was dated circa 1800.

The silver-gilt George IV inkwell illustrated is formed as the Round Tower of Windsor Castle, with a spreading base chased to simulate grass, and with an oak-leaf enriched border. It has two quill-wells and a lift-out inkwell. The maker was John Linnit (who also made the superb snuffboxes described elsewhere), but another larger variety of this type has been noted. This was a massive inkstand with a detachable tower, which contained various writing accessories such as a paper knife, scissors, compass, seal, ruler, eraser-holder, pencil-case, a gold snuffbox, and a tray with gold handles. It was by the London silversmith 'Hamlet' who worked in 1823, and weighed 180 ounces, being 15½" in diameter at the base.

The 'needlework' group is necessarily very small, as although various articles associated with this ancient craft are noted, most are not in precious metals. Nevertheless, even James I bodkins are interesting to the collector of small pieces, as they are rarely found, and when discovered appear to have much charm. The earliest mention in English literature of a bodkin occurs in the 15th Century work by Anthony Wydeville, Earl Rivers '*The dictes or sayenges of the philosophres*' published by Caxton in 1477: 'One of his disciples tooke a boddekyn and prikked him in his feete'. The first mention of a needle-case was in a 1440 lexicon where it was described as a 'nedyl case', and the London Gazette of 1686 advertised for news of a 'silver needle case with openwork' which had been lost.

An interesting Charles II toilet box containing scissors, boxes, inkpots and silk-winders (shaped quatrefoils) bodkins, and needlecases was noted; this was dated 1685. The Stuart bodkins all appear to come from the early years of James I's reign, and of the two specimens illustrated, one bears the mark of 'MH Conjoined' ascribed by Jackson to 1613. It should be explained that Jackson, when compiling his monumental work, took maker's marks from fully hallmarked articles, which thus enabled him to ascribe them accurately. This does not mean, therefore, that articles bearing similar marks will not be found either earlier or later than Jackson's ascription, and the maker's mark on the second example, which is 'RC in a rectangle' though not noted by Jackson is also a perfectly genuine mark, which, had he met it, would have been included in his pioneering work. Both these little bodkins have primitive engraving and one is pricked with contemporary initials.

Another interesting needlework accessory is the fine Stuart pincushion-cum-needlecase illustrated. The latter is finely 'scratch-engraved' with acanthus-leaf motifs, and comprises a three-lugged hinged thimble-case atop a tubular needlecase which opens at the other end. Both possess wrought-iron 'spring-catches' attached by a coarse silver chain to a silver-mounted circular pincushion covered in dark blue satin and velvet, in a frame of 'vandyke edging' also enriched with acanthus motifs, and secured by large-headed pins to steady the frame. The article had the maker's mark struck only on the needlecase: IA Crown above, which was not known to Jackson, but which has been seen on many small articles of the 1680–90 period, including spice-boxes, snuffboxes, nutmeg graters, etc.

Yet a third specimen noted consisted of a 'book-shaped' pincushion with domed padded covers. The centre contained a brass thimble, red flannel needle pad with very small fine needles, a three-leaved rag-paper notebook, a rectangular mirror encased in gilt wire, a shallow needle or patchbox and a folding satin wallet. A large-headed silver pin acted both as fastener to the 'heart-shaped' clasp and (when withdrawn) as an ordinary pin. On the back cover was mounted a tiny shaped scissors-case covered in tapestry bound in silver wire and containing a pair of contemporary fine steel scissors. It was dated circa 1640. The size was 2⅛" long, and being silver-mounted, the article was unmarked.

As might be imagined, the largest groups in the present survey are those which embrace personal use: the pre-occupation with food is a large part of man's life and it is not surprising that many fine articles associated with culinary use are encountered. The chapter on 'The Vessel' contains many fine articles, but many more are commonly met, and a brief survey of some of the more important examples is indicated.

One example is a fine porringer of the Commonwealth period: this is defined as 'a small basin from which soup, broth, porridge, and children's food is eaten'. An early reference occurs in the work of the 16th Century writer Thomas Nash, who, in his '*The Unfortunate Traveller*' 1594, says 'From Spaine, what bringeth our Traveller? A scull-cround hat of the fashion of an olde deepe porringer'. The term 'possett' is used in relation to the three fine little Queen Anne vessels illustrated in colour, and is defined as 'hot milk curdled with ale, wine or spices'. The 1606 comedy 'Sir Gyles Goosecappe' mentions, *inter alia*, 'forty posset cuppes caru'd with libberds faces and Lyons heads with spouts in their mouths to let out the posset ale'.

The 'caudle-cup' is also well known. Caudle was a warm drink of thin gruel mixed with wine or ale; in sweetened or spiced form it was given chiefly to sick people, especially women in childbirth. The early 13th Century '*Tale of Beryn*' (which followed Chaucer's '*Canterbury Tales*' but is by an anonymous author, circa 1400) says: 'Sit and ete thye cawdell that was made with sugir and with swete wyne'. The Liverpool Municipal Records for 1657 list 'one Cawdele Cup with a top'.

The term 'taster' is frequently encountered in English silver. An early reference occurs in an English will of 1420: 'A tastaur of seluer with myn owne marke ymade in the bottom', and the London Gazette for 1681 lists 'One silver Brandy Taster marked with 'R.A.H.', which had presumably been stolen.

English cutlery, in particular, is well represented. Many fine knives originated in Sheffield long before the city was known for its silversmithing interests. A story which would be comic if it were not tragic occurs in a 'Local Register' of Sheffield, and appertains to the assassination, in 1626, of George Villiers, 1st Duke of Buckingham, at the hand of John Felton, a disappointed officer, who, on reading that Buckingham was a public enemy (for his political misdemeanours) stabbed him as he left his house on the morning of the 23rd of August. 'The knife was found in the Duke's body, and on examining it, a corporation mark (the Sheffield cutlers' mark) was observed upon it, when enquiry was made to the London cutlers whether the knife had been made in London, who all agreed that it had been made at Sheffield, and the corporate mark would soon find out the real maker. An express was sent to Sheffield, and the poor cutler Thomas Wild, was sent to London, and taken to the Earl of Arundel's house. Wild acknowledged the mark was his, and that it was one of two knives which he had made for Col. Felton, who was recruiting at Sheffield, for which he charged him tenpence. The Earl was well satisfied of the truth and simplicity of Thomas Wild's testimony, and ordered him to be paid the expenses of his journey home' . . .

A little Charles II 'fruit-knife' is also illustrated, with a tubular handle and a steel blade bearing the London 'cutlers' mark' of David Treadwell, working in the mid-17th Century. A very similar set of three knives and one steeltined fork is in the Victoria and Albert Museum.

As is well known, the English fork originated in the second quarter of the 17th Century, and the simple fully marked London specimen in the Victoria and Albert Museum dated 1632 is still the earliest known example. This has two tines, but the type gradually developed into a three-tined implement.

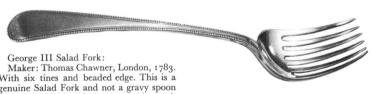

George III Salad Fork:
Maker: Thomas Chawner, London, 1783. With six tines and beaded edge. This is a genuine Salad Fork and not a gravy spoon cut in the bowl; this latter type is much more springy to the touch, as the support of the bowl-rim is lacking.
11".
Weight: 4 ozs.

Charles II small Knife:
Maker: EH in shield, circa 1670. With 'Cutler's Mark' of David Treadwell.
4¼".

From the collection of Captain T. E. Barlow.

Pair George III 'drapery and festoon' wine labels: pierced and bright-cut. Titles: Madeira and R. [red] Port. By Charles Reilly, London, 1792.
(2" in length).

George III 'scroll surmounted by fretted wreath' wine label: surrounding a shield bearing a crest and bright-cut. Title: Claret. By Samuel Bradley, London, circa 1785. This is a beautifully conceived label and in view of the delicacy of the 'fret', it is surprising that the article has survived undamaged.
(1¾" in length).

Pair George III 'goblet' wine labels: with projecting eyelets for the chains, and bright-cut around edges. Titles: Sherry and Red Port. By Hester Bateman, London, circa 1775.
(1⅝" in length).

George III 'goblet and festoon' wine label: pierced and bright-cut. The 'festoon' above caught up in a triple bow. Title: Port. By Hester Bateman, London, circa 1780.
(2" by 2¼").

Victorian 'Lady Bountiful' wine label: formed as cast escutcheon-shaped plaque, the top depicting a fairy with outstretched wings embracing bunches of grapes, the bottom depicting a lion's mask. Title: Claret. By William Sumner, London, 1878.
(2" by 2¾").

George III 'fouled anchor' wine label: this 'armorial' subject is generally unmarked (several varieties have been noted) and is circa 1770–90. Title: Sherry. The specimen illustrated was probably one of a set made to the order of Admiral Sir Hugh Palliser in 1774 (recorded in the Wakelin Ledgers, volume V) while he was Controller of the Navy, i.e. the Sea Lord in charge of ship construction and supplies. The Wakelin Ledgers are a series of complete goldsmiths' records kept by the firm which was founded by George Wickes in 1735, accepted Edward Wakelin as a partner in 1747, and descended to Robert Garrard in 1802; from that date the firm remained in the hands of successive heirs of the family of Garrard until the company was amalgamated with the Goldsmiths' and Silversmiths' Company of Regent Street in 1952. The Ledgers contain much important information which would otherwise have been lost to posterity.
(2" by 2½").

Victorian 'bugle' armorial wine label: with knotted cable and niello-filled title: Madeira. By George Unite, London, 1857. This label was probably struck in commemoration of the end of the Crimean War in 1856. The term 'niello' refers to an ancient decorative method whereby an alloy of silver, copper and lead was fused into an incised pattern on a silver article; the word itself is the Italian form of the Latin diminutive for 'niger'—'black'.
(1¾" in length).

The fork has been known from circa 1310, but not as a dining accessory, merely a pronged instrument for lifting hay, etc. John Fitzherbert's '*A Newe tracte or treatyse moost Profytable for all husbande men*' (i.e. farmers) was published in 1523: 'A good husbande hath his forkes and rakes made redye in the wynter before'. Two early references to culinary forks include a mention in an early will of 1463: 'I bequethe to Davin John Kertelynge my silver forke for my grene gyngour', and Ben Johnson's *Volpone* contains the following: 'Then you must learn the use and handling of your silver fork at meals'. This was written in 1605, well before the famous Thomas Coryat published his 'Coryats Crudities' in 1611 in which he mentions the use of forks noted during his travels in Italy.

James II Trefid Fork:
Maker: IO in heart-shaped shield, circa 1685. Of small size, silver-gilt and 'scratch-engraved' with foliate motif on stem.
4¼″.

George III telescopic Toasting Fork:
Maker: TID Conjoined, London, 1802. (Not identified.) Comprising five-draw sections extending to length of 34″. Two sections and the detachable tines fully marked. With suspensory ring.
12″.

Victorian Marrow-fork:
Maker: George Unite, Birmingham, 1844. An unusual combination.
7⅝″.
Weight: 1 oz. 10 dwts.

William & Mary Apple Corer:
Maker: RB, circa 1690. (Not identified.) The tubular handle of sturdy gauge engraved with foliate motif.
4¾″.

George I Barding Needle:
Unmarked, circa 1720. The looped handle extending into a channelled groove.
5⅜″.

An unusual item of culinary interest is the 'barding needle' illustrated. There has been a certain amount of dissension on the function of this article; some collectors have maintained that it is nothing more than a probe from a medical necessaire used by a surgeon to extract a bullet from a wound—the handle serves to steady his hand while he probes—and have insisted that the same instrument can be found in modern medical etuis. However, the fact remains that barding needles are known as far back as the late 17th Century; certainly, the term 'bard' which is taken from a technical term descriptive of a plate of horse-armour, is mentioned in early 18th Century household dictionaries. Richard Bradley's '*Chomel's Family Dictionary*' translated by him in 1725 contains the following definition: 'Bard—a thin slice of bacon used to cover a fowl' and Nathan Bailey's '*Household Dictionary*', 1736 states: 'Bard—broad slices of bacon, with which pullets, capons, etc. are sometimes covered before they are roasted'. This, exactly, is the function of the barding needle—to baste the roasting meat by inserting a silver of lard under the skin.

The most interesting aspect of this 'culinary group' though not actually connected with food, are the silver 'wine labels' or 'bottle tickets' as they were known in the early 18th Century, which were formed as 'pointers'. These dogs were known as foxhounds in the early 17th Century, and the earliest references to hunting as a sport occurred in correspondence regarding Lord Arundel who kept a pack of foxhounds between 1690 and 1700. As wine labels, too, these charming articles are rare, being firstly of Scottish origin dated 1817, and secondly of the 'Armorial' variety which is seldom encountered.

Set of four George III Scottish Wine Labels:
Maker: John MacDonald, Edinburgh, 1817. Formed as 'pointers'. Titles: Claret, Port, Madeira.
$2\frac{1}{4}''$.

Silver wine labels appear to have originated in the second quarter of the 18th Century, and the earliest known specimens have been ascribed to the maker whose name was long thought to be Samuel Dell, but who was shown to be Sandilands Drinkwater, who is stated by Chaffers (Gilda Aurifaborum) to have been elected an Assistant of the Goldsmith's Company in 1772, when the great Thomas Whipham was a Warden. These little 'bottle tickets' are escutcheon-shaped, and sometimes have 'flat-chased' vine motifs around

Pair George III Wine Labels:
Makers: Phipps and Robinson, circa 1810. (No date-letter.) Formed as wire scrolling initial letters—'B' and 'G'. Delicate floral chased motifs.
$1\frac{3}{4}''$.

the rims. The later varieties, of which there were many hundreds or even thousands, are very attractive, and some superlative examples are shown in colour. Hester Bateman and her family produced some very beautiful wine labels, as did the Phipps and Robinson partnership, (see the superb little 'wire initial' type illustrated) and Samuel Bradley, Mary Binley and Paul Storr, to name but a very few.

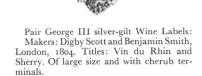

Left
Pair George III 'Cupids, Grapes and Satyrs' Wine Labels:
Makers: Thomas and James Phipps, London, 1816. Titles: Port and Madeira. 2⅛".

Pair George III silver-gilt Wine Labels:
Makers: Digby Scott and Benjamin Smith, London, 1804. Titles: Vin du Rhin and Sherry. Of large size and with cherub terminals.
2½".

George III Wine Spigot:
Makers: Phipps and Robinson, London, 1801. Formed as conical pourer with 'tap' near opening. Parcel-gilt and with reeded border.
5" by 4".
Weight: 10 ozs.
The term 'parcel-gilt' refers to the part gilding of the article; this is not 'wear and tear' but deliberate decorative intent.

From a private collection:
George II large Wine Funnel:
London 1739. No maker's mark. Semi-spherical with straight spout. Engraved with contemporary Coat-of-Arms.
3¾" in diameter by 4".
Weight: 5 ozs.

As may be seen, the most interesting group of all in this survey is connected with 'personal aspects'; not so much for its wide range, as for the pre-occupation with luxurious living which the Georgian silversmiths encouraged. An evil smelling room, for instance, could be sweetened by burning a pastille of incense in a silver pan with a perforated lid. The Countess of Aunoy's works contain the following: 'Certain Spanish pastils spread a fragrant odour round the room'. This was written in 1715. The wonderful little lady's parasol which is shown both folded in its little red morocco case and fully extended to its utmost 18″ in diameter with a four-slide telescopic handle was made by a master-craftsman in 1802, and is one of the finest examples of Georgian ingenuity extant which would do credit to a modern maker with all the latest tools at his disposal.

George III Folding Parasol:
Maker: George Giles, London, 1802. Fully marked on each part.
22″ by 19″ in diameter.
Formed as purple silk cover with yellow tassel fringe, and four-draw telescopic silver handle. The article, when folded, packs away into a morocco-covered tube 8″ long by 1⅜″ in diameter.
Locke's *Journal of Travel*, published 1675, speaks of his travels in France where he saw 'a pretty sort of cover for women riding in the sun, made of straw, something like the fashion of tin covers for dishes'.

Left
George IV Shaving Pot and Heater:
Maker: Archibald Douglas, London, 1829. Comprising: cylindrical shaving pot, with detachable ivory ring handle, and oval heater with 'steam-release' spouts forming handle and with screw-down lid. Mounted on a sliding runner-plate. Enriched with engine-turning and acorn and oak-leaf cast borders. Fully marked on every piece.
5½″ by 3″.
Weight: 30 ozs.

George III Churchwarden's Pipe:
Unmarked, circa 1790. Of three-draw telescopic form and with conical bowl.
Size extended: 8″. Diameter of bowl: 1″.

George III large Pocket Compass:
London, 1804. No Maker's mark. Of 'watch-type' the face marked with all bearings. The Compass by Watkins, Charing Cross, London.
2″ in diameter by ½″.

The very fine early Victorian telescope was made especially for presentation to Queen Victoria on her marriage to Prince Albert in 1840. As may be seen in the inset, the barrel of the telescope was enriched with gold piqué depicting the Royal Cypher and the Crown, and the silver-gilt mounts were finely engraved with the Royal Coat-of-Arms and trophies, banners, weapons, etc.

Victorian silver-gilt Telescope:
Maker: TH, London, 1840. (Not identified.) Formed as four-draw tube, in silver-gilt, the barrel mounted as tortoiseshell with pique enriched tube, depicting the Royal Cypher and a portrait of the Crown. The mounts finely engraved with trophies, banners, weapons, etc.

Size fully extended: 3 feet. On brass tripod stand and in contemporary fitted case.

The barrel was mounted with finely translucent tortoiseshell and extended to three feet long. It was mounted on a brass tripod and had its own contemporary fitted case. In spite of determined efforts, it was not possible to discover the history of this article—how it had left Her Majesty's collection and finished up in a Devonshire saleroom—as the Royal Records at Windsor contained no information whatsoever.

This last article was the epitome of opulent conception, a fitting example of the craftsmanship of the English workers in precious metals. They laboured for very little recompense, often at starvation point. Their ideas and designs were not always understood or appreciated. There were thousands of silver-smiths in little workshops all over England who all contributed something towards the proud heritage of the craft; their reward did not come within their lifetime, but occurs each time a little article is eagerly pounced upon by an avid collector, when an article which in the 1740's at most sold for one hundred pounds is sold at a saleroom for many thousands, when collecting societies enthuse over small and long forgotten trifles, or when a writer devotes his time and much energy to assembling an appreciation of their various and manifold talents.

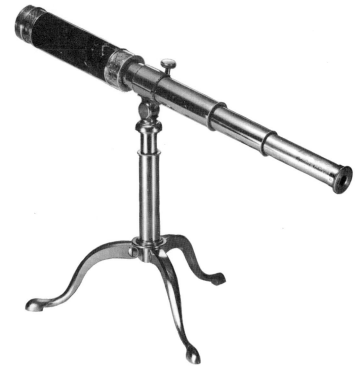

RARITIES & THE INVESTOR

Nothing has come as more of a surprise than the extraordinary rise in the price of candlesticks and other lighting appliances over the past five years. It cannot be surmised, for instance, as with many of the other articles, that the export programme has affected the availability, as for the most part, candlelight is not particularly popular as a lighting medium; it is inefficient, somewhat messy and, as has been explained, there are some peculiar prejudices and superstitions which, though now archaic, take a long time to die away. The answer must lie in either of two directions: a set of fine Georgian cast candlesticks enhance the decor of a gracious room with elegant furnishings, or, much more likely, wily 'stockpiling' by a few wholesalers can conspire to restrict the supply to such a degree that people have to become accustomed to a new price, which, once firmly established, becomes the norm and prices cannot then fall beyond this.

Candlesticks were sadly undervalued for years: this fact may be judged by comparing them with other articles of similar date and quality. From about 1957, when prices in general began to mount, the candlestick was still ignored as an investment medium. It was only when the supply was apparently curtailed that interest grew. It is an odd psychological caprice to ignore the obvious: as long as the candlestick remained reasonable in price (in 1958 a fine pair cost between £50 and £75, $140–210) nobody was interested, as soon as the prices soared, there was a flurry of buying. A comparable pair by John Cafe, Ebenezer Coker or William Cafe today realise between £500 and £650, $1,400–1,820 depending on condition and date.

Queen Anne and George I candlesticks are frequently by the famous Huguenot makers, Platel, Willaume, or Crespin, and this origin combined with the usually heavy gauge and fine patination makes them fairly expensive —between £1,650 to £3,000, $3,620–8,400 per pair, and comparable increases for sets of four. Pairs of candelabra of the George II-III era attain prices between £2,500 to £3,500, $7,000–9,800 and those of the George I period, if available (there never were very many) should realise exceptional sums. Even a fine pair of Victorian candelabra, highly sought today, should sell at £750 to £1,200, $2,100–3,350.

Lamerie and Storr candlesticks are usually heavily enriched with rococo or rocaille motifs and their price is fully in keeping with their quality. The Batemans, as is mentioned elsewhere, did not, as a rule make candlesticks, and if there are any at all, these were probably made by another silversmith to whom the job was 'farmed out' by the Bateman workshop. In passing, it might be pertinent to mention that there are instances of quite uncharacteristic articles with Hester Bateman's mark: the fine little faceted pepperette illustrated is much more in keeping with the work of John Schofield or Makepeace and Carter, and it is probable that these contemporaries were approached at a time when Hester's workshop was fully occupied in preparing an order which could not be interrupted.

Tapersticks, taperboxes and waxjacks have all shared the rising trend: a fine little Queen Anne taperstick which sold for £75, $210 in 1959 today achieves between £450 to £500, $1,260–1,400 and a pair sells for £900 to £1,500, $2,520–4,200. Chambersticks also reflect interest as they realise between £500 to £750, $1,400–2,100 for an early specimen, approximately £450, $1,260 for a Hester Bateman example and even George IV chambersticks of fine quality realise between £200 to £350, $560–980.

As mentioned in the chapter, Old Sheffield Plate articles offer excellent quality and fine craftsmanship, and candlesticks and candelabra in this medium are still very reasonably priced and offer a good investment proposition. The superb pair of 'rotunda' piano candlesticks, for instance, sell at the £75, $210 range, which is eminently reasonable in view of their charm and facility of design, and other small Old Sheffield candlesticks are equally low in price.

Pair George III Buckles:
Makers: George Smith and Thomas Hayter, London, 1792. Of large size, the borders pierced with 'heart-motifs'.
2¾" by 2½".
Buckles were known from the 14th Century, but of course, appear much earlier in Roman antiquities. These examples were used for shoes.

George III Tea-strainer:
Maker: JW, London, 1793. (Not identified.) On low circular collet foot, pierced with simple geometric motif in bowl and with short curling-back reeded handle.
3½" in diameter.
Weight: 2 ozs.
Tea Strainers did not arrive much before the end of the 18th Century. It is probable that 'mote-spoons' might have been used to remove tea-leaves before this date.

Candlesticks can, at any rate, be of some decorative use in the home, but the marked rise in values for inkstands cannot be as easily explained. The possible answer may lie in the 'status symbol' mentality of the sixties: a fine George II or III inkstand on an important looking desk implies prosperity, a feeling eminently to the satisfaction of many people. Again, there may even be a few who like to escape to the graciousness of the past from time to time, and may use the inkstand in their correspondence. It is not suggested that they take their practices as far as a past President of the Royal Academy of Art who refused to live in a contemporary setting, and insisted on 18th Century clothes and furnishings!

A good quality inkstand of the George II period, frequently silver-gilt and even without a bell, would realise between £750, $2,100 rising to £2,000, $5,600 for a Storr specimen or £3,000, $8,400 for a Lamerie example. Lesser varieties, of the George III-IV period are also well received, and a Hester Bateman inkstand, often possessing charm and elegance would realise between £450 to £600, $1,260–1,680, although inkstands from her hand (being rare), were always expensive.

An Old Sheffield Plate, 'globe inkstand', possibly not as fine as the example illustrated, would realise between £100 to £200, $280–560, and a silver globe, usually from the workshop of John Robins could achieve the respectable price of £750, $2,100. Victorian rectangular inkstands, in keeping with their elder brothers, are well up in price, and the plainer varieties are particularly popular. Inkwells, unless of Georgian origin, are not of interest and should be avoided unless the price is really attractive—with time even this is bound to rise.

Needlework accessories are few and far between, but a good quality bodkin of the James I–Charles I period sells today at between £50 to £75, $140–210, and a good pincushion is similarly valued. There are a few other items, chiefly from the George III era, such as lace-shuttles, needlecases, and thimbles which attract collectors, and the Victorian 'bobbin-eggs' (oval containers for bobbins, needles, a supply of pins as well as a thimble) sell well.

The charming little Queen Anne 'Posset-cups' which were, owing to their extreme rarity, included in this chapter rather than in the relevant chapter on vessels, should realise an excellent price. Sets of three or more are exceptionally uncommon, but would cost between £700 to £800, $1,960–2,240 if available. Culinary silver, that is, pieces used at the dining table other than cutlery, is uncommon, and anything in this range, apple-corers, barding needles, strainers (like the superb octagonal specimen in the colour plate) if of early origin, realise high prices.

Forks are very uncommon in the early period, so much so, that it is difficult to put a price upon them, certainly well into the 'three-figure' bracket, but more recent varieties, such as the telescopic toasting fork can realise between £50 to £75, $140–210, and a good salad fork such as the one illustrated, will sell for up to £25, $70. Small sweetmeat forks of the 'trefid' variety can sell for as much as £50, $140 for a partially marked specimen rising to £100, $280 for a fully marked one. Marrow-scoops are also well up in price, being between £25 to £40, $70–112 for an ordinary example, of the George II-III period, to between £100 to £125, $280–350 for a pair by Hester Bateman. Lamerie also made a few high quality marrow-scoops, but these would be expensive in view of the fact that many collectors would be quite content to own one piece bearing Lamerie's mark, and a small article would be very desirable.

Wine labels have greatly appreciated of late years. Perhaps the existence of a collecting society has made a difference, but fine quality articles of all kinds are in great demand today, and sooner or later, the wine label would have attracted attention, notwithstanding organised collectors or societies. On average a good wine label of the opulent variety realises between £15 to £25, $42–70, and a set of six by Paul Storr might achieve as much as £400, $1,120. Rare names on plain rectangular labels are a fascinating link with the past and prices are still comparatively reasonable. The field is enormously wide—there are many thousands of types, or perhaps variations, would be a better term—with superlative specimens from all the assay-offices and by as wide a variety of makers as any of the other articles. The Batemans produced some breathtakingly beautiful specimens, and examples from the early Birmingham silversmiths, Matthew Boulton and John Fothergill, for instance, are also charmingly enriched.

The most fascinating group of all is the 'ephemera': that is, articles belonging to no recognisable variety, but of fascinating form and with unusual functions: the George III 'wine spigot' shown is one of these, as is the incense or pastille burner. The 'bosun's call' is another Georgian rarity, although there are more Victorian specimens, and buttons are also interesting. There are a great many 'specialist collectors' today, who search for these 'out-of-the-way' articles, and fine prices are achieved for these. Many people limit themselves to one particular assay-office, or a special type of article in keeping with their interest. It is a peculiar paradox that what was regarded as useless in years gone by is now considered attractive and unusual.

To sum up on this and the other chapters dealing with investment opportunities it ought to be emphasised that the prices quoted are for the best specimens of their class with fine hallmarks and maker's marks (it is no use, for example, to acquire an article allegedly by Hester Bateman if the maker's mark is rubbed; if one pays for the maker, the mark *must be clear*) and in unrestored state. There are possibilities of purchasing items for less than is quoted here, but these are individual instances, not general trading circumstance. Saleroom catalogues may cite lower prices but these do not state whether the article is in perfect condition.

English silver today has innumerable admirers and this affection is reflected in the excellent prices which are paid and obtained. As was stated earlier, this is preferable by far to a static indifference.

FOR FURTHER READING

BANISTER, JUDITH:
English Silver, Ward Lock, 1965. Introduction to Old English Silver. Evans Brothers, 1965.

CAME, RICHARD:
Silver. Pleasures & Treasures Series Weidenfeld & Nicholson, 1961.

DELIEB, ERIC:
The Bibliography of Hall-marking, with Introduction. International Antiques Yearbook, Studio Vista, 1965.
Silver Boxes. Herbert Jenkins, 1968. Catalogue: Loan Exhibition of Tea-caddy Spoons, Goldsmiths' Hall, London, June 1965. Society of Caddy-spoon Collectors.

GRIMWADE, A. G.:
The Queen's Silver. The Connoisseur, 1953. And many learned articles in antique journals.

HAYWARD, J. F.:
Huguenot Silver in England. 1688 1727. Faber Monographs on Silver. Faber & Faber, 1959. And many learned articles in antique journals.

HOW, JANE PENRICE:
Collaborated with the late Commander How on 'English and Scottish Silver Spoons', privately printed, 1952, in 3 volumes. And many learned articles in antique journals.

HUGHES, G. BERNARD:
Small Antique Silverware. Batsford, 1957. And many other books and learned articles.

HUGHES, THERLE:
Small Decorative Antiques. Lutterworth, 1959. And many learned articles in antique journals.

JACKSON, Sir CHARLES J.:
English Goldsmiths and their marks, Batsford 1905, 1921, 1949.
An Illustrated History of English Plate. 2 vols. Country Life, 1911.

MAYNE, RICHARD H.
Old Channel Islands Silver, its makers and marks.

MILES, ELIZABETH B.:
The English Silver Pocket Nutmeg Grater. A Collection of fifty examples from 1693 to 1816. Privately printed, 1966.

NORMAN-WILCOX, GREGOR:
English Silver Cream Jugs of the Eighteenth Century. Los Angeles County Museum, 1952. And many learned articles in antique journals.

OMAN, CHARLES C.:
English Domestic Silver. A. & C. Black, First Edition 1934, reprinted many times. And many learned articles in antique journals. English Silver Toys. Apollo Miscellany, 1950.

PENZER, NORMAN S.:
The Book of the Wine Label. Home & Van Thal, 1947. Paul Storr. The Last of the Goldsmiths, Batsford, 1954. And many learned articles in antique journals.

STONE, JONATHAN:
English Silver. Cory, Adams & Mackay, Collectors' Guidebooks Series, 1965. And many learned articles in antique journals.

TAYLOR, GERALD:
Silver. An Illustrated Introduction. Penguin Books, 1956. Reprinted.

INDEX